Stepping Stones
to Jewish Spiritual Living

STEPPING STONES TO JEWISH SPIRITUAL LIVING

Walking the Path Morning, Noon, and Night

Rabbi James L. Mirel &
Karen Bonnell Werth

Jewish Lights Publishing
Woodstock, Vermont

Stepping Stones to Jewish Spiritual Living
Walking the Path Morning, Noon, and Night

Library of Congress Cataloging-in-Publication Data
Mirel, James L., 1947–
Stepping stones to Jewish spiritual living : walking the path morning, noon, and night / by James L. Mirel and Karen Bonnell Werth.
p.   cm.
ISBN 1-58023-003-2 (hardcover)
1. Jewish way of life. 2. Judaism—Customs and practices. 3. Spiritual life—Judaism. 4. Jewish meditations. I. Werth, Karen Bonnell, 1955–   . II. Title.
BM723.M54 1998
296.7—dc21
98-10939
CIP

First Edition
10 9 8 7 6 5 4 3 2 1
Manufactured in the United States of America
Book design by Sans Serif Inc.
Jacket design by Bronwen Battaglia
Jacket and interior line art by Michael Heffernan

Published by Jewish Lights Publishing
A Division of LongHill Partners Inc.
Sunset Farm Offices, Route 4
P.O. Box 237
Woodstock, Vermont 05091
Tel: (802) 457-4000 Fax: (802) 457-4004
www.jewishlights.com

You, the Eternal One, show me the
stepping stones, *the path of life;*
in Your presence there is great joy,
in Your ways there are pleasures for eternity.

—*Psalm 16:11*

We thank You and sing Your praises:
for our lives, which are in Your hand;
for our souls, which are in Your keeping;
for the signs of Your presence we encounter every day;
and for Your wondrous gifts at all times,
morning, noon, and night.

—From The Thanksgiving Prayer, the *Siddur*

CONTENTS

Contents

When we sat down to conceive this project, we were deeply aware that we wanted a book on Jewish spirituality that spoke to our post-modern consciousness while holding true to the Jewish tradition. Together, we discussed our vision, imagining a book that would be easily accessible, that would teach fundamentals of Judaism without overwhelming the reader, and that would invite folks from all walks of life to experience the rich spiritual expression of Judaism. To this end, we hope we have remained true.

We dedicate this book to . . .

All whose spirits yearn to experience the presence of God in everyday life through meaningful practices from an ancient tradition that helps us manifest in the world the love and light of the Eternal Oneness.

(kbw, jlm)

HOW TO USE THIS BOOK

We thank you for choosing *Stepping Stones to Jewish Spiritual Living* as part of your spiritual learning and enrichment. We hope that for many of you, the format of this book—a journey through a typical day—will help you engage with Jewish practices in a mindful and meaningful way. Although we present this material in the context of "one day," we fully realize that Jewish spirituality takes a lifetime to master (perhaps many lifetimes). Enjoy the breadth and depth of Jewish spirituality as presented here, and build your practices at a pace that is comfortable and suitable to your life. Know that with each step, your soul connects in yet one more way with the Eternal Oneness that surrounds, infuses, and supports us.

There are many ways you can use this book:

- As a practical guide to daily Jewish spiritual activities, meditations, and prayers—both traditional and creative.

- As a self-teaching tool that provides you with Jewish ideas and values.

- As a study guide for small groups that provides a springboard for discussion and practice.

- As a resource manual that lets you directly investigate specific subjects or activities applicable to your current life situation. For example, if you are working on your relationship with a sibling, look in the table of contents for the section on "relationships" and go directly to that material.

You might want to copy meditations or blessings and take them with you during your daily travels, reading and reflecting on them as you see fit.

We would consider it to be a great blessing to know that this material was used and reused, shared and reshared. Please communicate with us about how you've used this book and how it has affected you.

Rabbi James L. Mirel & Karen Bonnell Werth
c/o Temple B'nai Torah
15727 NE 4th St.
Bellevue, WA 98008
(425) 454-4510 (Karen)
(425) 603-9677 (Jim)
Fax: (425) 603-9699

CORNERSTONES AND FUNDAMENTALS

Judaism offers a rich tradition for the spiritual seeker: its spirituality infuses daily activities with holiness and purpose. While relating the spiritual journey to a typical day in your life, we will walk with you through brief sections that discuss Jewish thought and tradition. These are followed by sections that include methods, activities, devotions, and blessings to enrich your spiritual practice. Every page offers the reader another step, another area of focus, another perspective to bring the sacred into everyday life.

We use poetry, scripture, metaphors, and symbols throughout the book to enhance your journey from the intellectual to the emotional/spiritual realm. Allow yourself sufficient time to digest the writings of poets, prophets, great teachers, and rabbis as you move through the material. This may require a shift, while reading, from using your "rational mind" to opening your "listening heart" to help you appreciate the sustaining truths below the surface.

Trust in the Holy One with all your heart,
and do not rely on your own insight alone.
In all your ways know the Holy One,
and the Holy One will make straight your paths.

Proverbs 3:5–6

Hebrew is the historical language of the Jewish faith. Because of that, many traditional prayers are spoken in Hebrew. We've included Hebrew in transliteration to help you build a working Hebrew vocabulary. Most of the Hebrew is in italics and is followed by its English translation. We hope the Hebrew enhances your reading of the material and helps you feel connected to this ancient, sacred language.

Coupled with the sacred, traditional Hebrew, we have attempted to utilize gender sensitive language whenever possible. Judaism tries to honor the past while creating a future. As the Psalmist recognized, we must "sing to the Eternal One a new song" (Psalm 96:1). We are all singing new songs and using new words—knowing that we must create images and renew ideas about God so they reflect who we are as we speak from our heart. This re- newal can sustain your connection to that which is meaningful and traditional and which is essentially Jewish.

God loves novelty.
Reb Menahem Mendl of Kotzk

Each chapter is divided into time segments that focus on specific aspects of daily life. The material is arranged as follows:

- Sunrise: awakening, welcoming the day, morning routines, our bodies.

- Morning: transitions, work, ethics, the environment, money.

- Noon: mealtime, gratitude, and hospitality

- Afternoon: relationships with family, friends, and community.

- Evening: leisure—recreation, study, and prayer.

- Night: pain, death, loss, and healing.

- Midnight: mysticism, sexuality, creation, and *shalom*.

We ask you to continually generalize and reapply your learning, carrying practices from one chapter to the next in a way that makes sense for you. As described in this book, there are no restrictions on when or where to practice Jewish spirituality. Arrange and then, if necessary, rearrange freely the material so it best matches your day.

Also, each chapter contains two types of learning activity: Study, where we discuss concepts in Judaism that underpin spiritual practice; and Walking the Path, where we describe daily activities, provide guidance for contemplation *(kavanah)*, and suggest blessings *(brakhot)* to enhance your experience of the sacred. You will find traditional *brakhot* (blessings found in the prayer book, which in

Hebrew is called the *Siddur*) as well as more contemporary, creative blessings. We've written these as examples of spontaneous prayer. We hope these examples will help you find words that best express your feelings and deepen your own spiritual practice. Our goal is to transform mundane actions into acts of holiness—bringing the sacred, holy practices of Judaism into everyday life.

• • •

There's a contagious nature to spiritual practice. The more I dedicate a portion of my attention to the inherent holiness that surrounds life, the more I long to bathe in the peacefulness and connection that emerges from the effort. As I become more skillful at pausing and truly considering the miracle in those things I take for granted, I experience time with a renewed sense of fullness. When time "flies," moments are lived unconsciously. Awakening to the holiness of creation allows me to taste in this moment the eternal nature of my true self. This awareness changes the quality of my work and impacts the quality of my relationships. For me, this sense of Godfulness is the gift of life. (kbw)

• • •

We encourage you to pick and choose activities that appeal to you. Do one, do some, do them all. Above all, take your time and enjoy the process. The goal of living a spiritual life, of learning about Judaism, of coming to know the Eternal One is a lifelong process—ever deepening with each step you take on your path.

Experiencing God: The Eternal One, Our God

In history books, we are taught that the Jews were the first people to embrace monotheism, to insist that there is only *one* ultimate, interconnecting, Divine presence in the universe. History also records many stories of men and women who were searching for—and attempting to describe—the Eternal One. Today, we are no different in our attempt to know and describe the Ultimate, the Almighty, the Mysterious Presence—God.

Over centuries, many have wondered about, struggled with, and wished to express "what is God?" Often, our sense of God is a wordless feeling, an intuitive knowing that we belong to something greater than just our individual selves. As we look for adequate language to describe these intuitive knowings, our attempts to describe God often fall frustratingly short. Through this process we may discover, as have many before us, that God is indescribable and unknowable, that God is hidden, that God is No-thing.

God, You are my God; I search for You,
my soul thirsts for You,
my body yearns for You . . .

Psalm 63:1

The depth of primordial being is called Boundless. Because of its concealment from all creatures above and below, it is also called Nothingness. If one asks, "what is it?" the answer is, "Nothing," meaning: No one can understand anything about it. It is negated of every conception. No one can know anything about it—except the belief that it exists. Its existence cannot be grasped by anyone other than it. Therefore, its name is "I am becoming."[1]

The Jewish tradition provides many different ways of speaking of God. In the simplest form, we think of God as both transcendent (not realizable in human experience) and imminent (dwelling within ourselves). As you will see in the following paragraphs, the names or conceptions of God in Judaism express the incredible breadth and depth of humanity's relationship with the Divine. However inadequate, the many names of God are all attempts to depict the universal creative process, the infinite, and the eternal. By whatever name we call God, we are referring to that which is beyond naming.

Moses said to God, "When I come to the
Israelites and say to them 'The God of your
parents has sent me to you,' and they ask me,
'What is the name?' what shall I say to
them?" And God said to Moses,
"I Will Be What I Will Be."

Exodus 3:13, 14

You are called the Holy One of all.
You have no proper name since
You are the very essence of the divine names,
the perfection of the names.

Tikkunei Zohar

• • •

I grew up in a liberal religious home where "God" was something we talked about at worship services and mentioned before meals. My mom taught me that religion was a "personal matter" which I interpreted to mean private and not openly discussed, but something inwardly explored. I used to believe that God could "see" me when I was a child, and I went through a time of being embarrassed when changing my clothes (God was "male," of course). Later as an adolescent, I found that I could travel in my mind to a place of comfort and detachment, a place I felt to be close to God. I called this deep meditative place "the great beyond." As a young adult, I conversed easily and naturally with a "personal" God while exploring religious traditions from around the world. Today, I hold dearly to my sense of being a spark of the Divine—the essence that infuses all creation—while swimming in the river of Light, the infinite and eternal backdrop that supports life and moves creation forward. From this position, I do my work, love others, and I hope to contribute meaningfully to our world. (kbw)

• • •

In deep aloneness, you may have experienced your still mind entering an endless void of silent nothingness. This is a place the Jewish mystics might call *Ein Sof* ("without end"). This transitory moment of touching peace, of experiencing the sense of everything—and of nothing—escapes definition.

In moments of deep meditation or expanded awareness, we may feel awe at the immensity of the universe—the beginning and the end of All Existence, the force of Creation and Transformation: God. Out of this consciousness come several ways of conceptualizing the Source of All Life: God as King, God as Guardian, God as Mother of the Cosmos. These are all attempts to wrap the transcendent Unknowable in words. This is one aspect of the experience we call God.

Then there's the God of our everyday. There's the Presence in our faces, in our souls, in our hands. We all have a unique purpose—and our task is to discover

Who is like You, O Eternal One, among the mighty;
Who is like You, majestic in holiness,
Awesome in splendor, working wonders!

Exodus 15:11

that purpose and give it life. On days when we're solidly in the rhythm of life, we may be convinced that the Holy One is intimately involved in our every movement. Being in the flow, in the rhythm, brings a sense of intimacy with the Source of All Life. Instead of randomness, everyday events are illuminated with a sense of purpose. During these times, we can almost hear/feel/see a calling, a leading forward into transformation, into a creative process of "what can be." This is when it is easy to experience life as a blessing—and to be in the blessing of Creation.

In Judaism, *Shechinah,* which is often translated as "Presence," refers to the more intimate aspects of God. In the Talmud, the Rabbis call the *Shechinah* the *ruach ha-kodesh* ("Holy Spirit"). The *Shechinah* also refers to the feminine aspects of God. God is wholeness, both masculine and feminine—and the word *Shechinah* reflects the receptive, the feminine, the Sabbath, and the imminent Presence of God in the world that connects all life.

As we said earlier, the Jewish tradition provides many different ways of speaking of God. Most of these were originally in the Hebrew language. In many translations of the Hebrew Bible and the prayer book, the word "God" is used when the Hebrew reads *Elohim* or *Eloheinu.* Yet for many people, the English word "God" has uncomfortable connotations because it is often associated with a limiting concept of deity. This is true in Judaism as well, since there are many alternative references to God, especially in the mystical traditions.

In some traditional Jewish books or writings, "G-d" is written to refer to "God." The entire word "God" is not fully written out so the powerful holiness in that word can be honored. Many traditional books also prefer to say *HaShem* ("The Name") when referring to God or they use another euphemism for the Divine Name, *Adonai.* Either—or both—of these expressions may be helpful to some people. Feel free to substitute whatever word or name you feel comfortable with when you see "God" in this book. This is not a book of theology. It is a guide to bring you closer to your true self, closer to the Jewish tradition, and yes, closer to the One which many call God.

We have many ways of talking about the different aspects of God, but whether we are talking about *HaShem* or

> For I am God, and there is no other;
> I am God, and there is none like Me . . .
>
> Isaiah 46:9

Shechinah or *Holy Spirit,* we are talking about God—the Eternal One. This concept of "one God" is absolutely central to Judaism.

Kabbalah—"That Which Has Been Received"

Kabbalah (which is often translated as "reception") is the accepted term for the totality of Jewish mysticism. Mysticism refers to "the doctrine of an immediate spiritual intuition of truths believed to transcend ordinary understanding, or of a direct, intimate union of the soul with God through contemplation or spiritual ecstasy."[2] But what is *Jewish* mysticism? One way of thinking about Jewish mysticism might be the variety of ways Jews have attempted to draw closer to God beyond the normative means of prescribed prayer and formal *talmud torah,* or study. Jewish mystics and scholars described practices directed at accomplishing spiritual union with God, penetrating the veil between humanity and God, cleaving to God—all of which involved intense love and awe of the Holy One. Daily life

Out of this intense love evolved the metaphor, often used by Jewish mystical poets, of humanity being God's lover. One famous medieval kabbalistic poem speaks of God as "the Beloved of my soul." Another way of phrasing this is "soul mate." The lover/poet searches after the beloved/God. And like a starry-eyed lover, the poet only has the desire to do the "will" of the beloved—whatever that may be.

Various Jewish esoteric techniques include austere disciplines, meditation, hidden or obscure texts, and secret knowledge received from mystics. Historically, kabbalah also included some magic and occult practices akin to alchemy and divination—practices that most moderns would see as pure superstition. The important thing to keep in mind is that in its purer forms, kabbalah is simply a way to become close to God and to Holiness in *this* lifetime.

Kabbalah is not a unified, rational system. Rather, it is a complex overlapping grouping of several systems, each of which draw from different times, personalities, and places. One might hear references to classical, Lurianic, Sabatean, and Chasidic mysticisms. These approaches may use the same terms, but in radically different ways.

Their unifying principle is the desire to grow closer to God and to build an understanding of the workings of the universe.

• • •

Even as a child, I always had a sense of wonder when I would be alone outdoors at night. How could I, so small and insignificant, have meaning and relationship in the context of a universe so vast? How could God care about me? One night when I was about ten years old, I had a kind of mystical experience. In a way I can only barely recall, I suddenly knew that God was with me then and would be with me for the rest of my life and beyond. But I also became aware that I would need to continue to search, explore, and contemplate for the rest of my days in order to become more aware of my role in this amazing reality called life. Periodically over the years, this initial experience of God's Presence has been revived in moments of heightened awareness often in the context of my relationship with another human being. Through my love or respect for that person, I renew my faith in and love of God. (jlm)

• • •

In this book, we refer to Jewish mysticism as those practices that enhance our ability to experience closeness with God and recognize our intuitive knowledge of Divine Truth. Although we may find that studying mysticism and spirituality is difficult and elusive, by bringing it into the day-to-day we can begin to weave it comfortably into our lives. Keeping an eye on the sacred aspects of nature, relationships, technology, and creativity while filling our heart with holiness leads us into a spirituality that can be expressed in very concrete and real ways. We begin to see God everywhere in our everyday until we find ourselves *walking the Jewish path*. As the Baal Shem Tov, the great Chasidic master, wrote,

A king had built a glorious palace full of corridors and partitions, but he himself lived in the innermost room. When the palace was completed and his servants came to pay him homage, they found that they could not approach the king because of the devious maze. While they stood and wondered, the king's son came and showed them that those were not real partitions, but only magical illusions, and the king, in truth, was easily accessible. Push forward bravely and you shall find no obstacle![3]

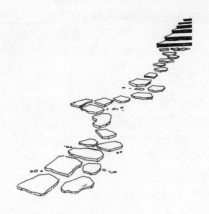

SUNRISE: DAWN—
AWAKENING TO LIFE

As the sun comes up, may I be praying . . .

• • •

When I was growing up, my dad used to say, "Another day, another dollar." Now as an adult, I also must work for a living. But each day before I head down that road, I engage in a number of practices that heighten my awareness and thankfulness for the life I live. "Awakening to Life" refers to all the ways that I attempt to remain conscious of God. In those precious minutes between opening my eyes and actually climbing out of bed, I enjoy knowing that today I have the opportunity to learn a little more about who I am in this world and how I will express my soul's purpose. This sets the tone and tempo for the day.

We begin this section by describing holiness: How can we live a life of holiness? How does holiness illuminate our work, our activities, our purpose? We explore the symbolism of the breath and light. Both of these are important to spiritual practice in many religious traditions, and in Judaism in particular. Then we turn to the mind, *to mindfulness practice and self-examination that prepare the spiritual traveler for further insights and deepening capabilities. Next, we focus on the body. Bathing and clothing our soul's home allows us to focus on the miracle of God's creation. Lastly, we take time for prayer. As Jews have done for thousands of years, we greet the dawn with prayerfulness in celebration of the Oneness: "Hear O Israel . . ." As you wrestle with God, listen as you walk your spiritual path and become all that you are capable of becoming. (kbw)*

. . .

Study: Our Purpose—How to Be Holy

"Everything in the universe," according to Z'ev ben Shimon Halevi, twentieth-century mystic, "is of a piece, like a seamless garment that God has wrapped about Divinity."[1] For centuries, Jews have recognized that in all of our daily experiences and activities, signals and signs can remind us of a deeper reality and our connection with God: "In all your ways know the Holy One" (Proverbs 3:6). Through this connection, Jews live as partners with the Ultimate One. This is the meaning and purpose of existence: to co-create the world that is constantly coming and to repair and heal the world that is already here. Connecting with God answers to a deep intuitive knowing that we are all part of an infinitely conceived, Divinely inspired plan.

> *I am so grateful to you God. For You have given me the privilege of waking to yet another day. Great is Your faithfulness.*
>
> The *Siddur,* the traditional prayer book

We learn to keep our eyes (our insight) and our hearts (our intuitive wisdom) open to God's touch in our lives: everything we do from the moment we wake up until we lie down is potentially a moment of Divinity. What changes it from mundane to sacred is our intention and inner devotion, our *kavanah.* By devoting our actions to God, we step into the sacred. This opens us to a deep sense of meaning and purpose, to finding our place in the intricate web of life. There are traditional ways to do this, such as prayers and *mitzvot* (sacred activities). There are also non-traditional ways, which are spontaneous, creative expressions of holiness. We encourage both.

"Our individual moments of faith are mere waves in the endless ocean of mankind's reaching out for God," wrote Rabbi Abraham Joshua Heschel.[2] God is in everything we do; our task is to reach out in moments of faith for the Presence already there.

An awareness of God seeps into all the activities of human life until this unseen Presence is taken as the true ground of being, more real than what we glibly dub "reality."

Rabbi David Wolpe

The living words of God are encountered in all our interchanges throughout the day: in the beauty of nature, in the advances of technology, in the process of self-care, in our interactions with others. This is where we find God. We can choose to awaken to God's creative, birthing influence or move mindlessly through life failing to truly live a moment with holy intention. Abraham Joshua Heschel wrote about it this way:

> How can I rationally find a way where ultimate meaning has a way of living where one would never miss a reference to supreme significance? Why am I here at all, and what is my purpose? . . . My assumption was: man's dignity consists in his having been created in the likeness of God. My question was: how must man, a being who is in essence the image of God, think, feel, act? The problem to my professors was, how to be good. In my ears the question rang: *how to be holy*.[3]

The question may seem simple: *how to be holy?* But the process is complex. It requires a willingness to go within, in deep aloneness, and wrestle with ourselves: our thoughts, feelings, wants, and needs. We may also have to wrestle with our world-view—the fundamental beliefs, logic, and reason offered by our families and community and ourselves about how the world works. These stories may prescribe limitations, deny possibilities that the everyday mystic will often go beyond in order *to be holy*—to live fully with congruence, harmony, and faith in Divine Truth. The current debate in the health care community regarding the healing power of prayer is one example of scientific truth versus spiritual trust. Meanwhile, we must do our own investigation and challenge our own beliefs. We must answer for ourselves what it means *to be holy*.

As with any change, there will be periods of smooth sailing. There will also be times of uncertainty and periods of darkness. As we trust in the process and reach out for whatever help we need, the darkness will be followed by the dawn—the light of spiritual insight. As we are changed, the way we walk through life will be different.

The biblical story of Jacob (Genesis 32:24–31) describes this process:

> Jacob was left alone. And a man wrestled with him until the break of dawn. When he saw that he had not prevailed against him, he wrenched Jacob's hip at its socket, so that the socket of his hip was strained as he wrestled with him. Then he said, "Let me go, for dawn is breaking." But he answered, "I will not let you go, unless you bless me." Said the other, "What is your name?" He replied, "Jacob." Said he, "Your name shall no longer be Jacob, but Israel, for you have striven with beings divine and human, and have prevailed." Jacob asked, "Pray tell me your name." But he said, "You must not ask my name!" And he took leave of him there. So Jacob named the place Peniel, meaning, "I have seen God face to face, yet my life has been preserved." The sun rose upon him as he passed . . . limping on his hip.

As we step further into trying to live in holiness and celebrating the sacred in everyday life, we find resources that facilitate our journey. These include teachers, friends, writings—creation in all its fullness.

We thank the Holy One for a world full of teachers and resources—a world full of holiness. We thank the Holy One for a world that renews hope and rebirths opportunity each and every day as the dark of night unfailingly gives way to the light of dawn.

> [The Eternal One] dawns on them like the morning light, like the sun shining forth upon a cloudless morning . . .
> 2 Samuel 23:4

We dedicate the ideas and guidance that follow to the dawn, to our *awakening*—the continual unfolding of Creation which brings us that which we are capable of becoming. Blessed is the dawn when we awaken to the Holy One!

Walking the Path:
Our Purpose—How to Be Holy

As you work through sections of "Walking the Path," we encourage you to keep a notebook or journal nearby. This can help you capture your thoughts and feelings as you study the material. Or you can finish your study time with a few minutes of quiet reflection in writing.

Be holy,
for I, the Eternal One your God, am holy.
Leviticus 19:2

KAVANAH: AWAKENING

Take a moment and consider what it means to say, "How can I be holy?"

- What would you wrestle with?
- What changes would you notice in your heart?
- How would your behavior change?
- How would those around you react?
- Would you feel a sense of struggle?

How would these changes toward holiness reflect the statement: "I am consciously preparing to become that which I am capable of becoming"?

• • •

I wrestled with my decision to become a rabbi over many years. As a young boy, the sense of awe and holiness I felt in the presence of my own rabbi and in sitting in the synagogue made me want to bring those feelings into my own existence. I remember one particular Yom Kippur eve as a college student. In the midst of a growing anxiety about my life and direction, I asked the rabbi of the synagogue in which I prayed if I could

Prove me, O Holy One, and try me;
test my heart and my mind.
For Your steadfast love is before my eyes
and I have walked in Your truth.
Psalm 26:2–3

remain in his study overnight, because I did not want to leave the holy place during that most sacred day. Without hesitation, he said, "Yes." During that lonely night, I resolved my years of questioning about what direction my life should take. I knew then that my destiny was to serve God and the Jewish people. (jlm)

. . .

CREATIVE BLESSING

"Blessed are You, the Eternal One our God, Holy Presence in the Universe, You are the force of all Creation that makes possible the transformation of life, my life, from mundane to holy. Help me to become all that I have been created to become."

Study: Breath—The Creative Force

As in other religions, the breath and meditations on breathing are very important to Jewish spiritual practice. Many scriptures and prayers focus on this precious gift from God: the breath that gives life, the breath that creates worlds.

By the word of God the heavens were made; by the breath of God's mouth, all their hosts.
Psalm 33:6

The rhythm of our own breathing contributes with all the other rhythms of the universe—the moon, the ocean tides, the seasons, the heartbeat—to the symphony of life. When we follow the breath, we enter the music of silence and hear the pulse of God throughout time.

On awakening each morning, we are brought back to our everyday conscious life; we are reborn to opportunity and experience. What is in front of us is never to be repeated. In *this* moment, we are alive—and in *this* moment only. (We can't go back to yesterday and we can't be certain of tomorrow.) Breathe deeply and fully. Let the breath of God enter your lungs. Breathe out and your breath returns to God. As Rabbi Abraham Isaac Kook (known as "Rav Kook"), the twentieth-century mystic, said, "In the flow of the holy spirit [the breath], one feels the divine life force coursing the pathways of existence, through all desires, all worlds, all thoughts, all nations, all creatures."[4] Breathe deeply and know that you bring oxygen into your lungs—and the Divine Presence into your life.

This simple act of breathing replicates our relationship with the Eternal One who gives life—the mutual giving and returning, the needing

God acts within every moment
and creates the world with each breath.
The Holy One speaks from the center of the universe,
in the silence beyond all thought.
Mightier than the crash of a thunderstorm,
mightier than the roar of the sea,
is God's voice silently speaking
in the depths of the listening heart.

Psalm 93, adapted from the Hebrew by
S. Mitchell, *A Book of Psalms*

and the needed. In Judaism, we believe we are *in* a relationship with God. As partners, we say, "I am not God, but God's presence is within me."

When we look at the traditional unspoken Jewish name for God, "YHVH," we realize that it is composed of four Hebrew letters. This name of God is not said today because of its holiness. We recognize that to say The Name is to limit that which is infinite and unlimited. The four letters (each of which can be a vowel) are *yod, hay, vav,* and *hay* and require nothing more than the movement of our breath to pronounce. As Rabbi Lawrence Kushner explains, "This word is the sound of breathing. The

If prayer is pure and untainted,
surely that holy breath
that rises from your lips
will join with the breath of heaven
that is always flowing
into you from above.
Thus our masters have taught the verse
"Every breath shall praise God":
with every single breath that you breathe,
God is praised.
As the breath leaves you, it ascends to God,
and then it returns to you from above.
Thus that part of God
which is within you
is reunited with its source.

Based on the re-reading of Psalm 150:6
found in Midrash *Bereshit Rabbah*

holiest Name in the world, the Name of the Creator, is the sound of your own breathing."[5]

To fully appreciate using the breath in Jewish meditation, we must start with understanding three levels of the soul. In Hebrew,

1st

STEPPING STONES TO JEWISH SPIRITUAL LIVING

nefesh refers to the lowest level and translates as "resting soul." This is where the soul interfaces with the physical being. The next level is

2nd

called ruach, which is translated as "the wind" or as "spirit." It is the force of God's breath, the move-

The spirit of God has made me, and the breath of the Almighty gives me life.

Job 33:4

neshamah = breath of God

3rd

ment of air felt as wind. It is associated with transition, the angelic realm, the Holy Spirit, speech, and prophecy. The Hebrew word *ne-shamah* refers to the next highest level of soul and translates as "the breath" of God. When we consider being so close, so intimate with another that we can feel their breath, we begin to appreciate this level of soul. It is through the *neshamah* that we experience the breath of God—a level of deep intimacy, of deep love . . . no words

The Holy One formed humanity from the dust of the earth, and God blew into his nostrils the breath of life; and man became a living being.

Genesis 2:7

are spoken, just aware-ness of the gentle touch of God's breath.

With this under-standing, we enter our meditation and begin the spiritual journey of

awareness. We become aware of the breath moving in and out, and we eventually ascend to a knowledge of the World of Love, an inti-mate awareness of the source of the breath—the Unity of All Life.

Walking the Path: Breath—The Creative Force

KAVANAH: AWAKENING *enthusiasm*

"I am preparing myself to fully experience the Divine Presence in my body, in my life. Let me know the miracle of Life with each inhalation and the return to God with each exhalation."

After reading the above meditation, close your eyes for a moment and focus on your breath, following it as you bring air into your lungs, fill-ing your chest and belly. Follow the breath as it returns to the Source on its exhalation. Say silently to yourself, "Miracle of Life" on the in-halation and "Returning to God" on the exhalation. Focus on your breathing in this way for three breaths. Repeat as often as you like.

> *In the Holy One's hand is the life of everything and the breath of all humanity*
>
> Job 12:10

Jewish meditation is an integral part of Jewish mystical traditions. Learning Jewish meditation will undoubtedly benefit your health and well-being, and will perhaps be a significant gateway to your growing spiritual practice.[6]

• • •

Some years ago, my physician suggested that I take medication for high blood pressure. I was 36 years old and determined to lower my own blood pressure without medication (recognizing that if I was un-successful within a reasonable period of time, I would agree to take medicine). Regular intervals of breathing meditation throughout the day (as brief as three breaths sometimes) became my first line of de-fense. In between clients in my therapy practice, while stopped at a red light, walking to the restroom—all kinds of opportunities to "breathe" mindfully emerged. What a gift—by punctuating my ac-tivities with a gentle pause of thankfulness, my everyday experience was infused with the sacred while my blood pressure returned to nor-mal. Mind, body, spirit working together. (kbw)

• • •

CREATIVE BLESSING

"Blessed are You, the Eternal One our God, Spirit of the world, with each breath Your Presence fills my life and connects me with all Creation."

Study: Light—The Sustaining Force

God's breath creates life and God's light sustains life: both breath and light are strong symbols of holiness. We could say, "Our souls are nourished by God's love, by Divine Light." The mystical tradition

And God said, "Let there be light";
and there was light.
And God saw that the light was good;
and God separated the light from the darkness.
And God called the light Day, and the
darkness the Holy One called Night.
And there was evening and there was morning,
one day.

Genesis 1:3–5

teaches that each of our souls contains a "spark" of the Divine Light—a piece of the Greater Whole. In this way, we are each related to one another and to all Creation.

The mystical teachings make plain that Creation is not a process of creating something new from nothing, but rather the expression in a new form of something that already existed: "There is nothing new under the sun" (Ecclesiastes 1:9). The Divine Light, the Holy One, already existed, and Creation is a spark of the Divine Light expressed in a new, human comprehensible form. Our purpose is to continue to create, to express the Divine Light that is within us in the "world of action," the physical world.

Light is an ever-present sacred symbol. Supernal light—God's light—is often considered synonymous with Life Energy. Light is associated with enlightenment,

Arise, shine; for your light has come,
and the glory of the Eternal One has risen upon you.

Isaiah 60:1

awakening, vision, aura, insight, wisdom, creation, possibility, eternity. Similar to the light or the aura (called *tzelem* in Hebrew) in our bodies, is the Eternal Light, *Ner Tamid*, which constantly burns in the synagogue and symbolizes God's eternal presence. With the light of insight, we bring clarity to a difficult situation and gain new perspective, a sense of holiness, and new growth: "Then your light will burst through like the dawn!" (Isaiah 58:8).

Blessed are You, Holy One, our God,
Divine Presence in the universe,
Who mercifully gives light to the earth and to
those who dwell upon it, and in Whose goodness
daily renews the act of creation.
How numerous are Your works, O Holy One.
All of them did You make with wisdom.
The earth is filled with Your creations.

The *Siddur*, the traditional prayer book

Each morning as we awaken, we welcome

the light as a faithful reminder of the Source of Light and Hope: "But for you who stand in awe of My name, the sun of righteousness shall rise, with healing on its wings" (Malachi 4:2).

We are God's agents, we are God's hope on earth. Through us and our actions, Divine love spreads into the world, and the Holy One awakens in the world of action. As we arise in the morning, the light of dawn reminds us that bringing love, bringing compassion, bringing peace—all ways of bringing *light* to the world—are not only God's doing, but also *our* work. As Rav Kook, the twentieth-century mystic, said:

> Then you gather everything, without hatred, jealousy, or rivalry. The light of peace and a fierce boldness manifest in you. The splendor of compassion and the glory of love shine through you. The desire to act and work, the passion to create and to restore yourself, the yearning for silence and for the inner shout of joy—these all band together in your spirit, and you become holy.[7]

Walking the Path:
Light—The Sustaining Force

KAVANAH: AWAKENING

As you greet the morning, open the shades with awareness that the light coming through the window is Divine light. Sunlight sustains life on the planet; Divine light sustains life in our soul. "The soul of humanity is the light of the Holy One" (Proverbs 20:27). Drinking up the light is another deep connection to the Holy One, an opportunity for reverence and thankfulness. "I am preparing myself to welcome the light of a new day which will provide countless opportunities for acts of lovingkindness and holy deeds. Holy One, help me make the most of this new day and all its potentialities." Breathe in with awareness of how life is sustained by the breath and the light.

May God be gracious to us and bless us and make God's face to shine upon us, Selah . . .
Psalm 67:1

• • •

God's Divine light shines in so many ways. The candles that I light for Shabbat, holy days, and Havdalah help me focus on the Divine in my life. As I light them, I close my eyes, but not completely. Through the tiny opening in my lids, the light is expanded and envelops the entire room. And God is in the light. On a summer's day, I walk to the shore before dawn. Gradually, the sky becomes lighter and the colors go from gray to a wonderful rose-pink. Then the first rays of the sun jut out over the top of the Cascade Mountain peaks, dramatic and bold, announcing the arrival of a new day. God is in the light. (jlm)

• • •

CREATIVE BLESSING

"Blessed are You, the Eternal One our God, Everlasting Light of the Universe, Your Light brings life energy to all Creation. Thank you, Holy One of Light. May I reflect Your dreams through acts of lovingkindness, today and always."

Study: Releasing Your Light, Repairing the World, *Tikkun Olam*

If we destroy a single life, it is as if we have destroyed an entire universe;
If we save a single life, it is as if we have saved an entire universe.[8]

The expression *tikkun olam* is used frequently today in a variety of Jewish circles. It has several different meanings and many shadings of those meanings. In its simplest and original context, it expresses our hope that one day the entire world will be "perfected" and there will be no difference between the mundane world of everyday

*Worship
is a way of seeing the world
in the light of God.*
Abraham Joshua Heschel

life and the "heavenly" world (or kingdom) of God. "On that day, God will truly be One because God's Name will be One" (Zechariah 14:9).

The kabbalistic mystics of the medieval period developed an entire cosmology based on the phrase *tikkun olam,* and retranslated the phrase from "perfecting the world" to "repairing the world." According to their schema—which is a metaphor for the act of Creation—the Divine Light of God entered the world in such a way that it shattered the vessels that would have held it. If not for this, Creation would have been perfect. Some of the broken pieces of light fell away from God's light and became the source of evil. Consequently, we see that evil was originally part of "good" and can be returned to "good." Each of us contains a spark of Divine Light and through our free will, can express the light as evil or as good. Our task and the task of all humanity is to carefully and creatively, through our actions and our way of life, elevate the broken pieces of light back to the source of God's Light—to the Oneness.

In this schema, every person works with God to repair the brokenness. Each vessel of trapped light is unique and each repairer is unique. The ultimate role of each of us is to release the specific vessel of captured light—repairing our own part of the world and realizing our true essence—that only each of us can.

Tikkun olam, repairing through the release of our unique light, is therefore the goal of our existence. It is in this mystical context that Judaism recognizes the idea of reincarnation: if a particular soul cannot fulfill its job of repairing its part in the world before death, then the soul will be reincarnated in another body so it will have the opportunity to complete its work or repair whatever injury to others may have occurred throughout its past. We are the only ones who can repair whatever it is that we have corrupted or destroyed.

Kabbalah tells how our motivation to repair the world comes from being aware of God's Presence and being concerned about all Creation.

> One man is equivalent to all Creation. One man is a World in miniature.
>
> Avot de Rabbi Nathan

We are not God, but through our acts of lovingkindness, the Divine Presence comes to light in the world.

Walking the Path: Releasing Your Light, Repairing the World, *Tikkun Olam*

ACTIVITY

Make a list of acts of lovingkindness that you plan to do today. Note two, three, or even four activities that will reflect the Holy One's light in the world through your actions. Notice how the process of listing these actions and connecting them to the mystical process of *tikkun olam* may change your feelings about doing them. Is there a shift from obligation or responsibility to a sense of purpose or blessing? Describe your feelings.

KAVANAH: AWAKENING

> "I am preparing myself to examine how my life's purpose—the ways that I can be more holy—relates to releasing light into the world. I want to fulfill my role of helping to repair the world in whatever small ways I can. I recognize that many generations of ancestors stand behind me supporting my steps. And I'm reassured that many will come after me to continue repairing the world. I honor all these beings as I consider my purpose and place in the Divine Plan."

• • •

> Often as rabbi and a counselor, I find myself staring into a face filled with pain, sorrow, or anguish. Something has been badly broken in this person's world. There has been profound loss of one kind or another. Most poignantly, this soul has lost the sense of God's loving Presence in his or her life. Through the gift of listening, through the act of praying together, through the process of sharing our tears, sometimes I am able to help this soul return to a sense of hope and recover the presence of God. These moments are the ones which speak to me of the possibility of repair in a broken world. (jlm)

• • •

CREATIVE BLESSING

> "Blessed are You, the Eternal One our God, Source of Endless Light, I pray that my life will bring joy and

14

*healing to those in my community and to the world; that
I fulfill my life's purpose in Your Creation."*

Study: The Practice of Mindfulness

Mindfulness practice requires that we focus our hearts and minds on
the present. By having the presence of mind to recognize thoughts—
thoughts of the past, thoughts of the future—we create a mental
space to be fully aware of the here and now so we can be fully alive in
the present. From this position, we can be aware of the importance of
the moment, the true miracle of our being, and connect with the Holiness of life.

As we awaken, we use mindfulness, heartfulness, and Godfulness,
to increase our awareness, and effectively live in a way that honors
Creation and strength-
ens and directs our steps *Love the Eternal One, your God with all your*
to the Holy One. When *heart, with all your soul, and with all your might.*
we keep our eyes, ears, Deuteronomy 6:5
heart, and soul focused
deeply on the present moment and on the Holy One, we notice life's
blessings and are deeply thankful for them. We relax into a sense of
peacefulness and purpose. Establishing time for mindfulness (prayer,
contemplation, meditation) lets us restore our composure and refocus
our energy, recalling our minds from all the distractions of the day, re-
minding us of our connection with the Ultimate Reality: God. The
mechanisms we use that help us tune into life and our partnership
with the Holy One become meaningful vehicles of spiritual expression. Over time and with faith, we begin to recognize that what may
seem like a world of coincidence and chaos is actually a profoundly
self-organizing process, which is also known as Creation. And we are
very much a part of that process.

You can begin mindfulness practice when you awaken in the
morning. Throughout the day, you can continue your mindfulness as
much and as often as you wish. In this way, you prepare yourself for
experiencing the Divine in all that you do. *Shabbat*, or the Sabbath,
represents an entire day set aside for mindfulness each week. It is a

Six days you shall work,
but on the seventh day you shall rest.

Exodus 34:21

day when we rest and separate ourselves from the mundane work world and open our hearts and mind to the Presence.

Walking the Path: The Practice of Mindfulness

KAVANAH: AWAKENING

As you begin your day, focus your attention on your activities so that you bring your heart, mind, and soul fully into each activity. Look deeply into what you're doing to see how your life connects with other parts of Creation. Notice how you fit into the Whole and be aware of your blessings. For example: As you make your bed, say softly or silently to yourself something like:

> "I am aware of the comfort that a bed provides me
>   and of Your bountiful blessings.
> I know many people in this world do not have the
>   comforts of a bed or shelter.
> I am thankful for the work that others have offered
>   through making this bed.
> I am mindful of the origins of the wood, metal, cotton,
>   and wool—all elements of the Earth,
>   which is Your Creation.
> I, too, am part of Your Creation.
> May I live my life in a way to be worthy of such
>   blessings."

Through mindfulness, we move from "taking the blessings in life for granted" to feeling interconnected with everything, from a world of chaos to knowing our place in Creation. We heal our greed, separateness, and self-centeredness with love, a wholeness, and awareness about how so many others in the Great Design contribute to our well-being. In this process, bed making (and any daily activity) becomes a joyful moment, a source of blessing!

The Eternal One is mindful of us;
the Eternal One will bless us . . .

Psalm 115:12

16

. . .

Going on a meditation retreat significantly improved my ability to be mindful. Being away from work and family let me focus on literally taking one step at a time: feeling my heel push into the dirt followed by the ball of my foot and my toes. I'm not sure I had ever slowed down enough to examine that motion and many others: brushing my teeth, eating a meal, dressing for bed, walking in the moonlight back to my cabin. I suppose this is why the Sabbath offers a whole day for mindfulness. Going on "retreat" in whatever form works for you— Shabbat, four hours on a Tuesday afternoon, or four days at the ocean—can really make a difference in your awareness, a difference which you bring back with you into your everyday life. (kbw)

. . .

CREATIVE BLESSING

"Blessed are You, the Eternal One our God, Creator of All, may I be mindful of Your ways. May I see Your design in all that I do. May I be thankful for Your blessings."

Study: Self-Examination—*Hitbonenut*

Spiritual awakening involves our willingness to look critically at motivations and intentions behind our behavior and practice. By committing to be honest with ourselves, and by practicing constructive self-examination, we begin to clear away the barriers to spiritual development: selfishness, self-importance, greed. Self-examination, or *hitbonenut*, is the key to making the exercises in this book true spiritual practices and not "feel-good pop psychology."

May my mindfulness be pleasing to God, for I rejoice in the Eternal One.

Psalm 104:34

You may be surprised that modern "Freudian" psychotherapy derives from traditional Jewish mystical practice. There is little doubt that Freud was aware of the introspection and self-examination practiced by traditional Jews in his day. The relentless self-examination of *hitbonenut* roots out those aspects of behavior and personality that keep us from drawing closer to the Holy One. *Hitbonenut* diminishes the ego's power over the soul, which longs for union with God, and it fo-

> Pour out your heart like water
> in the presence of the Holy One.
> Lamentations 2:19

cuses not only on the more obvious impediments to uniting with God, but also on the more subtle barriers such as self-righteousness, being overly pious, and the desire to negate the self out of pride.

Aryeh Kaplan, the influential late-twentieth-century kabbalist, talks about *hitbonenut* as the "self-understanding" which lets us see ourselves "as part of God's creation. When we see God's creation, and understand our own role as part of it, we can develop a deep and lasting love for God."[9] Out of our self-examination—a search for our true nature—comes deep insights into our place in the oneness of Creation, and a connection with Wholeness.

Walking the Path: Self-Examination—*Hitbonenut*

MEDITATION

Hitbonenut meditation is a form of meditation used to understand the self in relationship to God's Creation. Aryeh Kaplan described it as a "mirror in which one can see oneself in the light of true Reality."[10] Choose a single object of focus: a piece of bread, a leaf, an idea. Allow this object to fill your mind while moving beyond the object to its Source. You are like this object: a representation of the Source. Just as you see the Holy One, the Creator, beyond the object, the object becomes the mirror for you to see the Holy One that is beyond your self.

• • •

For much of my life, I've struggled with self-criticism and perfectionism. I've self-examined, analyzed, scrutinized—all in an effort to ensure I was OK. There's been an "up" side to this, which has to do with pushing myself to achieve and accomplish things that I may have never attempted without this internal drive. The downside has been the lingering question, "*Could I have done better?*" or, more often, the feeling that "*I could have done better.*" Today, I continue to self-examine, analyze, and scrutinize, but with a different awareness. I know now that my being is perfect: I am made in the Divine image. This is something I never have to prove. My self-examination goals are different: with gentle compassion, I review my behaviors and interactions with others. I work to identify my unskillful ways and make changes. I analyze my motivations for projects and performances. I ask myself, "*Am I self-serving? Or am I serving others?*" "*Is my deepest soul involved in what I'm doing?*" A natural joyfulness comes from doing the work of the soul, and I try to examine how I enhance or block my connection with God. Examining myself no longer means painful self-criticism. Rather, it means knowing the Divine Source of myself and fulfilling the purpose of my existence. (kbw)

• • •

CREATIVE BLESSING

> "*Blessed are You, the Eternal One our God, Divine Wisdom in the Universe, help me examine myself and root out the ways in which I separate myself from You. You are my Source of Life.*"

Study: Washing and Caring for the Body

Sanctify your limbs and adorn them with good deeds, making yourself into a throne for the divine presence, your body an ark for *Shechinah.*[11]

Many of us spend time in the early morning in the shower or washing up at the sink. We're offered the opportunity to care for a unique aspect of Creation—our bodies. When we're in front of the bathroom mirror, do we let ourselves, as Aryeh Kaplan described, "see ourselves in the light of true Reality"?

With very little effort, we can become aware of the miracle, the complexity, the holiness involved in the workings of our body, which is our soul's home. It is within the context of our body that heaven and earth come together. The mystics developed their entire schema around the shape and function of the human body, which for them was the ultimate representation of how God reveals Divine Reality. Each body part symbolizes an aspect of the Divine Essence and the flow of Creation's energy. It is said that the soul describes its experience according to the body: *the hand of God, the face of the Almighty.* Mystically speaking, these refer to expressions of certain aspects of God. Out of our awesome regard for the form and the workings of the human body, we attempt to find closeness with the Divine.

With this awareness, caring for our body takes on much spiritual significance. And although some of us may struggle with our bodies' imperfections, differences, illnesses, pain, or loss of function, we can pray for relief, for strength, for healing—we can bring love to the daily process of caring for our soul's home.

Walking the Path:
Washing and Caring for the Body

KAVANAH: AWAKENING

"Divine Presence, I offer praise for Life and for the health of body, mind, and spirit, which I sometimes take for granted. I acknowledge the miraculous intricacy of my being and my body. I affirm my spiritual and physical wholeness. I promise to try to love myself as much as You love me and to love others in the same way. I will especially attempt to love You with all my heart, my soul, and my strength, by walking in Your ways.

See yourself, and recognize your face and body as the signature of your soul. You are unique. Your soul's purpose is enacted through this body in whatever capacity is part of the Great Design. You carry both heaven and earth within you. Affirm this holy relationship.

Just to be is a blessing, just to live is holy.
Abraham Joshua Heschel

• • •

My moments of deepest relaxation and most profound calm are found in the water of my bath with only the light of a candle illuminating my body and the water. Here and perhaps here alone, I can put aside all the usual insecurities and dissatisfactions with the way God made me, and accept my physical being as it is, with all its faults. Becoming one with the water, I lose myself and find my Self—a being who senses but not with my eyes. Gently, I wash my body, which is not my own but belongs to the universe. I become aware that this body (the only one I will have in this life) is a Divine gift. I need no other affirmation. I am at peace. (jlm)

• • •

CREATIVE BLESSING

"Blessed are You, the Eternal One our God, Wondrous Fashioner and Sustainer of Life, I thank You God for giving me life. Help me to recognize my body as my teacher. Help me to gracefully tolerate my limitations and to grow in compassion through whatever pain I might experience. Help me love myself, my body, as one way of loving You. Help me use my mind and body in the service of Your Purpose in whatever ways are possible today."

Through morning prayers, we establish a respectful relationship with our bodies and with God. Our prayers may also focus on aspects of our bodies that have particular meaning to us and for which we are especially grateful. Create *kavanot* and blessings for aspects of your body that you wish to honor and celebrate.

Consider how it would be to go through the day without eyesight, as many people do. Consider not being able to see the words on this page. As Psalm 118:23 says, "This is the Holy One's doing; it is marvelous in our eyes." When you look in the mirror, take a moment to truly appreciate the blessing of your eyesight.

CREATIVE BLESSING

"Blessed are You, the Eternal One our God, Source of Wisdom and Insight, in this moment I experience your Presence in the blessing of my eyesight. May I use my eyes to see Your work in all Creation and in the faces of all those I meet today."

Our hands represent the tools we use to care for ourselves and others, to perform acts of lovingkindness, to work and play, to repair the world.

O God, strengthen my hands.
Nehemiah 6:9

Feet represent our ability to "walk with God," which we do to emulate God's ways, following the Divine path of love, compassion, justice and peace.

Thus says the Holy One: "Stand by the roads, and look, and ask for the ancient paths where the good way is; and walk in it, and find rest for your souls."
Jeremiah 6:16

You may have aspects of your body that you know are essential in your spiritual expression. Consider the gift of hearing, the power of speech, the faithfulness of your beating heart. Expand on these examples to fill your needs. The key here is celebrating your body and its capabilities, even when you're faced with pain and limitation, as Divine Creation—bringing you closer to oneness with the Source of All Life.

CREATIVE BLESSING (FOR WHEN THERE IS PAIN AND/OR DISABILITY)

The founder of Chasidism, the Baal Shem Tov, told his followers that "when a person has pain, whether physical or spiritual, he should meditate that even in this pain, God can be found. He is only concealed in a garment in this pain. When a person realizes this, then he can remove the garment."[12] We, too, pray and meditate to find God:

"Blessed are You, the Eternal One, Source of all Life, I awaken today with pain in my body. This pain is part of living in this world. It reminds me of so many people

around the world who also are in pain. Despite my illness or disability, I know that You are with me. I pray for strength and courage to live today to its fullest in celebration of the spirit that You placed within me. Please stay near me. You are my comfort and my strength."

Now, when you dress yourself and prepare to meet the world, do so peacefully and mindfully.

Eternal One, you have examined me and know me. . . .
I am awesomely, wonderfully made.

Psalm 139:1, 14

Study: Morning Prayer, the *Sh'ma,* and the Prayer Shawl, *Talit*

Morning prayers can be done formally or informally. Formally, the community gathers in synagogue for morning prayers, *Shakharit.* Informally, Jews individually pray around the world either in Hebrew or their native language. Our personal prayers are expressions from deep within the heart to the Holy One. Jewish prayer often praises and acknowledges the One: "O sing to the Holy One a new song; sing to the Holy One, all the earth!" (Psalm 96:1). They might request healing and guidance: "Do not hide thy face from me in the day of my distress! Incline thy ear to me; answer me speedily in the day when I call" (Psalm 102:2). Or they might express hopes for the future: "O thou who hearest prayer! . . . You are the hope of all the ends of the earth" (Psalm 65:2a, 5b).

There are times when a person's body
may remain completely still
while the soul serves God in silent prayer.
In such moments your prayer may be filled
with a burning and awesome love,
though one who sees you
might never guess the depth
of your inner service.

Zawa'at RIVaSH 13a;
Keter Shem Tov 39b–40a

Morning prayer may also include a time of listening to the "still small voice" (1 Kings 19:12) within us—the Divine Presence. The most famous and most ancient Jewish prayer (the *Sh'ma*) begins with "Hear, O Israel." Through our listening, we might actually hear the *voice* of God (although not necessarily through our ears as human language). As the first full line of the *Sh'ma* reads:

"Hear, O Israel! The Eternal (YHVH) is our God, The Eternal (YHVH) is One."

- *Hear:* To open ourselves completely—every cell of the body—to receive the message of the Holy One, to become aware of the force of Creation.

- *O Israel!:* Refers to the God-wrestler in each of us—that part of us which must come to know God on our own terms. As God told Jacob, "Your name shall no longer be Jacob, but Israel, for you have wrestled with God and humanity, and have prevailed" (Genesis 32:29).

- *The Eternal (YHVH) is our God:* Reflects our close personal relationship with the Eternal One.

- *The Eternal (YHVH) is One:* Proclaims the ultimate unity of the universe; the fact that God fills all Creation with transcendent Oneness.

The *Sh'ma* is the essence of the Jewish faith, the essence of holiness and the essence of *kol,* which is the mundane or the everyday. Through the *Sh'ma,* we declare the ultimate Unity of God and of all things and express our love and our closeness to God.

The *Sh'ma* calls us to a meditative state in which our very being becomes aware of the source of its origins. It can be used as a kind of *mantra* (a repeated phrase used to quiet, clear, and focus the mind) or as a *bakasha* (a Hebrew word meaning "a petition" that asks God for what we need). In essence, it is a statement of "being"—of God's being and our own. As Reuven Hammer writes in *Entering Jewish Prayer:*

We do not even pretend to be able to describe the Lord whose name represents existence and being. We say of Him the least and the most we can say—that of all that exists, of all we know and do not know, of all we experience, we make Him alone our God. . . .

His oneness means that the world in which we live is a harmony; it is a universe and not a battlefield of warring forces. Beyond it and beneath it there is unity of will and purpose.[13]

The weekday prayer book, the *Siddur,* is a source of other traditional and formal prayers. Spontaneous prayers are of just as much value in raising our awareness of and opening our hearts to God. And silence is the language of the Holy One. If you are uncertain about what words to use, meditation from your heart is certainly a beautiful alternative.

The Holy One sees into the heart.
I Samuel 16:7

For some people, ritual objects enhance the spiritual process. One of the most ancient of all Jewish ritual objects is the *talit,* the prayer shawl. The essence of the *talit* is a square or rectangular cloth with "fringes" attached at each of the four corners. The *talit* serves two basic functions:

- As a shawl, it envelops you, shields you from distractions and provides a kind of spiritual cocoon. Many people, when the *talit* is placed on the shoulders (or frequently around the head and shoulders), feel caressed by the Divine Presence.

- The fringes of the *talit* (which are tied in many small knots according to Jewish mystical practice) provide reminders of the obligations and responsibilities of daily life. Some see in the knots the entirety of the traditional 613 *mitzvot,* "commandments." For others, the fringes and their elaborate knots symbolize our unity with God.

The Holy One said to Moses,
"Speak to the people of Israel,
and tell them to make fringes on the corners of
their garments throughout their generations,
and to put upon the fringes on each corner a cord of blue;
and it will be fringes to look upon and
remember all the commandments of the Holy One . . ."
Numbers 15:37–39

Jewish tradition cautions against wearing a large or ostentatious *talit* in public because of the value of modesty, but you can wear any kind of *talit* in the privacy of your home. Indeed, you might find that placing a *talit* around yourself in the early morning *(Shakhar)* is a perfect way to begin the day. Jewish tradition often restricts wearing a *talit* to the daytime hours, but there are so many exceptions to that rule that you can really wear it whenever you wish to surround yourself with this symbol of holiness.

Walking the Path: Morning Prayer, the *Sh'ma,* and the Prayer Shawl, *Talit*

Taking time (even a few moments) for morning prayer after you wash and dress establishes a cycle that connects you to others around the world who are also beginning their days with the Holy One. Through prayer, we consciously establish a deep connection with the Divine before moving into the world.

If you are at home, choose a quiet, comfortable place for morning prayer. Others may join you if you wish. Sit in whatever position is comfortable and helps you create an atmosphere of devotion. You may prefer to stand or walk (as in doing a walking meditation).

Wrapping the *talit* around yourself can be one of the more uplifting experiences in your daily life. It is also a wonderful way to connect yourself with Jewish tradition and with your biological and spiritual ancestors.

Before placing the *talit* around yourself, consider saying the following:

KAVANAH: AWAKENING

"I am preparing myself to place the holy *talit* on my shoulders. May the Divine Presence envelop me in warmth and love. Let me find the energy and focus to concentrate on those aspects of my life which call out for blessing and praise. May I also be inspired to examine my life and find areas which are in need of improvement or healing. May this day be filled with love, energy, and peace."

CREATIVE BLESSING

"Blessed are You, the Eternal One our God, Divine Presence in the universe. As I wrap myself in the wings of Your Presence, be with me in my prayer time and help me know Your ways."

• • •

Most mornings, I say my prayers alone or as the leader of my religious community. I cherish those mornings in which I can be part of a minyan (a prayer group) and when I find myself being lifted up beyond the room to a higher plane. My voice blends with others and, if I choose to stop for a few moments, it does not matter. At these moments, I often feel that my prayers—tacit or spoken—have a special path directly to the heavenly throne. I can almost see the words flying (upward or inward) to their holy destination, each word a kind of messenger of my soul. I say Sh'ma and all of a sudden that word takes off and has a life of its own. It is not my prayer anymore, but a prayer from the heart of the world. (jlm)

• • •

ACTIVITY: RECITING THE *SH'MA*

If you're ever uncertain about what to say as a prayer and you'd like a simple, ancient prayer, recite the Sh'ma. It is especially useful when you're in need of prayer and other words fail you.

How precious is thy lovingkindness, O God!
And we take refuge under the shadow of Your wings.
We satisfy ourselves fully with the abundance
of Your gifts; and You give us all we can
drink from the streams of Your delights.
For with You is the fountain of life:
in Your light, we see light.
O continue Your lovingkindness for those that
know You and all who will come to know You,
and Your protection for those with a righteous heart.
Psalm 36:7–10

Here are several ways to say the *Sh'ma* aloud using Hebrew and/or English:

- *Sh'ma Yisrael Adonai Eloheinu Adonai Echad.*
- Hear, O Israel, the Lord Our God, the Lord is One.

- *Sh'ma*—listen. *Yisrael*—Jews. *Adonai*—The Lord. *Eloheinu*—Our God. *Adonai*—the Lord. *Echad*—is One.

- Attend My Soul—The Holy One My Sustainer—The Holy One alone.

- O God, help me listen to Your Presence in My Life and Find Unity with You.

- God, Oneness, Focus, Wholeness, Unity, Community. (These are interpretations of the words *Eloheinu, echad, Sh'ma, Adonai,* and *Yisrael*).

- Repeat *Sh'ma* over and over as a mantra with each out-breath.

Which version of saying the *Sh'ma* reflects the prayer of your heart?

In ease and rest shall you be saved; in quietness and confidence shall be your strength.

Isaiah 30:15

Try creating your own "version" of the *Sh'ma* that speaks to you.

As you finish with your prayers, breathe deeply and reconnect with the Breath of Life. Let this calm quietness anchor you throughout your day—something you can return to simply by closing your eyes and breathing deeply as you say softly to yourself on the in-breath, *Adonai* (the traditional written name of God), and on the out-breath, *shalom* (peace/wholeness). Walk your path with the Holy One, breathe, and know peace.

Conclusion: Finding Peace

With each sunrise, with each level of awakening, we begin anew our walk on the Path. The start of the day offers us a unique opportunity to reaffirm our purpose and to reset the tone for the journey. You may have already done many of the above activities: meditation, mindfulness, morning prayers. Or perhaps you prefer something simpler.

Expressing your spirituality takes many forms, and religion offers a prescription, a set of exercises, that if followed may prove invaluable in your search for meaning and connection to the One. Honor your process of discovery. Take risks. Listen deeply. And you will find what is meaningful to you.

God said to Abram, "Lech l'cha,"
Go to your self,
know your self,
fulfill your self.

Zohar I:78a

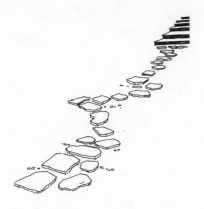

Morning: Going on Our Way, Doing Our Work

And God said, "My Presence will go with you . . ."
—Exodus 33:14

• • •

We now turn to the area of work, which is often the most time-consuming part of modern life. Here we'll suggest ways that work can become an integral part of the spiritual path rather than a task to be completed or simply a way to earn a living.

Work is also an area in which, quite often, we interact with people who may not share our values or concerns. We will suggest ways to accommodate differences and respect diversity.

The goal of this chapter is to enable you to begin each day with a sense of mission and an inner peacefulness. Having faced the day with gratitude and reflection through the exercises and prayers in the previous chapter, we proceed refreshed and energized into the world.

As you read this chapter, keep in mind a visual image of your front door. Each time you go out or re-enter your home, feel the sense of transition. Know that whichever way you are going, you are moving from one holy place to another. Each moment is an

*opportunity for growth and learning.
Work of whatever kind provides a
chance for you to make a difference in
the universe and to God.
The Hebrew word for "work," avoda,
is the same as the word for "prayer."
Each is a kind of service to the Divine.
Take the next step and begin reflecting on your daily life of work. (jlm)*

*Let me hear in the morning
of Your steadfast love,
for in You I put my trust.
Teach me the way I should go,
for to You I lift up my soul.*

Psalm 143:8

. . .

Study: The Journey— Hearing, Trusting, Following

Beginning the work day involves a change in your mind-set. There
are many journeys in the history of the Israelites. Common to all of
these journeys is hearing
God's guidance, strug-
gling with trusting what
has been heard, and fi-
nally, mustering the deep
faith required to follow the Eternal Guide, whether we are in the
wilderness or the Promised Land. Each of us is like those ancient Israelites as we engage in hearing, trusting, and following.

*O Holy One, in the morning You hear my voice;
In the morning I prepare . . . for You.*

—Psalm 5:3

Our journey through the day involves numerous opportunities to
participate in the Great Work of transforming the world, of participating in life with holi-
ness, and recognizing the
sacred in all that we do.
This requires us to listen
for God's guidance, to
trust in the Truth we
hear, and to follow the
path of Wholeness: free-
dom, justice, compassion, and love. Nothing is more important as we
journey through life and as we do our work.

*I remember the days of old,
I meditate on all Your works,
I think deeply on what Your hands have made.
I stretch out my hands to You;
my soul thirsts for You like a parched land.
Selah.*

Psalm 143:5–6

Walking the Path: The Journey—
Hearing, Trusting, Following

Take a moment in your car before turning on the ignition, or while you wait for your bus or train, and reflect on how you hope to be able to hear, trust, and follow the Eternal Guide in your work and your dealings with others. Breathe deeply and feel the Presence enter your body and renew your strength. Relax into the wonder of life.

ACTIVITY: HEARING THE "STILL SMALL VOICE"

As you hear the "still small voice" within, consider this true story: During a conference on the healing relationship between self and Spirit, an older woman remembered that, as she was traveling in Europe, she developed abdominal pain that was "quite disruptive, but not severe. I didn't want to go to a foreign doctor, and because I was a nurse, I felt that I could continue to simply deal with the discomfort. All

> *And though the Holy One*
> *give you the bread of adversity,*
> *and the water of affliction, yet your Teacher*
> *will not hide any more,*
> *but your eyes shall see your Teacher.*
> *And your ears shall hear a word behind you,*
> *saying, "This is the way; walk in it,"*
> *when you turn to the right hand*
> *or when you turn to the left.*
>
> Isaiah 30:20–21

the while, I kept hearing the voice in my head telling me, 'Drink more water, drink more water.' I've never liked water, but the voice continued to get stronger and stronger, yet I ignored it. The abdominal pain persisted. When I returned to the States, I went to see my physician. It turned out that I had a bladder infection and my doctor told me it was essential that I 'drink more water.'"

With a gentle laugh she added, "I'll never ignore that 'voice within' again!"

Think about a message that you may be receiving about your health, well-being, career choice, relationships, or other aspects of your life. These are often repetitive internal messages related to strengthening, growing, developing, creating—messages that will move your life in a new, positive direction. Are you experiencing a consistent message to "give up caffeine," to "take more 'down time,'" to "go to this conference"? Are you listening? Can you trust the message enough to listen to it? What do you think would happen if you did follow these messages from your "still small voice"?

ACTIVITY: THE BOOKSTORE

Go to a bookstore to find a book that you don't know you're looking for. Allow time to explore the shelves and selections. Be open to what catches your eye. Do this with as little logical concentration as possible. Your wanderings may not make sense, but if you find yourself wandering down an aisle containing books in a subject you've never been interested in, continue doing this just to see what happens next. Trust yourself—try not to tell yourself that you must be in the "wrong aisle." Spend thirty minutes noting which books get your attention. A book may "jump off the shelf" to you or "call" to you. Pick it up. Read three different pages in the book. Does it contain a message for you?

The bookstore is a metaphor for many aspects of life. Without understanding why, we're often drawn to those things or people or places that have a message for us. We may have a chance encounter that later we find was important to us. Getting comfortable with and learning to trust your intuitive guide is another example of *hearing, trusting, following.* Take time to identify recent experiences in your life that demonstrate the "bookstore" principle.

· · ·

I've often prayed, "Dear God, please send a fax!" I long for direct, unquestionable communications about where my life is going—and have come to accept that without some degree of mystery and uncertainty, God is probably not God at all. In other words, I'm not going to get a fax. I do get messages, though. My body speaks; pain and discomfort often contain messages that surface when I'm not paying attention and need to make a shift in my thinking or behavior. I've learned to pay attention to roadblocks to my progress, and work with the possibility that I'm trying to force something to change in an area of my life that's not ready. I also watch for doors opening, for opportunities to present themselves, for people to come into my life with information that I surprisingly need right as it's being offered. I listen to my heart, which dances when I'm doing work connected to spirit. I feel joyful, energized, and spiritually tireless. I'm developing trust in a deep sense of knowing that rests in my guts and I'm grateful for the budding clarity and awareness of guidance. (kbw)

. . .

Kavanah: Awakening

A Prayer for Leaving Home to Start the Work Day

Dear Eternal One, please open my eyes to Your
  teachings.
Lead me out of my darkness.
Help me let go of myself so that I can open my
  awareness and hear Your plan.
Forgive my impatient and aggressive ways.
Teach me compassion, strength, and love
  so that I work for justice and goodness in ways that
  honor harmony and growth for all life.
Make me an agent of healing.
Help me trust in Your ways.
Help me follow Your guidance
  as I work to bring this world closer to the days of
  Shalom, of wholeness, of peace.

Study: My Work, My Job—
Service to the Holy One

In Judaism, all work is service to the Holy One. This is God's world. Whatever we do adds to the holiness in the world or subtracts from it. Our goal is to "walk in the ways of the Holy One" in our work to emulate the Holy One, to follow the Divine Laws and the ways of Creation. Through this process, we heal the world through *tikkun olam.*

Yet surely my work is with the Holy One,
and my return, my compensation with my God.
Isaiah 49:4

In ancient Judaism, the ritual at the Temple in Jerusalem was

35

called *avoda*. This translates as "serving," and corresponds to serving a master. This word later also became associated with service in a secular sense. The Rabbis also spoke of *derekh erets*, to the "work" which is "the way of the land." By this, they meant coupling daily labor with Torah study to make a full life. They understood that honest labor of any kind was an ennobling pursuit. In later times, the expression *derekh erets* came to mean "basic decency." Although this may seem a departure from its original meaning, there is a connection, in the Jewish mind, between honest labor and basic decency. The former creates the sense of gratitude that enables the latter to flourish.

Walking the Path: My Work, My Job— Service to the Holy One

Before we begin our jobs, we are instructed by the Rabbis to pray to God that we are able to earn a livelihood.

KAVANAH: AWAKENING

"Dear God, I am going to engage in business with honesty and faithfulness to You and the Words of Torah, for the sake of bringing into the present all that can be. Eternal One, God of Truth, be with me. As I strive to work in accordance with Your Divine Plan, may I have success in all the work I do."[1]

• • •

There is an irony in choosing to become a rabbi. In doing so, you face the risk that your inner spiritual life will be usurped by the mundane tasks of being a "holy person." Too often, that has been the case. The ancient Rabbis of the Talmud often chose to engage in a secular occupation for just that reason ("torah im derekh erets"— "study with a practical occupation"). It is only when I take the time to renew my own inner life as a Jew and as a person that I can be most effective in my "job" as a rabbi. (jlm)

• • •

CREATIVE BLESSING

> *"Blessed are You, the Eternal One our God, Divine Presence in the Universe, I commit my work to You and my spiritual practice to walk in Your ways. Renew my work today. May my efforts provide in some useful way what the universe needs."*

The Bible and the Rabbis give specific guidance about the nature of work. Let's examine some of the guiding principles which we can use as we set off for work today.

Study: My Work, My Job—*Middot*, or The Seven Characteristics of Work

According to Deuteronomy (6:18), "You shall do what is right and good in the sight of the Eternal One." But, what is "right and good"? According to the Babylonian Talmud (*Hagiga* 12b), God's governance in the world is symbolized by the seven *middot*, the characteristics of God. They are peace, righteousness, justice, kindness, compassion, truth, and wisdom. Let's look closely at each of these:

> And I [God] will abolish the bow, the sword, and war from the land;
> and I will make you lie down in safety [Peace].
> And I will espouse you forever,
> I will espouse you to me in Righteousness and in Justice, and with Kindness
> and with Compassion. And
> I will espouse you with faithfulness [Truth]
> and you will come to know God [Wisdom].
>
> Hosea 2:18–20

Peace (shalom) In Judaism, peace is generally seen as the pinnacle of all values and the sum total of them all. *Shalom* means being at one with yourself and the world. *Shalom* means walking with God in life and in death. *Shalom* is found in our breath, and in our bearing. *Shalom,* in its fullest sense, is the ability to accept anything that life brings us, without losing face and without losing faith. In the workplace, *shalom* is found only when all those involved with their work have a sense of purpose. But personal *shalom* is possible even in a world of confusion and conflict.

Righteousness (mishpat)   This quality reminds us to follow rules and procedures, after reflecting on them and recognizing their rationale. It tells us that a society based on rules is necessary for fairness. Little things like putting back the tape or refilling the coffee pot may seem trivial, but if some people do it and some don't, a collegial work atmosphere can be damaged. Righteousness also focuses on the ways we correct broken relationships and environments. It encourages us to face difficult situations rather than ignore them.

Justice (tzedek)   This is the deeper sense of morality that is the cornerstone of work and life. A work environment, however fair and pleasant, can't be just if its ultimate purpose is harmful. A worker is obligated to ask, "Does the goal of my work add to the sanctity of the world and its creatures?" As in all things, ignorance about this is not a valid excuse. It is the obligation of business owners and directors and their employees to all understand the ultimate effect of the work effort.

Kindness (chesed)   "Love," "kindness," or "lovingkindness" are all attempts to translate the Hebrew word *chesed,* which is, essentially, an attitude. Its goal is to bring to every person and every situation the most positive and accepting heart. It may be found in trying to love the "other" as you do yourself. *Chesed* is found in a smile, a loving touch, a sympathetic look. *Chesed* is also found in the words we choose to speak and the voice in which we speak them. For people who have a close relationship to God, it is seeing God in each person and animal. Or it may be approximated by seeing in each person the value that you place in your closest human relations. *Chesed* means that you are my brother and my sister, my lover and my friend—even if we meet in a perfunctory business situation.

Compassion (rachamim)   Compassion is the deep empathy that we bring to a broken situation. It is the empathetic pain we feel when another being is hurting. It is the attempt to see the best in everyone, and to recognize that failure is a common bond between people. True compassion is not pity. Our pity pushes us away; our compassion draws us near. Compassion is most difficult when the other person pushes us away in hurt and anger. This is not unusual in a work setting. *Rachamim* helps us overcome our ego and understand the pain that causes people to act in ways that are counterproductive or hurtful.

Truth (emet)   Truth encourages us to get to the heart of the matter. It does not require us to say hurtful things. Truth may be something that we must keep inside ourselves and share with no one. Truth is that which tells us to go deep inside and discover our authentic self. Truth, even when unspoken, may be disquieting or painful, but it cannot be ignored. In the workplace, being conscious of the truth (what's really going on around us) may mean giving up position, salary, and security. It may take time to find, but once discovered it is a constant presence. Truth is what remains when everything else has passed away.

Wisdom (hokhma)   This quality enjoins us to be thoughtful and deliberate. It tells us to focus on the larger picture of our work. It can be reinforced at the beginning of each day by reviewing a professional oath or by reading a brief statement we might write about our purpose in pursuing a particular line of work. Wisdom also reminds us that work is only one aspect of our lives. The message of *hokhma* is balance. In traditional Judaism, wisdom is often personified as a woman who is the "receiver" or, in broader terms, a partner. Wisdom is also often synonymous with holy study in all its forms.

When we operate from these seven principles, we participate in the work of healing and we bring the world closer to the Days of *Shalom*—the manifestation of the Divine in the world.[2] We also recognize that one characteristic can come into conflict with another. Truth without compassion can be brutal. Wisdom may overwhelm peace if it's forced upon a situation. In work, as in life, there is the mitigating factor of "balance." It is in the balancing of needs, responsibilities, and legitimate desires that the work of life is found. When we balance spiritual introspection and healing, work and play, creating and resting, we follow the Divine Plan and *walk in the ways of the*

Holy One. We find that we are in the world in a way that minimizes the anger, conflict, and damage that are so easy to inflict when we are not balanced in work and relationships. By practicing the seven *middot* with balance, we bring holiness and healing into the world.

Walking the Path: My Work, My Job—*Middot,* or The Seven Characteristics of Work

ACTIVITY

As you think about work, consider the seven *middot* as described above. Make some notes about how you manifest each of these principles at work. Know that when you act in ways that express peace, righteousness, justice, kindness, compassion, truth, and wisdom you are repairing the world. Consider making journal entries for the next few days that reflect your growing awareness of *walking in the ways of the Holy One.*

KAVANAH: AWAKENING

As co-creators, we are responsible for the "world that is constantly coming." Through our behavior, we cause the seven Divine characteristics to manifest. If we doubt the importance of our actions and intentions, we separate ourselves from the Divine Force, the Eternal Oneness of which we are a part.

• • •

My daughter, who's dedicated to building a world in which animals are treated humanely, is a vegetarian. One evening at the dinner table (when she was just eight years old), she began to express her "truth" to her meat-eating (and meat-enjoying) father and brother. In her zealousness, she criticized their eating habits and tried to sway them to her way of thinking. They became offended and upset with her. The very compassion she wanted to teach them about was lost in the harshness of what she said.

This was an important teaching moment for all four of us. We've all had times when we felt certain about a truth or believed that an injustice was being perpetrated. In our attempt to get others to see our point of view, we've offended, judged, and alienated the very people we want to influence. Perhaps there are times when this is unavoidable. Our challenge is to struggle with keeping a balance to avoid forcing an issue, while trusting the growth process in hopes that we can live truth and seek justice in the spirit of peace and the wholeness of God. (kbw)

• • •

CREATIVE BLESSING

"Blessed are You, the Eternal One our God, Teacher of Universal Peace, in my study and practice be my Guide. May I deepen my capacity for lovingkindness. May I grow in wisdom. May I love truth and work for justice. May I bring peace."

Study: My Work, My Job— Honesty, Fairness, Truth

"You shall not have alternate weights, a larger and a smaller. You shall not have alternate measures, a larger and a smaller. You must have completely honest weights and completely honest measures, if you are to endure long on the soil that the Holy One your God is giving you."

—DEUTERONOMY 25:13–15

We recognize the issues of honesty and fairness in trade discussed in this Torah passage. The Torah gives very concrete and immutable directives about the essential importance of honesty and fairness in all our transactions. It is our job to reshape the world to conform more closely

Do not wrong one another, be in awe of your God; I YHWH [the Eternal One] am your God.
Leviticus 25:17

with what we perceive as the Divine ideal. We do this by trying to reduce the uncertainties of existence and by participating in life with consistent fairness and honesty.

There may be times when we operate from secular or economic standards and behave in ways that we know are not just, honest, and fair because "we can get away with it since no one will know about it. And if they do, who cares? Everyone does it."

O Holy One, who will sojourn in Your tent?
Who will dwell on Your holy hill?
The person who walks blamelessly,
and does what is right,
and speaks truth from the heart . . .

Psalm 15:1–2

But God tells us there are not different standards for honesty, fairness, and truth. We have the capacity to become conscious of the Divine Truth deep within our hearts, and to live by these standards every day, not just when it's convenient or to our advantage. Opening ourselves to deeper truth can be very powerful and very difficult, sometimes filled with a struggle between our ego's need for gratification, convenience, or power, and our soul's need to connect to the Holy One and Truth. Remember to be gentle and thoughtful with yourself. If you determine that some changes are needed in your work or the way you do business, make them without harshness or judgment. Trust in your ability to make positive changes, to become all that you are capable of becoming.

Walking the Path: My Work, My Job— Honesty, Fairness, Truth

We are taught that all of Torah (Divine Wisdom) is within us at birth. The Torah needed to be written down to assure that we would not forget its wisdom: studying Torah simply "reminds" us about what we already knew when we were born. We are also taught that each generation is responsible for seeking Torah's deeper meanings, the Eternal Wisdom, for its own time. It is our job to translate the Divine Wisdom of Torah for today's world—to enliven and renew the fire in our daily work.

ACTIVITY

Just as an acorn contains all the knowledge necessary to become the mighty oak, the seeds of humanity contain all the knowledge needed to grow into the Divine Image in which we were designed. We don't need to be taught Divine Truth, but we may need to be reminded of it. Consider the following statements. Can you imagine that all of us are born with this knowledge?

- Hold on to only what belongs to you. Do not steal.

- Share your abundance—and abundance will return to you.

- Use only what you need. Live simply and wisely.

- Respect all life. Do not kill anything needlessly.

- It is right that you were born. You are here to serve your purpose.

- Experience joy. It is your birthright.

- You are part of the whole called the Universe, all of which is God's Creation.

Write down other truths you think we were born knowing:

-

-

• • •

We live in an age in which relativism is a frequent byword: What is "true" for me may not be "true" for you. I often wonder if I can ever get beyond my own ego to see the world as others see it. In my better moments, I look at the person across from me and really try to see reality through his or her eyes. Truth comes when my identity and the identity of the other begin to merge. That is when I recognize that the Truth is not found within me, but within a larger context of the Divine where all egos and interests merge into a Unity. Getting there is not easy. (jlm)

• • •

KAVANAH: AWAKENING

Our spiritual path has everything to do with our search for Divine Truth and translating it into action. Consider the following meditation which is based on Psalm 51:6, and look deeply into your heart for the Truth that awaits your consciousness.

> Behold, You desire Truth in my inward being;
> therefore, teach me wisdom, O God, in my secret heart.

Study: My Work, My Job— Honoring Life

Another important guiding principle in Judaism is *choosing life*. In considering how we make a living, we'll want to discern how "doing our job" (making a living) reflects a commitment to strengthen our communities locally and globally, to support the well-being of those we work with and to honor life in all its many forms.

You have granted me life and steadfast love; and Your care has preserved my spirit.
Job 10:12

"Choosing life" means being concerned about how our work affects the environment: "The earth belongs to the Eternal One and the fullness thereof, the world and those who dwell therein" (Psalm 24:1). The sense that the earth sustains life makes its preservation the highest *mitzvah* (sacred behavior) since it is the only way life can be maintained.

Therefore choose life, that you and your descendants may live.
Deuteronomy 30:19

Judaism understands that holiness resides in the natural world. From the burning bush, God told Moses to "take off your sandals, for the ground on which you stand is holy" (Exodus 3:5). By

The earth mourns and withers, the world languishes and withers; the heavens languish together with the earth. The earth lies polluted under its inhabitants; for they have transgressed the laws, violated the statutes, broken the everlasting covenant.
Isaiah 24:4–5

extension, the Rabbis understood that all of Creation was as
sacred as its Creator.

You have given us dominion over
the works of Your hands;
You have put all things under our feet.
Psalm 8:6

Therefore, we are enjoined
to be a caretaker of God's Cre-
ation in our work. God has given to each of us stewardship of the
earth and directed us to "choose life." May we be conscious of this responsibility and fulfill our role earnestly.

Walking the Path:
My Work, My Job—Honoring Life

How we choose to make a living can reflect a deep consideration for
the impact our work has on life. This is quite different from choosing
our job only because of its income potential or choosing to do work
simply because of job availability. The opportunity to consider job
choice is likely to come up many times in our lives. Devoting time to
such deliberation may be very helpful the next time you consider a
job change.

ACTIVITY

Consider what it means to "choose life." List some ways you can
"choose life" in work. Be mindful of all the ways of preserving and enhancing the quality of life. Recognize our interconnection with the
entire world around you and list all the ways that you can care for all
beings and also honor the earth. What are your recycling/reusing practices? How does your work affect animals? What do you do to minimize any negative environmental results from your work? Does your
work strengthen the community? Does it somehow help the needy?

Now that you've listed how you "choose life" in work, how do
you feel about yourself? About your work?

Are there any changes you would like to initiate?

• • •

Standing over the bed of a young man who is attached to machines
and tubes and is fighting desperately for his life, I hold his hand and

pray. At moments like these, I am reminded how very precious and tenuous life really is. Every day, people die under a variety of circumstances. My work gives me rare glimpses into the deepest mysteries of human existence. While being grateful for the opportunities to serve others, I am often overwhelmed by the apparent unfairness of our individual fates and our tenuous hold on life. At those moments, my faith is my only hope for balance and strength. (jlm)

. . .

KAVANAH: AWAKENING

We're going to return now to the *Sh'ma*. As you may recall, the *Sh'ma* begins: "Hear O Israel, the Eternal One is our God, the Eternal One is One." Continuing to read in Deuteronomy (6:8), we come to these directions: "And you shall bind them [these words] as a sign upon your hand, and they shall be as frontlets between your eyes." We recognize that this scripture directs us to place *tefilin* (prayer boxes wrapped with leather) on our left arm and our forehead when praying. But spiritually, we're told that everything we do with our "hands" (every action we take in the world) bears witness to the Eternal Oneness, to the Essence of all that was, is—and ever will be.

We're requested to keep this knowledge between our eyes. This is the place that represents our "spiritual eye," which sees the wisdom and the understanding of God.

Open my eyes, that I may know wondrous things out of Your Torah.
Psalm 119:18

When we reach our hand out into the world, we are asked to be conscious of the Divine Oneness and "see" the unity and the interconnection of which we are a part.

Study: My Work, My Job— The Soul's Joyful Work

"It is God's gift to humanity that every one should . . . take pleasure in all his/her work" (Ecclesiastes 3:13). When we do what we love, when work emerges from our desire to create and to connect and to contribute to the well-being of others, we're truly working from our soul. Our work can reflect God's work because it offers repeated opportunities to bring into the present *all that can be*. True work contributes to liberation and freedom, justice and righteousness. True work repairs the world, honors life, heals the pain of hatred and oppression—and frees the heart to love fully.

Each of us is born to uniquely contribute work to our community. Part of the spiritual process is identifying and developing our work. The other part of the process is striving to live in accordance with the precepts and the *mitzvot* of Creation—the Eternal Words.

It may be frightening to accept responsibility for our work. "I just want to do my job," we might say. "I don't know how I can transform the world. I'm not a healer." But we forget that we are made in the image of the Holy One and that our job is simply a vehicle for expressing our purpose, for living in accordance with Torah and with Truth. The following story suggests how this can be done:

It has been shown you,
O humanity, what is good;
and what the Holy One requires of you;
to do justice, and to love compassion,
and to walk humbly with your God.

Micah 6:8

Rabbi Yitzhak of Vorki, his memory [is] for a blessing, told of how once he was together with his master, Rabbi David of Lelov at sunrise. The *rebbe* was enrobed in his *talit* and crowned in *tefilin,* ready to pray the Morning Prayer, when a Gentile came in, pounded on the table and asked that he sell him a quantity of liquor. [It seems that in the *rebbe's* house—this was before he became famous— there was a store where liquor was sold.] There was no one else in the house then to sell it to him, so the *rebbe* himself went with alacrity, measured it out himself, and put it before the man. [When asked about this by Rabbi Yitzhak, who was amazed at how the *rebbe* would leave off his preparation for prayer to do some business], the *rebbe* explained to him softly, "Listen to me, my sweet friend. My path in the service of God is 'Know Him in all your ways'. . . So when I went to measure out the liquor, my whole intention was to fulfill the Torah's *mitzvah* about honest measures and to give pleasure to God by this; and that is why I happily ran to do it with such haste."[3]

Rabbi Abraham Joshua Heschel said that the only sin is humanity's "refusal to be who we are." This is not a narcissistic sense of greatness, but a deep, humbling awareness of our capacity—the significance of our actions and our life. Too often, we believe that we are small and insignificant, that what we say and do has no effect on the world's pain and injustice. But as Heschel advised, "Know that every deed counts, that every word is power. . . . Above all, remember that you must build your life as if it were a work of art. . . ."[4]

Walking the Path: My Work, My Job— The Soul's Joyful Work

KEEP A JOURNAL

Write about the last project which brought you "joyful purpose." What was the source of joy? Were you using your gifts and talents? Were you enjoying the abilities of your body and mind? Were you serving, contributing, creating? Were you connecting what you were doing with Divine purpose?

Now, write about the mundane work you do each day: driving in the carpool, doing the dishes, crunching numbers, doing physical labor—whatever you find repetitive and joyless. Imagine doing that same task with intention to serve God—serving your children, your partner, your friend, your community, yourself. Imagine focusing on the wonders of creation as a way to experience the joy inherent in life. How does this change your feelings about "mundane work?"

KAVANAH: AWAKENING

Of the pious man, Heschel wrote, "It is not his destiny to accomplish but to contribute, and his will to serve shapes his entire conduct."[5] Let's examine our own motivations for work: What are we trying to accomplish? What sort of contribution do we want to make? To what and to whom? Are we working only to enhance our position and to satisfy ego's needs? Or are we considering how our work contributes to liberation, freedom, justice, and righteousness?

• • •

I've been fortunate that my "job" as a nurse and psychotherapist lets me express my "soul's work"; it's easy for me to bring spirit into my job. With recent changes in medicine brought about by managed care, however, I struggle with the lack of value placed on the thera-peutic relationship, which is very important to me. So, I've sought new ways to preserve the joyfulness and the spirit of my work. I've declined working with certain managed care companies. I've in-creased the number of courses and seminars I teach. I've joined the Adult Education Committee at my temple. And I write with my friend and rabbi. Finding ways to hold on to what's important takes energy and means some loss and change, but it's been well worth the effort. (kbw)

• • •

Creative Blessing (Based on Psalm 16:11)

"Blessed are You, the Eternal One our God, Force of Steadfast Love, You show me the path of life. In Your presence there is joyfulness; in Your right hand (my ac-tions which heal the world) are pleasures forevermore."

We've studied many of the Jewish values associated with work and we've considered how our jobs can be vehicles for spiritual work. Along with meeting our spiritual goals, we also work for "a living." In Judaism, it is honorable to make a fair livelihood. Let's turn now to spiritual practices associated with money.

Study: Money—Making a Living, Borrowing from the Earth

Land, livestock, and harvest were the "monies" of the ancient Is-raelites. These goods-of-the-earth determined "wealth." Today, we don't exchange a lamb for tools. We use money to buy commodities and goods. Few of us rely on our gardens for food; we simply choose food off the shelves at the local grocery store. And none of us would chop down a tree to make paper. Money lets us separate ourselves from our relationship with the earth, which is the source of the raw materials we depend on to do business and to sustain a liv-

But ask now the beasts,
and they will teach you;
the birds of the air,
and they will tell you;
or speak to the earth,
and the earth will teach you;
and the fish of the sea will declare to you.
Job 12:7–8

ing. Our spiritual work can make us more aware of the environmental impact of what we buy, how we spend our money and how we invest it.

Walking the Path: Money—Making a Living, Borrowing from the Earth

Learning to live more simply is a common outcome of the spiritual journey. As we reestablish a sense of connection with all life, we may develop uncomfortable feelings about unnecessarily consuming resources. We may dislike living disconnected from the environment once we are more aware of the impact we have on it.

KAVANAH: AWAKENING

For the Eternal One your God
is bringing you into a good land
a land of flowing streams,
with springs and underground waters
welling up in valleys and hills,
a land of wheat and barley,
of vines and fig trees and pomegranates,
a land of olive trees and honey,
a land where you may eat bread without scarcity,
where you will lack nothing,
a land whose stones are iron
and from whose hills you may mine copper.
You shall eat your fill
and bless the Eternal One your God

for the good land
the Source of All Life has given you.
                    —Deuteronomy 8:7–11

Eternal One, Source of all there is and ever will be,
speak to me from every corner of Your Creation. I want
to better recognize my relationship with the earth and
respond to the needs of my sisters and brothers, my
neighbors, and the stranger—Your creatures. Teach me
to live simply, to take no more than I need, to honor
and celebrate this wonderful habitat You have given for
my use and sustenance.

• • •

*Every once in a while, I put down a dollar to play the state lottery
game when the "payoff" is over $5 million. Fantasizing over what I
would do with the windfall, I reflect on whether I would continue in
my "day job" or just live a life of leisure. Invariably, I quickly understand that a good part of my self-image and esteem comes from
my profession, and that my life would be much emptier without it.
Yet, on a day-to-day basis, my work can be taxing, frustrating, even
boring. It also can be exciting, challenging, and spiritually reward-
ing. As in most things, my own attitude determines the tenor of my
life—and especially of my work. (jlm)*

• • •

Study: Money—A Trust from God

Our success, ultimately, depends on God. This is very important to
remember as we consider our ability to earn a living. We're told to
enjoy work, enjoy wealth, enjoy good fortune—and to remember that
the flow of milk and honey is from the Source of All Life. Like everything in life, money and wealth should be seen as a trust from God.
Use it well and wisely, but be ready to surrender it without protest.

Money and wealth do not necessarily corrupt, but, if we're not
careful, they can mask the higher goals of life. Materialism can

ensnare the unsuspecting heart. If we seek joy and satisfaction in money, we're likely to find ourselves on a vicious treadmill: acquiring money while starving our soul. Achieving a middle ground—enjoying work, enjoying money, living in accordance with God's ways—is one of the greatest challenges of life.

Beware lest you say in your heart,
"My power and the might of my hand
have gotten me this wealth."
You shall remember the Eternal One your God,
for it is the Eternal One who gives you power
to get wealth.

Deuteronomy 8:17–18

Walking the Path: Money—A Trust from God

KAVANAH: AWAKENING

Love not sleep, lest you come to poverty;
open your eyes, and you will have abundance.

—Proverbs 20:13

Remember that true spiritual abundance comes from opening our eyes to the Eternal One. If we mistake making money as the source of happiness, we will be profoundly poor in spirit. Acquiring wealth is all well and good, but "the beginning of wisdom is reverence for God" (Proverbs 1:7). May we have much wisdom in our relationship with money.

• • •

I have a piece of paper on which I have listed all the assets and liabil-
ities that I have accumulated over my first fifty years of life. It is
both comforting and a bit frightening to know that these numbers fit
so easily on a single page. Sometimes, when I feel insecure (and
these insecurities are often related to money), I take out that paper. I
try to remind myself that when I leave this earth, all those numbers
will be redistributed in a thousand ways, but the goodness I have
done and the love I have given will be undivided. Overcoming my
insecurities about money is a lifelong challenge. In some ways, I
hope that the single page will be blank when I die, that my heart,
soul, and pocketbook will be totally spent. (jlm)

• • •

CREATIVE BLESSING (BASED ON PSALM 16:8)

"Blessed are You, the Eternal One, Provider of insight and bread, I try to set You before me always and know that my good fortune, my sustenance, my life is from Your hand."

Study: Money—
The Flow of Abundance, *Tsedakah*

Explaining that abundance depended on the flow of money from one person to the next, the Rabbis told a parable about the difference between Lake Kinneret (the Sea of Galilee), in which fish and vegetation flourish, and the Dead Sea where nothing lives. Kinneret, they explained, receives water from the Jordan River, and then the Kinneret's own water flows back to the river. So the lake stays alive. The Dead Sea receives water from the Jordan, but does not give it forth. Since the Dead Sea takes without sharing, it deadens itself.[6]

Because we live in a culture that values how much money we make and does not assure a fair redistribution of wealth, we may be reluctant to give money away. Some people want to have "enough" money in the bank before they give any to others. Some may feel that they only have enough money to meet their own needs and can't give any money away. Others may not have enough money to meet their needs, and rely on others for sufficient money.

When you reap the harvest of your land, you shall not reap your field to its very border, neither shall you gather the gleanings after your harvest. And you shall not strip your vineyard bare, neither shall you gather the fallen grapes of your vineyard; you shall leave them for the poor and for the sojourner; I am the Eternal One your God.
Leviticus 19:9–10

Judaism gives us specific guidance about "social responsibility." Because we are all part of a greater whole, there are times when we give to others and times when we are in need from others. What we are able to give at any point in time and what we need from each other may vary, but the awareness of our interdependence drives our responsibility for giving in whatever ways we can. *Tsedakah* refers to giving money, food, clothing, or goods as part of our social responsibility: responding to the needs of others while being grateful for the opportunity to contribute. *Tsedakah* is expected of everyone in the community. Even the poorest person who receives from others can offer something if another person is in need. Giving *tsedakah* extends from our loved ones to the larger family, the community, and the global community, Jews and non-Jews alike. By eliminating poverty, we heal the world and move closer to the days of Wholeness. Until we eliminate poverty, we are responsible for sharing what we've been given.

> *All the tithe of the land,*
> *whether of the seed of the land or*
> *of the fruit of the trees, is the Eternal One's;*
> *it is holy to the Eternal One.*
>
> Leviticus 27:30

The twelfth-century philosopher Moses ben Maimon (who was also known as Maimonides or Rambam) proposed eight levels of worth in *tsedakah*. Arthur Waskow writes about them this way:

- "The highest level, providing someone with the wherewithal to make a living so as no longer to need *tsedakah;*

- "Next, giving in such a way that the giver did not know who received the gift and the receiver did not know who gave it. In this way, Maimonides thought, people would be doing *tsedakah* for its own sake as a religious act, not in exchange for honor or renown; and the dignity of the recipient would be protected against the tendency to kowtow to a donor;

- "Sixth, the recipient is known but not the donor (especially useful if the donor is not behaving honorably—perhaps has made the money in a lawful but not honorable way?);

- "Fifth, the donor is known but not the recipient (thus honoring the rich but preventing them from overawing the poor);

- "Fourth, giving from hand to hand, without being asked;

- "Third, giving from hand to hand, but only after the poor person has asked;

- "Second, giving in a friendly way, but less money than is appropriate; and

- "The lowest level, giving with a scowl."[7]

Giving *tsedakah* every day is important, and it is preferable to give a little often rather than a large sum infrequently. It is also important to preserve the integrity of the recipient. It's difficult enough to be in need; our task is to make receiving as comfortable as possible.

As the recipient of *tsedakah*, we realize that God's help comes in many different forms. We should make the best use of what we receive and be mindful of others who may also be in need. And we should remember that giving and receiving are best done with the intention to serve God.

If you pour yourself out for the hungry
and satisfy the desire of the afflicted,
then shall your light rise in the darkness and
your gloom be as the noonday.
And the Lord will guide you continually, and
satisfy your desire with good things, and
make your bones strong;
and you shall be like a watered garden,
like a spring of water, whose waters fail not.
Isaiah 58:10–11

Tsedakah can remind us that all we have belongs to God and that we are briefly holding it in trust. *Tsedakah* is an important way to resist the tendency to measure our lives by what we have rather than by what we do.

Share your bread with the hungry,
and bring the homeless poor into your house;
and when you see the naked, clothe him . . .
Isaiah 58:7

ACTIVITY

Consider having a *tsedakah* purse or *tsedakah* box to which you add money daily. You can carry a purse with you so money is always available to give to someone or some cause. The box can sit on a table or a desk in your home as a reminder to give each day.

Find an amount of money to give that is comfortable, affordable, and meaningful. To help you with this, the Torah offers a guideline called tithing: giving 10 percent of the money you earn. But only you will determine what is right for you.

. . .

My son has often expressed concern for people who are homeless and without adequate food. At age five, he came to me and explained that if everyone in the world who had money would give one penny, no one would be without food. Whether this would hold up to an economist's formula, Ben's heartfelt wish communicates the truth about tsedakah *and our responsibility for relieving the deep pain of hunger. (kbw)*

. . .

KAVANAH: AWAKENING

"More than what the householder does for the poor person, the poor person does for the householder" (Leviticus *Rabbah* 34:10). When we give *tsedakah,* we're offered an opportunity to serve the Eternal One. This is the gift that the poor person gives when we're able to help someone in need. We are returning to the Source of All Life that which belongs to all of us in the Eternal Oneness. Giving away money, time, and talents (within reason) helps create the flow of abundance that supports life.

Conclusion: Our True Wealth

Freud said that the true fulfillment of humanity is "to work and to love." Our work is about bringing quality to life, solving problems, experiencing pleasure, and recognizing the Divine in all that surrounds us.

The ultimate gift we pass along from one generation to the next is a sense of "values," and the value of life is not measured by the amount of money we have or what we can buy with it. The value of life comes from living life fully in the ways of the Universal Truth, the ways of the Eternal One.

Wealth and riches are in the Eternal One's house; and the Eternal One's righteousness endures forever.
Psalm 112:3

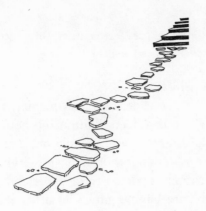

NOON: MEALTIME, GRATITUDE, HOSPITALITY

At noon I will pray and the Eternal One will hear my voice.

—Psalm 55:17

• • •

I often wonder at the Divine wisdom of making human beings so dependent on physical sustenance. We think of food at the most inappropriate times. When we think our hearts and souls "should" be directed toward some lofty point or when we "should" be overwhelmed by grief or remorse, there is still that constant nagging in our consciousness: "I am hungry. I want to taste food in my mouth." Though this may seem like a cruel trick that God plays on us, I finally see it as a wonderful gift. Yes, we may be a little lower than the angels, but even the holiest human being cannot go for long without food and water. This understanding keeps us humble and makes us realize that there is an infinite chasm between us and God. When we understand that, we can continue to strive for holiness without becoming self-righteous or pietistic. How wise is our Creator. (jlm)

• • •

Food is life: "Feed me with the food that is needful for me" (Proverbs 30:8). Food for our bodies; nourishment for our souls. In considering mealtime activities, we'll explore how, in Judaism, there is a deep relationship between food and the Source of Life—the Eternal One. In Judaism, eating is not simply a biological need for sustenance (although preserving life is, in itself, sacred). It is a spiritual opportunity to experience the Divine. The "foods of the earth" are Divine gifts. Our attitudes toward food and mealtime reflect our awareness of the sacred. On a spiritual level, we are asked to be mindful of our relationship with the Eternal Oneness, with our interdependence with all Creation as we choose, prepare, and consume the foods of the earth. This includes attention to the environment: how we care for the land and attend to our relationships, how we care for animals, how we share food with our neighbor and with the stranger.

Not by bread alone does a man [or woman] live, but by every word that proceeds out of the mouth of the Eternal One.

Deuteronomy 8:3

A righteous man has regard for the soul of his beast.
Proverbs 12:10

Study: Connecting to Our History

Food plays a central role in the practice of Judaism. The Creation story quickly turns toward eating forbidden fruit. This is only the beginning of much discussion of food and eating. In the days of the Temple, foods were brought for sacrifice to honor God, the Source and Sustainer of Life. By offering animals and produce through sacrifice, the ancient Jews honored their profound dependence on God, both physical and spiritual. They also acknowledged that *their* bounty was a gift from the Source of Life by returning some measure, often the best they had, through sacrifice. The process of

And you shall eat and be full and you shall bless the Eternal One your God for the good land the One has given you.
Deuteronomy 8:10

sacrifice at the Temple maintained a meaningful ritual that secured the connection between food—the blessings of the Eternal One— and the ancient Jews' deep gratitude for life.

After the Temple was destroyed, and sacrifices could no longer be made, the Rabbis, recognizing the profound importance of ritual practices, translated the "Temple sacrifice" into rituals for the home. The Rabbis faced a difficult task when translating Temple practices into home practices. Without the Temple, they concluded that actual "sacrifices" of food had to be symbolically replaced with "sacrifices" of words. As our ancestors became less dependent on their own foods and moved into cities throughout the Diaspora, as trade and commerce distanced them from the earth, their prayers at the "home altar" (their dining table) reminded them of the deep connection to God that food-as-offerings had once provided at the Temple altar in Jerusalem. As Rabbi Michael Lerner has written,

> Thus, each table becomes a mini-altar to God; each act of eating becomes an occasion to reconnect to the world and to straighten up our relationship to it. We wash our hands and bless God for that opportunity, bless the bread and thank God for having made this produce possible, and we end the meal with a long blessing thanking God for the food, for the abundant land, and for all the wonderful things in our lives.[1]

Blessings were prescribed; times for prayer were set. Each step of the way, the rabbis carefully considered how best to guide the Jew through a time of transition and loss. Rules, laws, prescriptions were all attempts to give the community something meaningful to hold on to, to identify with, to maintain hope and faith, to secure a Jewish way of life that would endure and reflect God's ways.

If you set your heart right,
You will stretch out your hands toward the Holy One. . . .
And your life will be brighter than the noonday;
its darkness will be like the morning.
And you will have confidence, because there is hope . . .
Job 11:13, 17–18

"This is the table which is before the Eternal One" (Ezekiel 41:22). It is in this context that we sit down to a meal: God is present. This is why we dress the Sabbath table in a white cloth and choose special adornments; why we have special prayers of acknowledgment and thanksgiving; why we wash our hands before eating; why we dip our bread in salt ("With all offerings you shall offer salt": Leviticus 2:13). These traditions are stored in our collective memories; they rekindle the deep gratitude for life that Jews have expressed to the Sustainer of Life for generation after generation.

Walking the Path: Connecting to Our History

One way of connecting to our history is taking an ancient ritual and applying it to everyday life. This is what the Rabbis did when they converted the Temple rituals of sacrifice to home rituals. Consider the following activities and rituals as part of your meal time of holiness.

ACTIVITIES

Washing the Hands

In Judaism, washing is an act of ritual as well as cleanliness, especially since the meal reflects the ancient sacrificial rite of the Temple. We come before God with "pure hands and a pure heart." The custom of using a vessel to pour the water over the hands symbolizes the ancient libation ceremonies. Even if we wash our hands from the tap, we can still be cognizant that we are engaging in a rite of purification.

Become aware as you wash your hands before a meal that you are doing so to come before the Eternal One with pure hands and a pure heart. To enhance mindfulness, you may prefer to place the water in a pitcher or glass and pour gently over one hand and then the other. The following is the traditional blessing:

TRADITIONAL *BRAKHA*

"Blessed are You, Eternal One our God, Divine Presence in the Universe, You make us Holy by mitzvot *(sacred activities) and have given us the ritual of washing hands."*

Traditionally a meal in Judaism begins with bread, which is dipped in salt or sprinkled with it. This is preceded by the blessing for bread, which symbolically blesses the entire meal. The centrality of bread reflects a deep human reality: Bread is, indeed, the staff of life. It was a constant in the Temple, as was salt. All animal offerings were made with salt, which drew forth the last vestiges of blood; blood was absolutely prohibited in these sacrifices since it contained the "life force." Bread and salt recall the rites of the ancient Temple, and affirm the table as *mikdash m'aht,* as a sanctuary in miniature.

On Shabbat, two loaves of bread are customarily used at dinner to remind us that the Israelites gathered a double portion of manna on Friday, so no gathering was necessary on Shabbat.

Begin your next meal by lightly sprinkling salt onto a small portion of bread. Then say the traditional blessing: *Baruch atah Adonai, Eloheinu melech ha-olam, hamotzi lechem min ha-aretz.* "Blessed are You, the Eternal One our God, Divine Presence in the Universe, who brings forth bread from the earth." Let yourself be connected to *mitzvot,* and to the ancient rituals that have guided the Jewish people for thousands of years and provide a spiritual gateway to the Divine.

• • •

At the Passover seder, food makes us cognizant that we are part of a great historical continuum. As a modern Jew, I hear the ancient words with a totally different consciousness than did my ancient forebears. But the taste of the matzah must be virtually the same to me as it was to them. And the maror, the bitter herb, I am convinced contorted their faces exactly as it contorts mine. By the fourth cup of wine, their heads were spinning just as mine does today. The taste of food is our truest link with the past and reminds us, as nothing else can, that "this [eating of the bread] is because of what the Eternal did for me when I went forth from Egypt." (jlm)

• • •

KAVANAH: AWAKENING

Pause to see the dining table as an altar, as a place of God's presence, and consider the following:

I wash my hands in innocence, and go about Your altar, O Eternal One, singing aloud a song of thanksgiving, and telling all Your wondrous deeds.
Psalm 26:6–7

"Rabbi Levi Yitzhak of Berditchev told how Queen Esther made a meal with such holiness and purity that holiness rested on each and every dish of food, and on the table and all its utensils."[2]

Bring holiness to your table.

Study: Mealtime:
What—and How—We Eat Matters

The deep relationship between food and the Source of All Life continued to unfold as the Eternal One guided our attention toward food through restriction and consciousness. As Genesis 2:16–17 says:

> "Behold, I have given you all plants that bring forth seeds that are upon the face of all the earth, and all trees in which there is tree fruit that brings forth seeds; you shall have them for food."
> But God said, "You shall not eat of the fruit of the tree which is in the midst of the garden . . ."

In the beginning, the Eternal One spread before us a vast array of plants for food. It is conceivable that, before the flood of Noah's time, God had hoped we would be satisfied with a vegetarian diet. (In fact, the prophet Isaiah imagined a return to vegetarianism in the "world to come": "The wolf shall dwell with the lamb . . . and the lion shall eat straw like the ox . . . and none shall hurt or destroy in all of God's holy mountain" [Isaiah 11:6–9].) But, after the flood, God expanded the menu to include "every moving thing that lives shall be food for you; and as I gave you the green plants, I give you everything. Only you shall not eat flesh with its life, that is, its blood" (Genesis 9:3–4).

The Eternal One couples abundance—"I give you everything"—with specific prohibitions called the laws of *kashrut,* the dietary laws. There are many interpretations of these laws. As we look at what many of them have in common, we identify acts of "self-control" and themes of "separation." Much of what we do regarding food involves being conscious about it and maintaining self-control while separating the everyday from the sacred and the holy. One way that we can stay compassionate and conscious when eating animal foods is to follow the laws of *kashrut,* which insists that animals be killed in the most pain-free manner by a holy person who follows the mandate *Tsa'ar bal'alei hayim,* "Do not cause sorrow to any living creature."

One of the deepest aspects of the Jewish tradition is the idea of *kashrut.* For the ancient Rabbis, who like many Jews today understood the laws of Torah as pure acts of Divine will, these restrictions and requirements were the source of much speculation. Suffice it to say, whether you view the Torah as divinely revealed or merely divinely inspired, no explanation of

> *The Eternal One is good to all,*
> *and God's tender mercies are over all God's creatures.*
> Psalm 145:9

kashrut on the basis of logic will ever be definitive. Therefore, for some people, keeping *kashrut* is the ultimate manifestation of obedience to God; for others, it is an existential choice about being a Jew.

In either case, deciding to follow the laws of *kashrut* influences growing, purchasing, preparing, and eating food. While *kashrut* may not be an organizing principle for other Jews, they may follow other food restrictions which are also based on ethics and may also require intentionality, such as a variety of "vegetarianisms" or fasting.

All of the above limit in a conscious way what and how we eat. By doing that, we create a sense of autonomy and discipline which may add to the sense of what it means to be human or to be a Jew. The process of choosing, purchasing, preparing, and blessing food—and finally eating it—has many opportunities for spiritual expression.

Through our relationship with food, we can connect ourselves (body, mind, and spirit) with the plant and animal kingdom, the earth (sea and soil), the cosmos (sun and rain), and the Eternal One. When we plan a meal, when we eat with intention, when we separate our minds from everyday pressures and hubbub and enter into the sacred, we take the time to enjoy the miracle of Creation and the unity of life at each and every step.

Walking the Path: Mealtime:
What—and How—We Eat Matters

We will now walk you through a variety of activities, meditations, and blessings for meal preparation and mealtime. These examples are in no way exhaustive and we encourage further study in those areas that interest and inspire you. The first activity focuses on the Oneness of Creation and how Truth awaits in each food we eat. In the next activity, we consider how restriction, separation, and self-control enhance spiritual practice. The third activity investigates why we might follow *mitzvot* (sacred activities) as part of our spiritual practice. From there, we move to meal preparation and mealtime.

Activity: Finding God in a Piece of Bread

"The Kibriner Rabbi turned to his Hasidim and said: 'Do you know where God is?' He took a piece of bread, showed it to them all and continued: 'God is in this piece of bread. Without the mani-

You gave them bread from heaven for their hunger . . .
Nehemiah 9:15

festation of His power in all nature, this piece of bread would have no existence.'"[3]

With a piece of bread, say a prayer of thanksgiving and spend a moment contemplating its origins. Look into the bread to see the baker, the measuring cups, the warm ovens baking the bread; look deeper to see the wheat mill and the raw grain; and look deeper yet to see the wheat fields, the rich soil, the clouds offering rain, the sun making growth possible. See the farmer planting the fields in spring and see the farmer's parents nurturing him or her from childhood. Continue back as far as you like, realizing that "in the beginning" there was only God. This is the unfolding story of Creation and the Eternal One's power of transformation; this is knowing that God is in a piece of bread.

Traditional *Brakha*

Baruch atah Adonai, Eloheinu melech ha-olam, hamotzi lechem min ha-aretz.

"Blessed are You, the Eternal One our God, Divine Presence in the Universe, who brings forth bread from the earth."

ACTIVITY: RESTRICTIONS AS PART OF SPIRITUAL PRACTICE

Fasting for a meal or a day is one way of creating intention in spiritual practice. You may choose to give the food that you purposefully choose not to eat (or the money that represents it) to others. "Is not this the fast that I choose. . . . Is

[A]iding the poor and hungry weigh as heavily as all the other commandments of the Torah combined.

The Talmud

it not to share your bread with the hungry?" (Isaiah 58:6–7).

Fasting, while essentially a spiritual exercise, can make us more understanding about poverty and hunger. But remember that someone who can buy food can never truly understand how pernicious hunger can be. Through this humility, we can open ourselves to the deep cry for help from the hungry that echoes around the world—and we can do whatever is necessary to provide relief.

ACTIVITY: *MITZVOT* AND *KASHRUT*

Following the laws of *kashrut* helps us focus on the holiness of meal preparation and eating. If we accept *mitzvot* as tools to enhance our spiritual development, then they will assist us with sensing "a vision of supreme revelation." Through following the laws of *kashrut,* we walk the spiritual path in a manner that is authentically Jewish. This requires us to submit to rules that supercede our indi-

Mitzvot, in all their minutiae, constitute an endless, moving series of images depicting a vision of supreme revelation.

Rabbi Adin Steinsaltz

vidual autonomy. By relinquishing self-determination and replacing it with the discipline of following the Jewish laws, we may develop a deep devotion and intensity that leads us further along the spiritual path in a profoundly Jewish way.

Review the laws of *kashrut* and consider following those aspects that have meaning for you, that bring a sense of discipline to your practice—aspects of the laws that bring attention to the holiness of mealtime. Associating eating practices with the laws of *kashrut* may help you meaningfully connect to the Jewish tradition and a sense of holiness. Consider writing in your journal about your experiences and feelings about keeping kosher.

• • •

For one week every year during Passover, choosing food becomes a central preoccupation. So many favorite choices—perfectly acceptable during the 51 other weeks—are now forbidden. Even those Jews who are most strict about keeping kosher, who are vegetarians or even vegans, now find that there is another level of restriction. The rationale for the restrictions of Passover have no deep moral basis. These are things we do solely on the basis of our choice to follow Divine tradition. Through these few days each year I learn, once again, that I am an agent of choice, and that, in some small but significant way, I shape my life through what I eat—at Passover and every day of the year. (jlm)

• • •

KAVANAH: AWAKENING

PRAYER FOR YOUR FOOD

O God, sustain and feed, through Your kindness, all Your creatures, from the mighty wild ox with its gigantic horns to the tiny eggs of the smallest insects. Give me my daily bread, and let all those in my house have the food they need easily and not with difficulty, by permissible ways and not forbidden ones, so we can do Your will and study Your Torah and fulfill Your *mitzvot*. Let me not be in need of the gifts of flesh and blood, or of their loans, but only of Your helping hand, which is full, open, holy, and ample. "The eyes of all wait upon Thee, and Thou givest them their food in due season. Thou openest Thine hand and satisfiest every living thing with favor" (Psalm 145:15–16).[4]

Practice mindfulness as you take food out of your cupboard, refrigerator, or garden, or the "ready-made" section of the grocery store, to

satisfy your hunger. Rec-
ognize your anticipation
of taste, your awareness
of nutritional need—all
gifts from God. Notice
the choices you make
and why. Slow down. Do

And the Eternal One will guide you continually,
and satisfy your desire with good things,
and make your bones strong; and
you shall be watered like a garden,
like a spring of water, whose waters fail not.
Isaiah 58:11

you sense the Eternal One's guidance? Be aware of your relationship
with the food you will eat and your relationship with your Sustainer,
the Eternal One. Reflect on how preparing this meal and fueling your
body lets you fulfill your work of repairing the world.

Be creative as you take the time to prepare a sacred space for your
meal. Consider performing a ritual before the meal that is meaningful
to you (for example, saying a prayer as you wash your hands), then
follow it with a blessing:

"Blessed are You, the Eternal One our God, Divine Pres-
ence in the Universe, by whose word everything—the
All—comes into being."

Now begin eating mindfully. And enjoy!

Traditionally a meal is followed with Torah study. After
completing the meal, reflect for
a few minutes on how the nourishment you've just received is
similar to the spiritual nourishment you can receive when
studying Torah.

My son, eat honey, for it is good,
and the drippings of the honeycomb
are sweet to your taste.
Know that wisdom is such to your soul;
if you find it, there will be a future,
and your hope will not be cut off.
Proverbs 24:13–14

ACTIVITY: STUDYING TORAH SWEET AS HONEY

Core, pare, and slice an apple. Pour honey into a small bowl for easy
dipping. Before leaving the
table, choose a portion to study
from Torah or from another inspirational holy book. Reflect
on its meaning. Punctuate your
study time with occasional

Oh how I love Thy Torah!
It is meditation all the day. . . .
How sweet are Thy words to my taste,
sweeter than honey to my mouth!
Psalm 119:97, 103

And the Eternal One said to me,
"Son [or daughter] of humanity,
eat what is offered to you; eat this scroll,
and go, speak to the house of Israel."
So I opened my mouth, and the Eternal One gave me
the scroll to eat. And the Eternal One said to me,
"Son [or daughter] of humanity,
eat this scroll that I give you and
fill your stomach with it." Then I ate it;
and it was in my mouth as sweet as honey.

Ezekiel 3:1–3

pauses so you can mindfully eat a slice of apple dipped in the honey. Let your spirit move effortlessly back and forth between these two realms of delight: the nourishment of the body and the nourishment of the soul! Celebrate.

Completing the meal, we offer another blessing in celebration of life. In this way, mealtime is filled with thanksgiving, joy, and sharing.

CREATIVE BLESSING

"I offer thanks to You, Eternal One, for the sustenance of the food I have just enjoyed. Thanks for the variety of tastes and aromas. May I never take for granted the simple, profound gifts which are mine everyday. May the fullness I enjoy not prevent me from remembering those in need. Help me find the balance between enjoying the goodness of life and the responsibility to share what I have with others. Thank You God."

Study: Hospitality—Sharing Food with Others

Genesis tells of Abraham and Sarah's hospitality to three strangers: "And the Eternal One appeared to him by the oaks of Mamre, as he sat at the door of his tent in the heat of the day. He [Abraham] lifted up his eyes and looked and behold, three men stood in front of him. When he saw them, he ran from the tent door to meet them, and bowed himself to the earth, and said, 'My lords, if I have found favor in your sight, do not pass by your servant. Let a little water be brought, and wash your feet, and rest yourselves under the tree, while I fetch a morsel of bread, that you may refresh yourselves, and after that you may pass on—since you have come to your servant'" (Genesis 18:1–5).

For the Eternal One satisfies him who is thirsty,
and the hungry the Eternal One fills with good things.

Psalm 107:9

This story shows the importance of hospitality, of inviting others into our home and sharing our food with them, particularly those in need: the traveler, the stranger, the poor.

Now, we will learn how to serve the Eternal One by serving others in this life.

In our collective consciousness, we remember that the Eternal One took care of us when we were hungry in the desert. Through our empathy, we try to understand the shame and deprivation that plagues people who don't have basic human necessities. We wish that all can come and eat, that all can be clothed, that all can have shelter.

If your enemy is hungry, give him bread to eat;
and if he is thirsty, give him water to drink.

Proverbs 25:21

When we participate in activities that help others, we feel our "light rise . . . as the noonday" and are profoundly grateful to the Source of Life for the opportunity to help. And the work of *tikkun olam*, healing the world, moves forward another step.

Walking the Path:
Hospitality—Sharing Food with Others

ACTIVITIES FOR SHARING FOOD AND HOSPITALITY

Inviting a guest for a meal is one way to share your blessings with others. For the holidays, men and women in the armed forces often need a place to have special meals while stationed away from their families. Consider inviting a new family in your neighborhood for a simple meal and a welcoming. There are many ways we can share our hospitality. Be creative. Do what reflects you as a person: Sharing food from your garden, bringing fresh zucchini bread into the office for the coffee break, volunteering your living room for a group meeting. In many ways, you can practice sharing and hospitality.

KAVANAH: AWAKENING

Consider the following:

"The Eternal One had visited the people and given them food" (Ruth 1:6).

"The Eternal One loves the sojourner, giving him food and clothing" (Deuteronomy 10:18).

We are reminded that giving to others is a holy act. When we visit others and bring them food, when we give food to those in need, we are following in the ways of the Eternal One.

From a kabbalistic perspective, when we read in the scriptures that the Eternal One feeds the hungry: "Happy is he whose help is the God of Jacob. . . . Who gives food to the hungry" (Psalm 146:5, 7), we understand that we can manifest God's intention. We are the ones who can feed the hungry. Our role in the Creation story is to be midwives to the Divine goal to end hunger and to repair the world.

• • •

We often go away on the weekends to the San Juan Islands. Good friends of ours go there, also. Over the years, many memorable Shabbat dinners, Passover Seders, and lots of casual meals have been served around a large table. Our families have shared stories and laughed. Food preparation is generally a group effort involving contributions from both households. After blessings, we enjoy the blending of flavors from unplanned menus. The children "accidentally" drop scraps of bread for the dog or run off while the grownups solve world problems over one more serving of salad. Dishes are washed by hand while tea is brewed. This scenario is repeated the next day at lunch when leftovers resurface. The cooperation, hospitality, sharing, and love that goes into these meals have built lasting memories. We are blessed with this opportunity—the getaway, the food, the friendship, the history we're building together. This is God. (kbw)

• • •

Meditation

"He who gives . . . will not want" (Proverbs 28:27).
"Cast your bread upon the waters, for you will find it
after many days" (Ecclesiastes 11:1).

Can we have faith in the circle of giving and receiving?

Conclusion: Feeding the Soul

Food for thought, food for body, food for spirit—manna from the
Eternal Provider. The Jewish attitude toward food is complex. One of the greatest challenges of any ethical system—religious or secular—is to

For I will pour water on the thirsty land,
and streams on the dry ground;
I will pour my Spirit upon your descendants,
and my blessings on your offspring.

Isaiah 44:3

transform eating into a spiritual expression. May we take the opportunity that food preparation and mealtime offer to connect deeply
with our Sustainer, and be thankful for Life and all Creation's gifts.

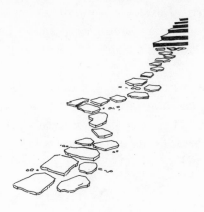

AFTERNOON: RELATIONSHIPS—
FAMILY, FRIENDS,
COMMUNITY, GOD

> If the spirit of people delights in someone, so does the
> spirit of God. . . .
>
> MISHNAH AVOT 3:11

• • •

Everything lives in relationship. Nothing exists without the Other.
Everything that is taken, received, given, accepted comes from That
which permits, offers, holds, returns all that is and all that ever will
be.

Others support and surround our spiritual journey. Whether we
are talking about our relationships with parents/caregivers, siblings,
friends and enemies, lovers, community—or our relationship with
God, nature, or the universe—we are describing the soul's many
teachers.

Hillel taught that the entire Torah can be summarized in the pas-
sage, "Love your neighbor as yourself" and that the rest of Torah is

"just commentary." This simple five-word instruction contains the most profound learning any human being can ever investigate. Loving another and loving the self are both aspects of the same love: loving God.

In this chapter, we discuss the complexity and blessings of relationship, the healing power of words, and the sacredness of communication. Through psyche and soul, words spoken and unspoken, relationship to others, to time and to place, we ultimately find our way to God. (kbw)

· · ·

Study: The Nature of Relationships

"Then the Eternal One God said, 'It is not good that the man should be alone'" (Genesis 2:18). Being "in relationship" with others was part of the Eternal One's plan from the beginning. This is not to say that having time alone is not essential, but only to recognize that we were created with needs that only relationships can satisfy. The nature of relationship is complex as we learn from the following stories.

> At that time says the Eternal One,
> I will be the God
> of all the families of Israel,
> and they shall be my people.
> Jeremiah 31:1

In Genesis, we read, "God created humanity in the likeness of God, male and female, and blessed them, and named them Man when they were created" (Genesis 5:1–2). This teaches that we are created in God's likeness—male (Adam, which means "of the earth") and female (Eve, which means "life itself"). Within each of us and together as a species, we hold the possibility of living with balance: masculine and feminine, action and restraint, wisdom and understanding, love and power, grace and judgment, creation and destruction, beauty and compassion—the balancing forces of the Infinite Oneness.

> Love your neighbor as yourself.
> (Leviticus 19:18)

We know that holiness is an ideal; the development of holiness, of Divine balance, is difficult to attain. So we may stumble and pick ourselves up again. Relationship offers us an opportunity to learn from what causes us to stumble. In this way, relationship becomes our teacher. Each conflict and each time we close our heart to another provides us with a mirror to learn about ourselves, love, compassion, mercy, and understanding. Through these, we strive to heal the imbalance and strengthen our relationship with the Holy One.

We realize that each relationship reflects our relationship with God. As we strengthen one, we strengthen the other, just as that which is above is as that which is below. Rabbi Abraham Isaac Kook taught that "all existence is the body of God,"[1] and Rabbi Abraham Joshua Heschel wrote, "You are not alone, you live constantly in a holy neighborhood; remember: 'Love your neighbor—God—as thyself.'"[2] "Dealing with other people is the first and most important measure of our respect for—or disregard of—God."[3]

The Baal Shem Tov established an important maxim: when we detect a mean quality in a man, we do so because we possess it ourselves.
Abraham Joshua Heschel

Relationships are like concentric circles: relationship with self and relationships with others all circling in the boundlessness of God. The mystics remind us that we never act in the human world alone; our ways with each other are our ways with God. All our actions cause a ripple throughout the world—and this affects the creation that is constantly unfolding. As Moses Cordovero, the sixteenth-century kabbalist, wrote:

Yet in my flesh shall I see God.
Job 19:26

> Who am I? I am a mustard seed in the middle of the sphere of the moon, which itself is a mustard seed within the next sphere. So it is with that sphere and all it contains in relation to the next sphere. So it is with all the spheres—one inside the other—and all of them are a mustard seed within the further expanses. And all of these are a mustard seed within further expanses.[4]

Walking the Path: The Nature of Relationships

KAVANAH: AWAKENING

"God, and God alone, remains Himself in all His relationships—never becoming someone else, never becoming *the other*."[5]

Through relationships, we become who we are. We adapt, we change, we grow, we learn, we love, we struggle, we reject, we hate. Only when there is an "I" is there an "other"—the person who is opposite us, whether that person is family, friend, stranger, enemy. Each relationship helps us find truth, question certainties, challenge rules, and search for holiness. And here is the paradox of the spiritual path: relationship teaches us about the boundaries of self in the context of seeking God, the Infinite and Eternal.

For I am the Eternal One, I do not change.

Malachi 3:6

ACTIVITY

As Heschel wrote, "[O]ne of the goals of the Jewish way of living [is] to feel the hidden love and wisdom in all things."[6] As you consider an important, positive relationship that is in your life, contemplate how this person has enriched your life and strengthened you. Then allow yourself to see deeply into this person and let the boundaries of self and the other melt away and uncover the Divine love and wisdom you share. Send love from your heart and wishes for God's blessing to this person.

Now contemplate a difficult, painful relationship that has taught you something about yourself. Perhaps it taught you how you *don't* want to live your life. See the other person in front of you and attempt to appreciate their offering to your life—the opportunity to examine those qualities that you share in common, the insights that you've gained, the struggles that you've grown from. See deeply into this person. Let the boundaries of self and the other melt away and uncover the Divine love and wisdom you share. If you feel able to do so, send love from your heart and wishes for God's blessing to this person.

• • •

Every day, my phone rings and I hear a voice that I have never heard before asking me for help. That is the reality of being a rabbi

or being in any helping profession. While I can always not answer
the phone, I usually do. By doing so, I enter into a new relationship.
To me, this is a wonderful metaphor for life: the unknown soul is
reaching out and I am the only one in that moment who can answer.
What is my responsibility in such a situation? It is to listen, and then
to respond out of my heart. Relationships are based on the principle
that we need each other. Every day, I remind myself how fortunate I
am that I am needed and that I am able to respond. (jlm)

• • •

CREATIVE BLESSING

*"Blessed are you, Eternal One our God, Teacher of Rela-
tionship. Help me through healthy self-examination to
prevent the pain and suffering of thoughtlessness, and to
bring understanding and compassion to others."*

Study: Communication in Relationships

We learn from the *Sh'ma,* which means "Listen," that the first step in
any significant relationship is the act of listening. But the first part of
listening is to be quiet. Being quiet is not easy. It does not mean simply not speaking. It also means
opening your ears and your heart.
It means trying to clear from your
mind the inner dialogue which can
be distracting when we want to listen to the voice of another. To be a

*These are things that you shall do:
Speak the truth to one another,
render . . . judgments that are true
and make for peace.*

Zechariah 8:16

good friend, lover, parent, or co-worker, we must truly listen not only
to the words, but to the heart of the other.

Listening can be a way of receiving someone's words so we can
understand, feel, appreciate their meaning. This builds a bridge between hearts. We

Let thy ear be attentive, and thy eyes open to hear . . .

Nehemiah 1:6

listen for joy and
pain; we listen to

what is being said—and to what is not being said. By doing so, we
can bring peace, understanding, and reconciliation.

Listening in the middle of conflict can be especially challenging. Our feelings may be hurt and we may be angry. We may want to defend, blame, strike back at whomever we're clashing with. At such times, the ability to step back, breathe deeply, and silence ourselves until a thoughtful response is formulated is essential. We remember, just as Abraham demonstrated by arguing with God over the destruction of Sodom and Gomorrah, that "allowing others the dignity of different views is holy."[7]

> Then the Eternal One said, "The outrage of Sodom and Gomorrah is so great, and their sin so grave! I will go down to see whether they have acted altogether according to the outcry that has come to Me. . . ." The men went on from there to Sodom, while Abraham remained standing before the Eternal One. Abraham came forward and said, "Will You sweep away the innocent along with the guilty? What if there should be fifty innocent within the city; will You wipe out the place and not forgive it for the sake of the innocent fifty who are in it? Far be it from You to . . . bring death upon the innocent as well as the guilty. . . . Far be it from You! Shall not the Judge of all the earth deal justly?" And the Eternal One said, "If I find within the city of Sodom fifty innocent ones, I will forgive the whole place for their sake."
>
> Genesis 18:20–26

The negotiating between Abraham and God is typical of the kind of interchange that underpins the Jewish values of discussing, debating, arguing, negotiating—all in search of Truth.

Judaism does not see conflict as negative. Conflict drives progress, just as the world itself emerged from chaos. But unresolved conflict is the source of much unhappiness and can be as oppressive as any reality on earth.

I, I am the Eternal One. . . .
Put me in remembrance,
let us argue together;
set forth your case,
that you may be proved right.
Isaiah 43:25–26

It is important to see conflict as something to resolve as constructively as possible. Can we trust in our personal integrity? Can we hear our "still small voice within" offering wisdom, insight, understanding? Can we trust our abilities to heal the wounds caused by conflict and have new faith in others, in the world, in God?

*The mind of the wise
makes his speech judicious. . . .
He who is slow to anger
is better than the mighty.*
Proverbs 16:23, 32

When conflict is unresolvable, we're left with a sense of helplessness and pain that can only be assuaged through trusting that healing will come by removing ourselves from the situation. We apologize for our part in the conflict and breakdown in a relationship. We continue to examine ourselves and trust that insights gained and our intentions to resolve conflict will flourish in the future.

We continue to live by our principles. We continue to work for justice and pursue truth and search for understanding. We set limits. We defend the oppressed. We speak up clearly and consistently. We do this because we are here to repair and restore in a framework of *shalom*—of peace—and in the Spirit of God.

The lessons of power and intimidation in relationship are difficult to learn. Hurtful anger directed at the heart of another may leave deep wounds.

Not by might, nor by force, but by My spirit . . .
Zechariah 4:6

Learning to use our anger purposefully, constructively—to speak in a way that *brings healing*—is an important part of our spiritual path.

Learning to appropriately tolerate someone else's anger is also a spiritual concern. As Rabbi Abraham Isaac Kook wrote:

> Tolerance is equipped with a profound faith, reaching a point of recognizing that it is impossible for any soul to become altogether devoid of holy illumination, for the life of the living God is present in all life. Even in areas where we encounter destructive actions, where ideas take the form of negation, there must, nevertheless, remain hidden in the heart and in the depths of the soul a vital light of holiness. . . . Out of this great and holy perception and faith is engendered tolerance, to encircle all with the thread of compassion. *I will gather together all of you, O Jacob* (Micah 2:12).[8]

We find guidance in the laws of *lashon ha-rah*, which means "the evil tongue." The Torah teaches, "Do not go about as a talebearer among your people" (Leviticus 19:26), "Keep far from a false matter" (Exodus 23:7), and "You

The tongue of the wise brings healing.
Proverbs 12:18

shall not take vengeance nor bear a grudge against any of your people" (Leviticus 19:18). We typically think of *lashon ha-rah* as "gossip"—talking about another person in a hurtful way, whether true or untrue. But our sages taught not to judge another person until we've walked in their shoes. This is similar to how God judged the people of Sodom and Gomorrah—not from heaven above, but rather by walking among the people in an attempt to understand their actions.

We examine all of our behaviors and practices that bring hurt and suffering to others. Sometimes our pride or our wounded self-esteem prevents us from saying words that could heal. Only we can move beyond pride and wounding to help create a world of peace and well-being. On this issue, Moses Cordovero taught:

> I have found an effective potion for the cure of pride. This consists of training yourself to do two things. First, respect all creatures, recognizing in them the sublime nature of the Creator, who fashions human beings in wisdom and whose wisdom inheres in each created thing. Second, train yourself to bring the love of your fellow human beings into your heart, even the wicked, as if they were your brothers and sisters, even more, until the love of all human beings is firm in your heart.[9]

The Rabbinic ideal of the good person is someone whose "yes" is "yes" and whose "no" is "no." We are occasionally confronted with situations when lying may seem to be a more gentle way of handling a situation or a less stressful way of solving a problem. When we recognize these incidents as opportunities for us to stretch for truth and honesty, we're challenged to ensure that our words carry the integrity of our heart, even when that's difficult or inconvenient. When we speak honestly and kindly, we are saying that we would like our relationship with the other person to grow in an atmosphere of truth, compassion, and kindness.

By the word of the Eternal One the heavens were made, and all their host by the breath of Its mouth.
Psalm 33:6

In the mystical tradition, it is words that are responsible for creation. "And God said . . ." (Genesis 1:3) announces the onset of Creation. In describing the sacred Hebrew alphabet of 22 letters, the *Sefer Yetsirah* says, "God engraved them, carved them, weighed them,

I will change the speech of the peoples to a pure speech, that all of them may call on the name of the Eternal One and serve the Source of All Life with one accord.

Zephaniah 3:9

permuted them, and transposed them, forming with them everything formed and everything destined to be formed."[10] Words, spoken and unspoken, create relationship. It is in the context of relationship that we form the "I" and the "Other." It is the context of listening to the Eternal Words and praying that we discover God. May we approach the deep listening of our hearts and the expression of our words with the holiness that was intended by God.

Walking the Path: Communication in Relationships

KAVANAH: AWAKENING

The Talmud interprets Psalm 95:7, "If only today you would listen to My voice," a wistful prayer of the Almighty, as a Messianic prophecy: The Messiah would come immediately if we would only harken to God's commanding presence, if we would listen sufficiently to the Eternal One.

On another level, the Rabbis teach us that we have considerable control over our own spiritual and cosmic destiny and that we can influence our own as well as our collective future. Even the "Messiah" depends on our actions, which means we can influence the Creator—and the Divine plan.

On a very personal level, our inner state of being is the critical factor in life—and not the external realities around us. The quest for "inner peace" is found in the metaphorical "coming of the Messiah." Each of us can help his or her own "Messiah" arrive today and every day.

Through our communication with self, with others, and with God we bring about the world that is constantly coming.

• • •

I recently decided to choose a Psalm to use as a daily prayer. I've always been fond of Psalm 23, but I was ready to learn another.

Starting at the beginning of the Book of Psalms, I read each one.
When I arrived at Psalm 139, I knew this was my new daily prayer.
There is much about it that I love and some of it that I don't. It's the
last two verses I want to share with you here: "Search me Almighty,
and know my heart, try me and know my thoughts. And see if there
be any unskillful way in me, and lead me in the way of eternity."
This is clearly the prayer of my heart: that God will help me recog-
nize my intentions, open my heart with compassion and forgiveness,
scrutinize my thoughts and communications and help me know my
unskillfullness so that I can correct my actions and live in God's
way. How I communicate verbally and nonverbally reflects the de-
gree to which I do this homework. Each day I ask for God's guidance
and believe that for me, this is the road to inner peace. (kbw)

• • •

Meditation

Holy One . . . my heart is heavy.
My daily existence has become a source
    of deep sadness and disappointment.
Give me the strength to face conflict
    with dignity and forthrightness.
Let me speak openly, but with compassion.
Give me the patience to hear the opinions of others
    without being defensive or overly sensitive.
Help me discover the true nature of this conflict
    and then act in an appropriate manner.
Help me distinguish between matters of principle
    and matters of power.
Let me be understanding of others' shortcomings—
    and of my own.
If, after making the best effort I can, I am not
    succeeding, help me remove myself
    from a situation without bitterness or anger.
Help me refrain from pettiness or recriminations.
Help me remember that I am created in Your Image.

Study: A Loving Partnership

"The most important prerequisite of love is appreciation," wrote Rabbi Abraham Joshua Heschel. When we consider the qualities of a strong, loving relationship with another person—listening heart, trust, kindness, love, support, appreciation, commitment—we recognize the same deep love and closeness that we yearn for in our spiritual life with God.

The Eternal One, your God, is in your midst,
. . . the Eternal One . . . will renew you in love . . .
Zephaniah 3:17

To be cherished, cared about and cared for, to be honored and celebrated, to be truly loved—and to be able to return all this to another person—is a beautiful experience. We extend our affection in loving, nurturing ways: a gentle smile, a hug, an arm around a waist or shoulder. These are simple, nonverbal ways of saying, "I'm glad you're in my life." But they have a different significance when our beloved is ill and needs help physically. Bathing, wrapping a wound, preparing special foods, rubbing a sore back—all these may try our patience, but they teach us the meaning of "being there" for someone in need.

From the realm of the heart—the seat of our emotional life and strength—we listen deeply and we care. We practice walking in our lover's shoes, attempting to understand, to see through his or her eyes, to feel that we are one with his or her heart.

I have trusted in Thy steadfast love;
My heart will rejoice . . . I will sing . . .
Psalm 13:5–6

We learn to speak with compassion, to solve problems with insight. We also build trust, which may be difficult to create, but can easily be broken.

In the mind, which is our intellectual realm, lies our respect and appreciation for our beloved. When we look at him or her, we see many strengths and capabilities, and we celebrate how our differences enhance our lives and challenge us to grow with one another. We've come together partly because of common values and we continue to be with one another as our thinking changes with experience and time. We reach out to one another—mind to mind—inviting the other into understanding, and seeking to understand.

In the spiritual realm of relations resides the mystery of meeting another person. Here is the complexity of our individual personalities, the sum total of the challenges we'll face together, the changes we'll go through. In the spiritual realm, we strive for creativity, acceptance, unity. It is here that we willingly compromise for the good of the partnership (unless compromise would be self-destructive). We also learn to balance our willingness to change with our willingness to tolerate difference; we learn in ever deeper ways how to be compassionate, trusting, merciful, caring, peaceful; we learn how to truly love. Sheldon Kramer, psychologist and kabbalist, wrote:

Happy is the one who finds wisdom, and the one who gets understanding.
Proverbs 3:13

> The commitment to oneself as well as to a partner requires maturity to withstand the rocky road of tolerating profound inner and outer struggles. Sacred love comes from knowing one's beloved in the totality of his or her strength and weaknesses, appreciating and supporting the other deeply, through heartfelt compassion.[11]

The awareness of gratitude engendered by the spiritual life spills over into our relationships. As we thank God for the miracles of life, we are reminded to offer similar words of affirmation to friends, family, and especially to our partners and lovers. We warmly affirm others for their uniqueness. Sharing the rituals of *Shabbat* or a simple prayer at a meal each day reminds us to bless each other for the many gifts that we bring to each other.

On the other hand, if spiritual solitude takes us away from each other for a while each day, we may understand that this can heighten our appreciation for the other person.

The excitement of being in love at the beginning of a relationship does not need to fade. Take the time in the early phases of a relationship to meet each other physically, emotionally, intellectually, and spiritually. This will set the stage for a fulfilling relationship. Each day we have countless opportunities for genuine romance. These are best achieved when each person's efforts and enthusiasm are nearly equal and mutual. "Behold, you are beautiful, my love, behold, you are beautiful!" (Song of Solomon 4:1).

Walking the Path: A Loving Partnership

ACTIVITY: RESOLVING HURT FEELINGS

Most of us share positive feelings with our partner or lover. Difficulty may arise when anger, pride, or defensiveness interferes with taking corrective steps. Our hurt and suffering seems to justify creating hurt and suffering in our partner: "Now you see how it feels!" Yet, in our heart, we know that creating more pain, more hurt, more suffering does not help us or help the relationship to heal. Talk with your partner about trying a new approach when either of you has hurt or angry feelings. Including him or her in your plans creates greater possibility for success and cooperation. Consider saying this when you have a difficult feeling to express: "Darling, I hurt so much—please help me." Know that the strength of true love is to be able to agree with your beloved that when you need help, the other will respond with something like: "Please tell me what hurts you. Let me know how I can help." Commit to each other to open your hearts and try to reduce the other's hurt and suffering. Listen deeply, consider compromise, look for solutions that do not blame anyone. Recognize that your efforts are as much for yourself as they are for the other—because the two of you are one.

• • •

The idea that we are partners with God in repairing the world forms the basis of my relationship with my wife, Julie. Julie and I have been together since we met over 25 years ago. Although neither of us would speak of love at first sight, something clicked and has kept us going all these years. I consider myself extremely fortunate because I can still say that my happiest moments are those when it is just the two of us together talking about life. We see ourselves as partners repairing the broken places in our lives and in the lives of those around us. We begin with ourselves because we cannot help our children— or anyone else—if we are consumed by our own pain. Over many years, we have tried to be there for each other in times of stress or anxiety. Each of us knows that we cannot be whole without the unconditional love and support of the other. Many things have changed over the years, but we know that we are still partners in this adventure called life. I pray that I will continue to be Julie's best friend and loving partner. (jlm)

• • •

KAVANAH: AWAKENING

I am grateful today for the earthly, yet spiritual companionship of my dear _____. She/He provides for my physical and emotional needs, and reminds me that I am special and worthy of being loved. Help me be a good friend and partner to _____. Let me forgive his/her foibles and idiosyncrasies—and recognize my own. May I try each day to bring a little more happiness and fulfillment into a life that has added immeasurably to my own. I am grateful to and I am grateful to You for helping us be in each other's lives.

Study: Parent-Child Relationships

We open this section with the story of the *akedah,* the binding of Isaac by his father, Abraham. We'll explore this difficult story in an attempt to understand the possibilities for transformation available to us as either parent or child in the parent-child relationship.

I [the Eternal One] will love you freely . . .
Hosea 14:4

God put Abraham to the test. God said to him, "Abraham," and he answered, "Here I am." And God said, "Take your son, your favored one, Isaac, whom you love, and go to the land of Moriah, and offer him there as a burnt offering on one of the heights which I will point out to you." So early next morning, Abraham saddled his ass and took with him two of his servants and his son Isaac. He split the wood of the burnt offering, and he set out for the place of which God had told him. On the third day, Abraham looked up and saw the place from afar. Then Abraham said to his servants, "You stay here with the ass. The boy and I will go up there; we will worship and we will return to you."

Abraham took the wood for the burnt offering, put it on his son

Isaac. He himself took the firestone and the knife; and the two walked off together. Then Isaac said to his father Abraham, "Father!" And he answered, "Yes, my son." And he said, "Here are the firestone and the wood; but where is the sheep for the burnt offering?" And Abraham said, "God will see to the sheep for the burnt offering, my son." And the two of them walked on together. (Genesis 22:1–8).

The specter of a parent and a child walking together on the most painful of journeys is haunting. Having heard the voice of *ha elohim* (which can be translated as "the gods" or "the God") to sacrifice Isaac, Abraham obeys. Thus begins one of the Torah's most troubling narratives. We can only imagine Abraham walking for three days, coming to grips with the voices of his ego (self) and Divine Guidance (Self) that he hears, trying to discern what motivates him, what he will do, and what Truth is.

While commentators have offered every possible justification for the motivation of God, as well as the response of Abraham and Isaac, perhaps it is sufficient for us to reflect on what is so difficult in the relationship between parents and children. Why is the greatest source of satisfaction also the source of the greatest anguish?

As the exemplary parent, Abraham is torn between the need to be true to his own faith and values while at the same time fulfilling his role as a loving and devoted father. The Bible provides an ending which obviates the choice: At the last moment, God retracts the requirement to sacrifice Isaac. But day-to-day life is not as neat.

They arrived at the place of which God had told him. Abraham built an altar there; he laid out the wood; he bound his son Isaac; he laid him on the altar, on top of the wood. And Abraham picked up the knife to slay his son. Then an angel of the Eternal One called to him from heaven: "Abraham! Abraham!" And he answered, "Here I am." And he said, "Do not raise your hand against the boy or do anything to him. For now I know that you fear God, since you have not withheld your son, your favored one, from Me" (Genesis 22:9–12).

The first time a parent says "no" to a child marks the beginning of a lifetime of parental messages which have a similar function. As children grow older, the form of the message may become more so-phisticated, but its substance is the same.

Can a child hear a "no" without also hearing that *"You* are a 'no' (or 'no-thing')"? How do parents distinguish between "no, because you will hurt yourself" and "no, because you will hurt me" when the feelings are often the same? A child's feelings, thoughts, and wishes may be sacrificed in honor of the parent's needs—whether they be for safety or control. Both parent and child work within the confines of a powerful bond that ensures survival, is complicated by judgments and approval, strengthened by love and challenged by loss. Parent and child grow together, teaching each other, filling voids, fulfilling dreams, sacrificing, thriving, conflicting, and longing for love.

How often as parents do we suffer from a confusion of feelings that emerge from childhood as we try to do what's best for our child? Are we responding with a solid sense of who we are and what we know makes sense? Or are we responding to the voice of a parent (one we may still be trying to please years after our own childhood) that remains loud and strong in our mind? Inadvertently, we often pass on the pain and suffering of misunderstandings or unskilled par-enting that we received in our own childhood.

As we become conscious of our motivations, examine our ac-tions, and listen for Truth, our relationship with our parents and our children can evolve. This can help us resolve issues with our parents that we were once sure were insolvable, and we can separate our egos from our children in ways that allow them the fullness of their birthright.

The ultimate goal of the parent-child relationship is to pass on enduring values about faith, integrity, and compassion. The most im-portant of these is found in the Bible (Jeremiah 31:3): "You love us with a monumental love." Though God and parents often must say "Thou shall" and "Thou shalt not," if given in an atmosphere of *un-conditional* love and acceptance, they do not diminish a child's self-esteem.

If we are to successfully communicate love and heal past wounds we must consciously come to grips with the voices of self/Self that we hear: Are we hearing our own egos or the voice of our parents (self), or the voice of wisdom, the voice of God (Self)? We must discern what motivates us, what actions we will take, and what Truth is.

When Abraham looked up, his eye fell upon a ram, caught in the thicket by its horns. So Abraham went and took the ram and offered it up as a burnt offering in place of his son. And Abraham named the site *Adonai-yireh,* whence the present saying, "On the mount of the Eternal One there is vision" (Genesis 22:13–14).

Walking the Path: Parent-Child Relationships

ACTIVITY: FOLLOWING ABRAHAM'S PATH

The word "sacrifice" resonates deeply with parents. We're aware of the emotional, financial, time- and energy-related sacrifices made to honor a child's needs and well-being. When we were children, we sacrificed when we "gave up" certain drives and desires to meet requirements or expectations of our parents. Now that we are parents, the word "sacrifice" resonates within us when considering the discipline and commitment required to develop our spiritual selves—time and energy that could otherwise be devoted to meeting ego needs.

The greater the learning, the greater the reward.
Mishnah Avot 5:22

Consider the following interpretation of Abraham's spiritual path and his role as a parent to Isaac and a child of God:

As a parent, Abraham was torn between the need to be true to his own vision, faith, and values, while at the same time fulfilling his role as a loving and devoted caregiver. He was put in the ultimate psychological/spiritual dilemma of whether to follow his spiritual path by obeying God—or listen to his heart and protect his relationship with his son. For Abraham, Isaac was not only his son; he represented his entire future.

While traveling for three days of travel in search of Mount Moriah, Abraham was forced to confront his doubts and fears and the depth of his love for his son and God.[12] All the while, he remained true to his faith in God. Through binding Isaac to the altar and raising the knife, he experienced the ultimate in "non-attachment":

"Isaac is not mine—everything belongs to God." When the angel of the Eternal One called, Abraham responded, "Here I am." The angel said, "Do not raise your hand against the boy." As Abraham lifted his eyes (to look to God), he saw the ram that he would sacrifice in place of Isaac. Through this process, Abraham was prepared, in yet another way, to fulfill his immense spiritual role.

Now imagine that you are walking for three days so you can sacrifice the single most important person in your life so you can be closer to God. Ask yourself:

- Of what am I letting go?

- How do I feel?

- What's holding me back from letting go?

- What would I have to do, believe, or feel to be ready to let go?

- What does the angel of God say to me as I prepare the sacrifice?

- What do I *see* when I look toward God? What is my spiritual insight?

- How does this experience change me?

Many times in life, we feel torn between irreconcilable choices. We often can wade through the tension—holding opposite points of view or opposing needs, exploring the meaning of the choices—to a place where we find the Godfulness in the dilemma, the Godfulness that will obviate the need to sacrifice some aspect of ourselves or someone else. And we emerge from the process with new understanding and stability.

Recognize at a deep level that for both parents and children, the relationship they share offers many opportunities for growth and spiritual development. Perhaps this is one reason that the metaphor of the parent-child relationship has been so frequently applied to our relationship with God. The more we can bring the

"You are children unto the Eternal One your God . . ."
Deuteronomy 14:1

sacred into parenting, and the more we see the Godfulness in the relationship between parent and child, the more wisdom and stability we will find.

• • •

Our daughter, Ali, was born 13 days after that magic "due date." Her birth was induced. I had been waiting eagerly for her arrival for months. I didn't have post-partum blues, but I did have a tremendous sense of loss even as I gained this beautiful relationship with our first-born. In the first few nights after her birth, alone with her in the nursery, the depth of my feelings about her vulnerability echoed in the emptiness of my womb and from the fullness of my heart. I was surrounded by the sense that she could be taken from me now, that I could not protect her in the same way that I had during nine months of pregnancy. I realized that this precious being was a gift on loan— and was not mine at all. (kbw)

• • •

KAVANAH: AWAKENING

"Have we not all one father/mother/Creator?
Has not one God created us?"
                                        Malachi 2:10

Everlasting Father, Everlasting Mother, Birther of the Cosmos, how do we experience God as "father," God as "mother," God as "parent"? Is our experience like that of a young child relying on God to watch over and care for us? At times, are we the adolescent who claims not to need God? Are we the young adult away at school, too busy to think about God believing that we know more than God? Are we the older adult who thrives on a renewed relationship with Wisdom and Truth? Most likely, we are all of these. Consider your relationship with God and imagine how you

It is the way of the father to be compassionate and it is the way of a mother to comfort. The Holy One said: "I will act like a father and a mother." Pesikta de-Rav Kahana 19:3

might deepen that relationship and bring greater closeness between you and the Divine.

CREATIVE BLESSING

"Blessed are You, Eternal One our God, Source of Eternal Love. May my life thrive under the influence of Your monumental love. May I return to You all the love I feel in my heart through acts of lovingkindness each and every day."

Study: Siblings—My Brother, My Sister, and I

At the core of our relationship with our sibling is fear that our parents will favor him or her. Ancient Judaism required the eldest son to inherit a double portion of his father's legacy. But all the children were given a share of the inheritance. It is difficult for us moderns to understand why Jacob and Esau competed for Isaac's blessing. But the birthright went only to one son, and with it a lion's share of the inheritance and leadership of the next generation. This is a metaphor for the universal phenomenon of competing for parents' love and attention, for the "real" or "perceived" favoritism that divides so many siblings. As Elie Wiesel wrote in *Sages and Dreamers*:

> Every human being reflects the image of God, who has no image: mine is neither purer nor holier than yours. Truth is one, but the paths leading to it are many. In the eyes of the Father, all His children are worthy of His love. In my eyes, the Other is the center of the universe, just as any Other ought to be in his or her eyes.[13]

The story of Jacob and his twelve sons teaches us how easy and natural it can be to favor one child over another: "Now Israel [Jacob] loved Joseph more than any other of his children" (Genesis 37:3). The story continues until Joseph's brothers are so angry at him that they conspire to kill him: "Come now, let us kill him and throw him into one of the pits; then we shall say that a wild beast has devoured him, and we shall see what will become of his dreams" (Genesis 37:20).

The story has multiple meanings. As parents, we can benefit from the message that how we love and feel about our children is of ultimate importance in their developing relationships with others. Hopefully, we can create an environment that provides healthy boundaries and respects their unique gifts, their rights of privacy and place, and their way of contributing to the family. This is no small task. Begin by being conscious of your actions and reactions, and the messages you deliver. Out of respect can grow a deep and lasting friendship.

We recognize that we are given our siblings; we do not choose them as we choose our friends. Sibling relationships offer an opportunity to practice a love based on shared history and heritage. We may have many feelings about our siblings, but they do play an important role in shaping the experience of family. They can be a natural support network and the people we most want to share lifecycle events with. Or, they can feel like strangers to us. Even worse, they can feel like our enemies.

When relationships with siblings are strained or broken, it may be best to simply "let go." This can turn a broken relationship into a healthy one. Hopefully, we can leave the door open to a sibling who wants to mend a relationship; when we soften our hearts toward another, we create a pathway for connection.

Walking the Path:
Siblings—My Brother, My Sister, and I

KAVANAH: AWAKENING

> "You shall not hate your brother/sister in your heart, but you shall reason with your neighbor, lest you bear sin because of him."
>
> —LEVITICUS 19:17

Are brother, sister, and neighbor one and the same? Perhaps the lessons about siblings in Genesis are truly lessons about relationships among the children of Creation. For do we not share the same history and heritage and are we not ultimately of the same lineage? Is the story of Cain and Abel about two brothers? Or about two tribes, two peoples living in tension, but sharing the same planet?

> And when they were in the field, Cain set upon his brother Abel and killed him. The Eternal One said to Cain, "Where is your brother Abel?" And he said, "I do not know. Am I my brother's keeper?" Then the Eternal One said, "What have you done? Hark, your brother's blood cries out to Me from the ground!"
>
> Genesis 4:8–10

Are we our brother's and our sister's keeper? Perhaps our family is the first classroom where we learn about being the "keepers" of others—all in preparation for learning to care for the entire family of humanity.

Thus says the Eternal One of hosts,
"Render true judgments, show kindness
and mercy each to your brother [and sister],
do not oppress the widow,
the parentless, the sojourner, or
the poor; and let none of you imagine evil
against your brother [and sister] in your heart."
Zechariah 7:9–10

The mystics recognized that when God created humanity, Divine Oneness manifested as our experience of duality: right and wrong, yes and no, wave and particle, free will and destiny, self and other, us and them. This became the birthplace of competitive needs, opposing views, and paradox. On a spiritual level, we live with the struggle of Cain and Abel within ourselves. What we experience as someone else's problem is often an unexamined aspect of ourselves—split off and hidden—as if killed and buried. As we are able to reclaim and heal these aspects of self and return wholly to God, we know peace. Out of this deeper understanding of self, we can help heal our brothers and sisters around the world.

• • •

Our daughters, Chava and Shoshana, have taught me so much over
the years. Now that they are on the brink of adulthood, I see in them
many traits I wish I had in myself. One of the things I admire most
is their true devotion to each other as sisters. Separated in age by
three and a half years, somehow they relate to each other as equals.
They have done this since they first became aware of each other.

They are so different in every area—looks, interests, and abilities—but they are united by their sisterly bond. Somehow, I can face my own mortality with greater comfort knowing that (with God's help) these two will always be there for each other—and that nothing can ever come between them. (jlm)

• • •

CREATIVE BLESSING

"Blessed are You, Eternal One our God, Birther of Life, help me look deeply into the eyes of each person I meet so I can see our shared history, our shared heritage in the family of humanity. Help me remember, 'She is my sister' 'He is my brother,' so I can be the kind of 'keeper' you hope me to be. Thank you for such a diverse and beautiful family!"

Study: Friendship

"Acquire for yourself a friend."
—MISHNA AVOT 1:6

"Friendship or death."
—BABYLONIAN TALMUD, TA'ANIT, 23A

One of the most satisfying interludes during any day is a time of sharing with a true friend, whether in person or over the phone. The sound of a familiar voice or the sight of a friendly face can be a balm for life's many pressures and obligations. Elie Wiesel wrote that a friend is:

"More than a father, more than a brother, a traveling companion; with him, you can achieve what seemed impossible, even if you must lose it later. Friendship marks a life even more deeply than love. . . ."[14]

Friendship is forged over time. It is based on trust and, like all enduring relationships, it is given freely and without condition. Friends are interested in our lives; they are often the ones with whom we share a common purpose. Friends are not easy to acquire and, over our entire lifetime, we may have few enduring friendships. The nature of friendship is as varied as life itself, but a friend's most important quality is to "be there" in time of true need.

The Eternal One was with Joseph and showed him steadfast love.

Genesis 39:21

In the Bible, the relationship of Jonathan and David is one of the best examples of deep friendship. When Jonathan's father King Saul, in a fit of jealousy, seeks to kill his rival David, Jonathan protects his friend at peril: The spear that his father throws in anger and frustration narrowly misses him. One hopes that there will never be a need to choose between family and friend, but this story shows how friendship may have to withstand severe challenges.

In the Book of Ruth, we see a similarly deep friendship develop between Naomi and her daughter-in-law, Ruth:

> And she [Naomi] said, "See, your sister-in-law has gone back to her people and to her gods; return after your sister-in-law." But Ruth said, "Entreat me not to leave you or to return from following you; for where you go I will go, and where you lodge I will lodge; your people shall be my people, and your God my God; where you die I will die, and there will I be buried. May the Eternal One do so to me and more also if even death parts me from you." And when Naomi saw that she was determined to go with her, she said no more. So the two of them went on . . .
>
> Ruth 1:15–19

Walking the Path: Friendship

EXERCISE

Oil and perfume make the heart glad, so doth sweetness of a friend.

Proverbs 2:9

Think about a good friend and some of the times when that friendship meant the most to you. Imagine how it would feel if the friendship had not existed. Silently express your gratitude for what your friend has meant to you. Write a letter of gratitude to your friend that expresses some of these feelings. Try to be open to new ways of expressing your emotions. Let your friend know that you will always be there in time of need.

ACTIVITY

"Jacob resumed his journey and came to the land of the Easterners. . . . Jacob said to them, 'My friends, where are you from?'"

Genesis 29:1, 4

Friendliness is communicated by how you greet someone. As you move through the day, consider greeting those you see

When one person greets another it is as if he greets the Divine presence.
Mechilta/D'Rabbi Ishmael

with the intention of creating friendship. Take the initiative to say "Hello." If you know their name, use it in the greeting. Names distinguish us from other people; by calling someone by their name, you affirm their personhood, their uniqueness, their essence.

• • •

I've known Robin since I was three years old. She lived down the street from me. We played Barbie dolls, dress-up, and Beatles together, teased each other mercilessly, were best friends throughout childhood's ups and downs. We've gone our separate ways only to find each other again. We lived in the same college town and visited each other across the country in times of need. She knows my family, just as I know hers. There are few, if any secrets, between us. We share nearly forty years of history. I have a handful of very good friends, but only one—Robin—has been a friend for almost my entire life. There isn't anything I couldn't share with her. She would celebrate in every joy; she would hold me in my deepest sorrow. And I would do the same for her. (kbw)

• • •

KAVANAH: AWAKENING

"God spoke to Moses as a person to a friend" (Exodus 33:11).

I am preparing myself to walk in the ways of the Holy One, to be a good friend. I recognize the importance of affirming, helping, standing by and walking together in friendship. I pray to be a good friend to those in my life.

Study: Our Relationship with Community

All life is within community and each of us is inextricably connected to those around us. Community can have many meanings and many

And they shall be my community, and I will be their God.
Jeremiah 32:38

forms. Within community, we hope to be nourished and sustained so we can create, reach our goals, and be transformed. Within community, we may experience the "whole" becoming greater than the sum of the parts. The power of community has been an essential theme in the story of the Jewish people.

And be ready by the third day; for on the third day the Eternal One will come down upon Mount Sinai in the sight of all the community.
Exodus 19:11

Our ancestors stood as a community before God at Mount Sinai, when the Eternal One honored the importance of sharing an experience with others and expressing communal support for the sustenance of the individual and the whole:

> So Moses came and called the elders of the community, and set before them all these words which the Eternal One had commanded him. And *all the people answered together* and said, "All that the Eternal One has spoken we will do and we will hear." And Moses reported the words of the community to the Eternal One. And the Eternal One said to Moses, "Lo, I am coming to you in a thick cloud, that *the community may hear* when I speak with you, and *may also believe* you for ever."
>
> Exodus 19:7–9

I will rejoice in Jerusalem [in holiness], and be glad in my community. . .
Isaiah 65:19

Today, the importance of sharing experience and expressing communal support is personified in Judaism by the idea of *minyan,* the quorum of ten which is traditionally required for a prayer service.[15] Without a *minyan,* some prayers are not to be recited aloud. This is a metaphor for the void we feel when we are not fully supported by family and friends. God is not enough to overcome our existential loneliness. We need each other.

Jews often have a sense of comfort and security when they meet members of the Jewish community, whether they are home or halfway around the world. Finding out that someone is a Jew often breaks down barriers between people. When we travel and seek a synagogue or a Jewish community center or a Jewish museum, we seek comfort and familiarity in a strange place. Even in our everyday world, we may be attracted to cues that indicate that someone is Jewish. This elicits a sense of kinship, an understanding, a bond. Community may also provide comfort and security that reminds us of extended family. The Hebrew word for "family," *mishpacha,* derives from the root for the word "confluence" and "flowing": we *flow* together connecting one person to the next. We may experience *mishpacha* with all the Jewish people; and we spiritually long for a *mishpacha* with all humanity, since the universal river connects all Creation.

Community is also our context for *tikkun olam,* repairing the world. Here, our responsibility to others comes to bear. In our prayers we say, *Sh'ma Kolenu*—"hear *our* voice"—indicating our collective, communal responsibility and power. Whether we pray alone or with others, we pray *for* the community, which reminds us that we belong to community.

In Judaism, we recognize that communal empowerment is fueled by individual action, which is really individual responsibility coming together for the sake of the community. As Heschel wrote, "We must continue to remind ourselves that in a free society all are involved in what some are doing. Some are guilty, all are responsible."[16] The West was founded on principles of individual freedom; we may find it difficult to consider ourselves responsible for the actions of others in any way. Yet, as Einstein wrote, "To be a Jew means to bear a serious responsibility not only to his own community, but also toward humanity."[17]

Do not separate yourself from the community.
Mishnah Avot 2:5

The group that each of us shares our lives with is surrounded by the larger Jewish community, by the larger secular community, by a national community. All these are surrounded by the global community, the cosmic community, and finally the Infinite Community. We belong. We are responsible. Our individual actions are not restricted to a select few, but extend to all humanity and to all God's Creation. Our soul's work keeps alive the community's Tree of Life, circulating the sap of life, and moving us toward the Days of *Shalom*, of Peace. As Abraham Isaac Kook wrote,

> There is one who ascends with all these songs in unison—the song of the soul, the song of the nation, the song of humanity, the song of the cosmos—resounding together, blending in harmony, circulating the sap of life, the sound of holy joy.[18]

The shadow side of "community" is cult. This occurs when we insist that each person in our group adopt the same thinking and behavior as the group norm, and when the group's certainty about truth cannot be challenged or changed. Judaism has a long history of challenging, disagreeing, adapting, changing, questioning, of wandering through the desert of uncertainty and searching for the Promised Land of understanding. As a dynamic religion, Judaism moves us forward toward the world that is constantly coming.

I will give them a heart to know that I am the Eternal One; and they shall be my community and I will be their God, for they shall return to me their whole heart.

Jeremiah 24:7

In the face of challenging and questioning, Judaism has maintained certain traditions for thousands of years. This is every community's challenge: finding a balance in which growth constructively intertwines with essence, a balance which maintains tradition and purpose within the context of creation. Doing this requires tolerance and respect, pursuing justice and embracing the diversity of the Eternal One's family.

It is possible to have a path and a discipline that enhances spiritual progress without hierarchy, that does not create an "other" whom we perceive as "less than" or "bad." Rav Kook claimed that the highest sensibility of the Jewish soul is the quest for universality.[19] If so, then we must ask ourselves: Do any of us have the authority to exclude others from God's holy community?

Community does not come about spontaneously. *Pirke Avot,* "The Words of the Elders," tells us, "Find a Master, Acquire a Friend." We need to recognize our own responsibility in creating community. Often this consists of seeking out an already existing community and trying to be part of it; or we

> *And many nations shall join themselves*
> *to the Eternal One in that day,*
> *and shall be My community;*
> *and I will dwell in the midst of you . . .*
> *Zechariah 2:11*

may need to create community for ourselves. At such times, we need to look inside for the courage to reach out, even when it may mean rejection.

To become a member of the Jewish community, we only need to follow the wisdom of Torah and God's Eternal Oneness: "Let not the foreigner who has joined the Eternal One say, 'The Eternal One will surely separate me from the Eternal One's people'. . . . I will bring them to My holy mountain, and make them joyful in My house of prayer . . . for My house shall be called a house of prayer for all peoples" (Isaiah 56:3, 7). Becoming a Jew-by-choice involves deliberately deciding to walk the Jewish path. Spiritually, all Jews are "Jews-by-choice" since we must choose—moment-to-moment—how to live our lives as Jews.

> *O that I had in the desert*
> *a wayfarers' lodging place,*
> *that I might leave my community*
> *and go away from them.*
> *Jeremiah 9:2*

Judaism is lived most fully with family and community. Yet, there are times when we are completely alone. It is important to develop spiritual coping mechanisms to be able to feel God's embrace at those times. Remember *Sh'ma Kolenu,* "hear our voice,"

> *The Torah was given in public, openly, in a free place.*
> *. . . it was given in the wilderness publicly and openly*
> *in a place that is free for all, everyone willing to accept*
> *it could come and accept it.*
> *Mechilta D'Rabbi Ishmael*

and know that even when praying alone, we are in community. Prayer and meditation are the paths to God and wholeness, whether in the company of others or alone.

Walking the Path:
Our Relationship with Community

ACTIVITY: COMMUNITY SERVICE

One way to strengthen our ties to community is through service, which is also a *mitzvah*. Giving back time, energy, and talents to the community is an important way of repairing the world.

They will call My name,
and I will answer them.
I will say, "They are my community";
and they will say,
"The Eternal One is my God."
Zechariah 13:9

When considering what kind of service to perform, make a list of sentences that begin: "What I love to do is. . . ."

As you review what you've written, notice themes and commonalties. This will help determine the kinds of projects that can use your talents and gifts.

Blessed is every one who stands in awe of the
Eternal One, who walks in God's ways!
You shall eat the fruit of the labor of your hands;
you shall be happy,
and it shall be well with you.
Psalm 128:1–2

If involving yourself in service is new, you may want to start with a small project, something "do-able" and close to home. With experience, you will have a clearer idea of the time and energy you can commit to bigger, more ambitious projects.

KAVANAH: AWAKENING

In Zephaniah (3:14), the Jewish community is described as God's daughter: "Sing aloud, O daughter of Zion; shout, O Israel! Rejoice and exult with all your heart, O daughter of Jerusalem!" This calls us to honor the feminine aspects of community: relationships, nurturing, sustaining, feeding of the spirit, receiving of Godfulness into the world. For all these aspects of community, we sing!

• • •

I was fifteen when I left my "religious" homeland and wandered
away from the religious community I'd been raised in. In retrospect,

this crisis was a necessary step of exploration and growth. In college, I visited other religious groups and was invited to be a part of their communities. These were resting points, not my destination. When I was planning to marry a man who was Jewish, I recognized my need for a religious home. I also acknowledged the many fond memories of growing up in a thriving religious community and I wanted similar opportunities for our children. I studied Judaism, a religion tolerant of my questioning and questing, a religion that spoke directly to my heart. I converted in September 1984. At first, I found my way into the Jewish community with all the uncertainties and self-consciousness of a stranger in a strange land. Now, years later, after time and effort, I am at home in my chosen religious community. I continue to travel in the realm of world religions, returning home to Judaism with renewed commitment and deeper understandings. (kbw)

• • •

CREATIVE BLESSING

"Blessed are You, the Eternal One our God, Provider of Universal Community, we are thankful for our place in Your holy community. Guide us as we create the sense of community with our fellow sojourners that reflects Your magnificent light."

Study: Our Relationship with Place— The Land of Israel

While Jacob traveled, he "came to a certain place, and stayed there that night, because the sun had set" (Genesis 28:11). When he awoke, Jacob said, "Surely God is in this place, and I did not know" (Genesis 28:16). In his darkness, Jacob could not see God; after "awakening" with the dawn, Jacob knew in a way that transcended his five senses that God was in this place.

Once Jacob became aware of God's presence, he exclaimed:

"How awesome is this place! This is none other than the house of God and this is heaven's gate." So Jacob rose early in the morning, and he took the stone which he had put under his head and set it up for a pillar and poured oil on the top of it. He called the name of that place Bethel [the house of God].

Genesis 28:17–19

The Talmud and the Midrash often call God *Ha-Makom*, literally, "the Place." In a famous midrash (which is an inquiry into the biblical texts), Rabbi Huna asks: "Why is God called *Ha-Makom*, 'the Place'? Because He is the place of the world, and the World is not His Place." This means that God precedes the world.

> Walk about Zion, go round about her, number her towers, consider well her ramparts, go through her citadels; that you may tell the next Generation that this is God, our God for ever and ever. God will be our guide for ever.
>
> Psalm 48:12–14

God is in every "place" and it is up to us to know God's Presence. This is a fundamental goal of spiritual life: To know God's presence in space and time.

Rabbi Abraham Joshua Heschel described the Sabbath as "a palace in time" . . . a sacred place that we retreat to from the mundane world. The mystic looks for ways to change the quality of time by infusing the sacred—the timeless—into the moment. On the Sabbath, we have a taste of the end of all days, the eternal time and place of *Shalom*. And we are reminded that every place, every time, indeed every aspect of creation is holy. When we call one particular place "holy" or one particular day "holy," we recognize that this is a relative term.

Jewish tradition emphasizes God's presence in *every* place and *every* moment: "Thus says the Eternal One: I will return to Zion, and will dwell in the midst of Jerusalem, and Jerusalem shall be called the faithful city, and the mountain of the Eternal One of hosts, the holy mountain"(Zechariah 8:3). Living in a world of limits, we map our universe by using the concept of "place" and we organize our experiences in "time." Zion is a place, Jerusalem is a place, the "holy mountain" is a place; "will return" indicates a time in the future that will follow "now." If we could transcend our mind's limits, we could see the land of Israel as having no boundaries and expanding throughout all of God's Creation. If we could live our lives in such a way as to *know* God's presence, we could penetrate linear time to see that God is returning in this very moment to Zion.

While the land of Israel is a concrete representation of "sacred ground," we must remember that spiritually it is without measure and without location. It is a land for all people in God's holy nation.

"Israel," the name given to Jacob, means "one who wrestles with God." The people of Israel represent "God's first-born" (Exodus 4:22). Israel is a birthplace (Psalm 68:26) and a place of *shalom,* of wholeness (Psalm 125:5). In the world to come, there will be no need for limits since the land of Israel will be *all* places *and* contain *all* holiness.

> *O that my people would listen to Me,*
> *that Israel would walk in My ways!*
> Psalm 81:13

May Zion always be in our hearts: "For the Eternal One has chosen Zion. . . . 'This is My resting place for ever; here I will dwell'" (Psalm 132:13–14).

Walking the Path: Our Relationship with Place— The Land of Israel

ACTIVITY

- What makes a place "holy"?

- How do you define "sacred space"?

- Make a list of features that describe "holy place" and "holy time." It might include music, a building, nature, people, religious words, dancing and movement, solitude, day or night, home or away.

- How do you feel in a holy place?

- How do you perceive time?

> *In Your presence is the*
> *fullness of joy.*
> Psalm 16:11

- Where and when are you most likely to know God's Presence?

KAVANAH: AWAKENING

Rabbi Adin Steinsaltz, the twentieth-century mystic, wrote of the Jewish people: "[W]ith the acceptance of Torah as an inner way of life, as an inner map, they encumber themselves with the responsibility and obligation of a priesthood not confined to a particular time or place, but for all of life."[20]

Accepting the responsibility of priest/priestess—serving the Eternal One for all life—we dedicate our lives to being mindful, to living in such a way as to bring awareness of God's presence in each moment, to each place and to each creature. "The Eternal One has sworn and will not change, 'You are a priest [and priestess] for ever'" (Psalm 110:4).

• • •

There are many Israels in my mind: There is the ancient land of Canaan where my ancestors Sarah and Abraham walked with their clan and flocks, discovering the place that would become their home. There is the place I came to 4,000 years later as a teenager and found my first love—and my own inner soul as a Jew. Israel is also the name of the country filled with conflict and genuine tragedy I read about daily in the newspaper. Israel is a Rorschach test for the Jewish soul: Place the black outline of the country on a white piece of paper and you will receive as many different responses as there are Jews, even more since, like me, each person has many different responses. But the most important Israel is the one I carry around inside of me: the Israel that forms me even as I create it. (jlm)

• • •

CREATIVE BLESSING

"Blessed are You, Eternal One, the All that is Place and Time, You have provided within me the potential to be a priest/priestess—one who serves You and brings sacredness to life. Please be with me as I strive to know Your presence."

Conclusion: Our Relationship with God

Every moment in our lives has a potential for *brakha* (blessing) or *klala* (curse). The Torah teaches us the power of choice. The presence of so much pain and violence in our world teaches us that these choices can be easily abused. But by training our heart and soul to be increasingly mindful of the consequences of our every act and word, we grow closer to the image of God in which we were created. This is the enduring work of the examined life.

Judaism recognizes the importance of human connection. Every relationship in life is potentially life-affirming. Every encounter can be sustaining. As Martin Buber wrote, "All real living is meeting." In a very real sense, every encounter with another human being is a relationship since it is an encounter with God's Presence. The skills developed as we interact with other people are the most crucial ones for happiness and wholeness. In many respects, this is what defines our lives and defines our relationship with God.

> *And the effect of righteousness will be peace, and the result of righteousness, quietness and trust for ever.*
>
> Isaiah 32:17

> But now thus says the Eternal One, the One who created you, O Jacob, the One who formed you, O Israel: "Fear not, for I have redeemed you; I have called you by name, you are mine. When you pass through the waters I will be with you; and through the rivers, they shall not overwhelm you; when you walk through fire you shall not be burned, and the flame shall not consume you. For I am the Eternal One your God, The Holy One of Israel . . ."
>
> Isaiah 43:1–3

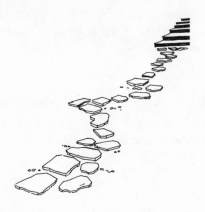

EVENING: LEISURE—
RECREATION, STUDY, AND PRAYER

And Isaac went out to meditate in the field toward
evening.

—GENESIS 24:63

• • •

Our Rabbis taught: Do not say when I have leisure I will study—
perhaps you will never have leisure.

There is a deep irony in the fact that we have to plan to be spontaneous. But we do. As I look through my date book for the month
to come, I invariably designate certain days as D.O.—"day off." By
that, I mean that I will schedule nothing on that particular day.
About 90 percent of the time, something unavoidable comes up and,
at least part of that day, I find myself busy. Very often when I am
able to keep my word to myself and reserve an entire day for leisure,
I get pangs of guilt by early afternoon.

I suspect that this chapter is as important as all the others in this
book combined, especially for those of us who are "workaholics."
Please approach this chapter knowing that self-care and renewal are

the basis for caring for others and renewing the world, that studying a page of Talmud and praying and meditating renew not only us, but also the world around us. (jlm)

• • •

During each day, there are different kinds of time, especially since some activities (such as work) may require more concentration and more energy. As we move toward evening, we'd like to consider those activities that bring relax-ation, rest, renewal. For this time, we'll stop serving oth-ers and focus on our own needs, recognizing that when we are strengthened and renewed, we can better serve others—and the Holy Oneness.

For everything there is a season, and a time for every matter under heaven.

Ecclesiastes 3:1

The mystics teach that we are each "a world in miniature." As we care for ourselves, as we reestablish a balance of energy and renew our spirit, our efforts are reflected throughout the worlds of God's Creation!

Study: Renewing the Spirit— Personal Endeavors

Carving out time during the day for our renewal and enjoyment may be very difficult when we are faced with many responsibilities. Hope-fully, we can find ways to enjoy—to infuse with joy— activities throughout the day by staying mindful. As Nehemiah (8:10) wrote, "Joy in the Eternal One is your strength." In Judaism, the goal is to find the joy—the Godful-ness—in every aspect of daily life.

I know that there is nothing better for them than to be happy and enjoy themselves as long as they live.

Ecclesiastes 3:12

But some of us struggle with feelings of guilt and/or selfishness when we plan activities that only serve us and not others. We have filled our days so often with the business of life that we wonder whether it is valid to spend time that produces no tangible income and focuses on caring only for ourselves.

But taking time to renew ourselves is part of the spiritual path. Whether we choose to exercise, study, meditate, play music, or pray, we must spend some time refreshing ourselves. And by committing the time, creating the rhythm, and entering the discipline, we become more proficient at personal renewal and experience its benefits. We move toward a "balanced" life: work *and* play, activity *and* rest, making money *and* enjoying the fruits of our labor.

Having leisure time involves discovering those activities that renew your spirit and strengthen your mind and body. Explore your creativity, stretch your body, expand your mind. All these renew your spirit.

Walking the Path: Renewing the Spirit— Personal Endeavors

ACTIVITY

The Mishnah offers this caution: "Do not say when I have leisure I will study Torah—perhaps you will not have leisure." Often the most difficult barrier to adding a spiritual practice or an exercise regimen or a new activity to our schedules is blocking out the time for it and holding that time as "sacred." Psychologists have determined that it takes about six weeks to incorporate a new activity into our schedule before we recognize it as "routine." So we are faced with the following challenge: How can we schedule a new activity into a time slot that (seemingly) doesn't exist?

> Fix one hour during the day when you will behave completely according to the Torah.
> *Hayei ha-Musar*, III

Imagine you have just been given a twenty-fifth hour for the day. What would you do with it? Examine your schedule and see if you can't find a place for this twenty-fifth hour in the twenty-four that you already have. Create the space you need to renew your body, mind, and spirit.

KAVANAH: AWAKENING

Behold I am ready to fulfill the *mitzvah* of renewal of body, mind, and spirit. Make me aware of Your nearness at all times. Help me embrace myself in love and let me give myself permission to turn inward. As I take deep breaths, help me let go of the need to always live for others. Let me now live for myself, however briefly.

• • •

Reading and writing, time at the water's edge, walking alone and simply being alone are all ways to spiritually renew myself. Of course, I could pray and meditate, but spiritual renewal happens in many more ways than these intentional activities. Quiet (with the exception of beautiful music or nature's sounds) is important. This often requires separating myself from my loved ones and others: Going to my office where I can be undisturbed, going for a walk, or turning off the phone allows me to pursue an activity or a thought without interruption, to enjoy the silence that restores my spirit. An aesthetically pleasing environment also helps! I love fresh flowers, scented candles, gentle colors. All of the above can offer many opportunities throughout the day for spiritual renewal—whether for a moment or an hour. (kbw)

• • •

CREATIVE BLESSING

"Blessed are You, Eternal One, Force of Renewal and Transformation. You have blessed us with the many rhythms of life. You have punctuated our day, our week, our month, our year with time for rest and renewal. We are grateful for renewal of body and spirit."

Study: Renewing the Body— Recreation ("Re-Creation")

Recreation has been defined as "refreshment of strength and spirit after toil."[1] For some people, playing may be as intensely active as working, but there is a world of difference, whether the "playing" is reading a novel or a magazine or playing a competitive game of tennis or chess. There can be a spiritual side to playing a sport. For instance, in tennis we can lose ourselves as we swing a racquet and truly become one with the tennis ball. There is a poetry in the movement of our body and the flight of the ball. Time often stands still; there is no sense of past or future. There is, instead, only the moment and the motion.

Some of this is found in sedentary activities, as well. The expression "losing yourself in a book" is an accurate description of the act of reading. Books speak to us—or is it the Presence that speaks to us through books? Reading and exploring words, poetry, and meaning connects us with the writer as we listen for how his or her message applies to our lives.

The same can be said of doing or enjoying art or listening to music, or attending a film, a play or an opera. Art and music can be vehicles to the Divine: "Music is the gateway to the soul." They can remove us from time—and heal us. Al-

> But as for me, I will sing of Your strength
> I will sing out loud . . .
> rejoicing in Your Chesed/*Lovingkindness*
> Psalm 59:16 as translated by
> Rabbi Sheila Peltz Weinberg

though ephemeral, the blending with the Greater Self inspired by art and music brings us back, again and again, to touch the sacred.

Walking the Path: Renewing the Body— Recreation ("Re-Creation")

EXERCISE

During whatever recreation you choose to do, let yourself focus and be mindful of the re-creative aspect of what you are doing. What are you re-creating? Is it physical or internal strength, endurance, beauty, ideas, melodies, energy, self?

Take a moment with your journal or just your thoughts and see if you can put into words what "re-creating" means to you.

Activity: Music

The Baal Shem Tov, the founder of Chasidism, taught that "through music, you can reach joy and d'vekut, intense love of God, with the Infinite One, blessed be He."[2] Consider how your choice of music affects your feelings and your ability to be mindful. Try listening to a piece of beautiful music and be the music and be the notes. This can be particularly wonderful when listening to music sung in a sacred language, such as Hebrew. You can become the Hebrew, whether you understand the words or not. Let the words and music wrap around you like a prayer shawl, and feel surrounded and infused with love. This is a moment with the Holy One.

Then sang Moses and the Children of Israel this song for God.

Exodus 15:1

• • •

Recently, I spent several days at the seashore. Each morning, I looked forward to walking along the beach, listening to the breaking of the waves, feeling the water on my bare feet, experiencing the rising sun on my back or on my face. It was a magical time. I reflected on the difference between looking out on the seashore and experiencing it more directly through the physical act of walking. The blessing of walking is the sense of oneness that comes from being part of the physical universe as opposed to experiencing it vicariously through a single sense, such as sight. I am grateful for the ability to be at one with my universe through this simple act. (jlm)

• • •

Kavanah: Awakening

"Restore us to Yourself, O Eternal One, that we may be restored! Renew our days!" (Lamentations 5:21). Whether we are taking a walk, playing a sport, reading, listening, or relaxing, we can do so while being mindful of the miracle of Life, the Eternal One. We enter into these activities knowing that in caring for our bodies, minds and spirits, we further our opportunities to

The ecstasy produced by melody . . .

is in the category of spontaneous ecstasy alone,

without any choice or intellectual will whatsoever.

Rav Dov Baer

participate in God's creative plan. Through renewal, we can participate in other areas of our life with new vigor and peacefulness which would not be possible without pause, reflection, and recentering.

*[T]hey who wait for the Eternal One
shall renew their strength,
they shall mount up with wings like eagles,
they shall run and not be weary,
they shall walk and not faint.*

Isaiah 40:31

Study: Renewing the Mind— Torah and Other Jewish Holy Books

The central act of being a Jew is *talmud torah,* Torah study. Since Talmudic times, it has commonly been viewed as the single most important Jewish activity. This idea is captured by the phrase *"v'talmud torah k'neged kulam,"* "Torah study balances them all"— Torah study is the sum of all the other *mitzvot,* or sacred activities. As Elie Wiesel has written:

And you shall meditate in [Torah] day and night.

Joshua 1:8

[W]e have repeated certain sentences so often in four thousand years that they have become immortal. . . . That is the profound beauty of Scripture: its characters are not mythical; their adventures are not imaginary; they vibrate with life and truth, and thus compel those of us who approach them to enter their lives and search for their meaning. . . . Read and reread the sources and you shall marvel at their depth; you shall see that underneath each face there is another face, that beneath each story there is another story.[3]

Many people have traced the predominance of Jews in many academic fields to the high emphasis placed on Torah study in Jewish culture. While this cannot be empirically demonstrated, there is a strong sense that this academic success is a natural outgrowth of traditional Jewish priorities.

For I give you good instruction; do not forsake My Torah.

Proverbs 4:2

"Torah" can refer specifically to

Open my eyes, that I may behold
wondrous things out of Your Torah.
Psalm 119:18

the first five books of the Hebrew Bible. In this sense, Torah may be described as a roadmap to God. Legend says that we know the entire Torah prior to our birth. At birth, an angel hides the wisdom, causing us to forget all that we know. Consequently, we never "learn" Torah, but simply "recall" what was forgotten.

Another legend describes the dynamic, energetic power of Torah by teaching that it was written as "black fire on white fire." This implies that nothing is static. Instead, everything undergoes creation, change, and transformation—even Torah. And the mystics teach that there is a specific portion of Torah that we are here to manifest, to interpret, to live. They also remind us that the stories of Torah are simply garments wrapped around the deeper truths which we must unwrap. With all this said, there are times when parts of Torah may simply seem unexplainable, or irrelevant, maybe even offensive and wrong. We realize that with Torah, as with other aspects of life, there will always be parts we don't understand, or don't accept, or perhaps parts we'd like to change.

"Torah" in general refers not only to the *chumash,* the five books that begin the Hebrew Bible, but to all authentic Jewish religious texts, especially the Mishnah and the Talmud. In modern times, we associate Torah study with all aspects of learning about Judaism.

It is the tree of life to those who grasp it, and whoever holds on to it is happy.
Proverbs 3:18

The daily service contains a beautiful prayer that captures the essence of what Torah study means in Jewish tradition: "Eternal our God, make the words of Your Torah sweet to us, and the House of Israel, Your people, that we and our children may be lovers of Your name and students of Your Torah. We praise You, O God, Teacher of Torah to Your people Israel."[4]

The sweetness of the words of Torah reflects both the aesthetic qualities found in it and the overriding sense of gaining insight into the Divine will. Ideally, the study of Torah brings us closer to God and provides a guide to the religious life.

Your word is a lamp to my feet and a light to my path.
Psalm 119:105

Another aspect of traditional Torah study

that makes it special, if not unique, is studying with other people. The Mishnah speaks of the desirability of studying with a *rav*, a master or mentor, as well as with a *chaver*, a peer or friend. As the Rabbis said, "If two sit together and occupy themselves with words of Torah, the *Shechinah* [God's presence] abides in their midst" (*Mishnah Avot* 3:2).

But studying by yourself is also possible because of the assistance offered by *perushim*, or commentaries, which are printed and added to the basic texts. Commentaries (notably those by Rashi, an eleventh-century French exegete) are invaluable tools for delving into the biblical and talmudic texts.

Fortunately, virtually every important Jewish text is now found in an excellent English translation. These are often annotated and explained by first-rate scholars. They may have particular philosophical bents, such as Chasidic, Reform, Orthodox, Conservative, Reconstructionist, or Renewal. This proliferation of Jewish publications is one of the more robust aspects of Jewish American life.

When you open a book to learn and when you close it, kiss the book.
Derekh Hayim, 5–61

Like many other aspects of life, Torah study is best accomplished by practice and diligence. Finding a comfortable chair, a good light, a quiet time, and the needed discipline helps us be students of God's Words. In many respects, Torah study is a kind of prayer—and certainly a spiritual discipline of transcendent value. It can elevate even the most mundane moment to a higher plane, and it can connect us to our past in a way that no other Jewish activity can.

Walking the Path: Renewing the Mind— Torah and Other Jewish Holy Books

Those unfamiliar with Torah study might imagine scholars hovering over Hebrew books, quoting and debating with great authority. We might think, "I've never done anything like that." Or worse, we might tell ourselves, "I can't do that. I don't know how." But there is a way to enter into *talmud torah*, Torah study, with ease and a sense of ability. You are not required to know someone else's definition or interpretation (although these may be inspirational); you are here to understand your own experience of the particular Torah you are studying. Torah study is often more "art" than "science" and you are the artist creating new insights into ancient text.

The Torah of the Eternal One is perfect,
reviving the soul . . .
the precepts of the Eternal One are right,
rejoicing the heart;
the commandments of the Eternal One are pure,
enlightening the eyes;
the ordinances of the Eternal One are true,
and righteous altogether.
More to be desired are they than gold . . .
Psalm 19:7–10

Our first step in preparing for Torah study is to create a space and time separate from the mundane world. We enter into a sacred space, a space of great honor and pleasure, a space near God. Like the Garden of Eden, it is a space not of this world, but of the world to come.

The purpose of the laws of the Torah is to promote compassion, lovingkindness, and peace in the world.
Moses Maimonides

Consider what sensory cues will help you enter the Presence of God:

- Saying the blessing and wrapping yourself in a prayer shawl.

- Studying in a place that has few, if any, distractions.

- Imagining that you are studying with your teacher (who may be a living or even an ancient rabbi whose teachings and life you've studied).

- Seeing the Hebrew letters of the Tetragrammaton (*yud, hay, vav, hay*) printed on a card. This is the unspoken, most holy name of God.

- Lighting candles.

- Seeing a plant or flowers symbolic of the Garden of Eden.

The Holy One is near to all who call upon the One, to all who call upon the One in truth.
Psalm 145:18

- Smelling spices and scents—which can remind us of the fragrance of the Garden.

• • •

My "mind" is constantly being flooded with thoughts, ideas, and in-
formation. Sometimes it is difficult to distinguish between my own
ideas, those received from others, and those thoughts which perhaps
come to me from the Mind of God. I am often amazed at the variety
of intellectual concepts that I encounter each day. People living in
the same universe experience our world in so many different ways.
The challenge for me is to keep an "open" mind and receive the ideas
of others, while at the same time affirming the core concepts which
define my essential being. Therefore, it is a great gift that I am given
a regular opportunity to express my ideas in writing, while also
blending with them quotes from other people or sources, and to
present these ideas in a public forum through the act of delivering a
drascha or sermon. (jlm)

• • •

KAVANAH: AWAKENING

From our mystical tradi-
tion, we are given an-
other beautiful concept,
d'vekut, which Yitzhak
Buxbaum, author of *Jew-
ish Spiritual Practices,*

And when the highest point and the world
that is coming ascend, they know only the
aroma, as one inhaling an aroma is sweetened.
Zohar 3:26b

translates as "God-consciousness imbued with
love." The ultimate goal of d'vekut is such intense love of God that
no separation exists between self (ego) and the Self (Divine Presence). There is only direct awareness of God, and we become a
dwelling place for the Divine Presence. *D'vekut* is an ideal state that
can inspire our whole being, our every thought, our every move:
"And you shall love the Eternal One your God with all your heart,
with all your soul, and with all your might" (Deuteronomy 6:5).

About Torah study and d'vekut, the Baal Shem Tov taught, "You
should learn Torah . . . in a low voice, and should shout in a whisper,
and say the words . . . with all your strength, as it says, 'All my bones
shall say: Oh Eternal One, who is like You!' (Psalm 35:10). For the
shouting which is from d'vekut should be in a whisper."[5]

This intensity of fiery devotion brings on an altered state of consciousness—God-consciousness—and through deep love we enter

the sacred as Elijah did when taken from earth in God's fiery chariot: "And as they still went on and talked, behold, a chariot of fire and horses of fire separated the two of them. And Elijah went up by a whirlwind into heaven" (2 Kings 2:11).

As you study Torah, may you be aware of your potential, may you cultivate love and devotion, may you reach for God in all of your awareness.

MEDITATION: LIGHT

As you begin your study time, take a moment to imagine the light of the *Shechinah,* the Divine Presence, above your head. Let the light flow through you, infusing you with the love of God's Presence. Feel the joy in your heart, the swelling of emotion in your chest, the awesomeness of coming before God. Remove the everyday world from your spirit, just as you remove a garment, and free your spirit to enter the Garden. Sanctify your space, your study, your prayer. Know that the light and the glory of *Shechinah* continues glowing all around you as you study.[6]

Oh send out Your light and Your truth;
let them lead me,
let them bring me to Your holy mountain
and to Your dwelling!

Psalm 43:3

Where is God?
In the heart of all who seek Him.
Rabbi Abraham Halevy bar Hasdai

BLESSING OVER TORAH:
AS YOU BEGIN YOUR STUDY (TRADITIONAL)

"Blessed are You, Eternal One our God, Divine Presence in the Universe, who has sanctified us by Your commandments and commanded us to occupy ourselves with the words of Torah."

STUDY

You may want to begin your study with a prayer for understanding. Each study session will be an opening into the unknown and, at times, the unknowable. Approach study with gratitude for whatever insights you'll gain.

If you are studying a Torah story, imagine becoming the characters. Step into each role and notice your thoughts and feelings when placed in their situation. Think about everything you know about a concept, an idea, a symbol in the story, and try to apply it to your life. Recognize that stories speak to each of us differently, depending on what we need to hear. This is the magic of study, and this is why the same stories have spoken to a hundred generations.

As you complete your study time, you may want to say a prayer of thanks for the understanding offered and the insights gained.

BLESSING OVER TORAH: AS YOU END YOUR STUDY (TRADITIONAL)

"Blessed are You, Eternal One our God, Source of Divine Truth, who has given us Your Torah of truth, and has planted everlasting life in our midst. Blessed are You, Eternal One, who gives the Torah."

TURNING STUDY INTO ACTION

Do what is taught: *Naaseh v'nishmah*, "We are ready to do whatever You tell us." The value of learning is turning that knowledge into action in our everyday life.

The Merciful One! Have mercy upon us and permit us to understand, to discern, to heed, to learn and teach, to observe, perform, and fulfill all the words of instruction of Your Torah in love.

The *Siddur*

Study: Renewing the Heart—Prayer

Here is a wonderful Chasidic tale about prayer:

There was once a simple herdsman who did not know how to pray. But it was his custom to say every day: "Lord of the world! You know that if you had cattle and gave them to me to tend, though I take wages from everyone else, from you I would take nothing."

Once, a rabbi was passing and heard the man pray in this way. He said to him, "Fool, do not pray in this way." The herdsman asked: "How should I pray?" Then, the rabbi taught him the Sh'ma and other prayers so that he would no longer say what he was accustomed to.

After the rabbi left, the herdsman forgot all the prayers and did not pray. And since the rabbi told him not to pray as he once had, he said nothing. And this was a great catastrophe.[7]

The ancient Rabbis taught that prayer is "service of the heart." Heschel wrote that prayer "makes the heart audible to God." Jews believe that when we speak truly from the heart, our words go directly to God.

Let Your ear be attentive, and Your eyes open, to hear the prayer of Your servant which I now pray before You day and night . . .
Nehemiah 1:6

From deep in our hearts, the truest prayers emerge. The painful realities of life, its joys and wonders, its challenges and blessings are all expressed in the fullness of the heart. And we are reassured over and over again that God knows the heart: "I, the Eternal One, search the heart . . ." (Jeremiah 17:10).

The heart is symbolized by *t'feret*, the life center which is one of the ten aspects of God in Jewish mysticism's "Tree of Life." It is associated with the unspoken name of God *"YHVH"* and with the aspect of God that spoke at Sinai. The heart is considered the stable center of our being: It harmonizes that which is above with that which is below. It is the center of God's love and mercy, which is reflected in our own desire to compassionately respond to other people's pain. The heart is the gateway to Divine Truth. With it, we can enter the gates of Jersalem—the gates of prayer—with sacred intention; through it, we can experience the power of healing, love and union with all Creation.

For the Eternal One knows the secrets of the heart.
Psalm 44:21

It is often assumed that Jews pray at certain times or in certain places, and it is true that normatively Jews pray frequently according to a prescribed liturgy. But the Rabbis wrote a midrash on Psalm 4:4

about prayer that expresses the many ways that the Eternal One hears our prayer:

> Said the Holy One to Israel, "I have told you that when you pray, you should do so in the synagogue in your city. If you cannot pray in the synagogue, pray in your field. If you cannot pray in your field, pray in your house. If you cannot pray in your house, pray on your bed. If you cannot pray on your bed, meditate in your heart."[8]

Traditional Judaism sees prayer in terms of *mitzvot,* deeds that indicate acceptance of the rule of God for Jews and all humanity. There are also a great variety of prayers, each of which has a specific purpose. Prayer may include praise, petition, and/or thanksgiving. The basic prayer formula, *"Baruch atah Adonai Eloheinu melech ha-olam,"* "Blessed are You, Eternal One our God, King of the Universe . . . ," is the traditional essential language that glorifies and thanks God.

Even though Judaism has significant formal liturgy and prescribed prayer, it is clear that throughout Jewish history, individual and spontaneous prayer was commonplace, such as when "Moses cried to the Eternal One, 'Heal her, O God, I beg You'" (Numbers 12:13). In his book *Entering Jewish Prayer,* Reuven Hammer describes the healing effect of spontaneous prayer this way:

> The hoped-for results of such contemplation will be that my resolve will be strengthened to live in a way that is morally correct and in accord with the highest ethical traditions of mankind. By making myself sensitive to the world and appreciative of the gifts I am given, I am challenged to be worthy of them and to take nothing, including life itself, for granted. Prayer may take effort, but its rewards are great.[9]

Judaism recognizes the validity of petitional prayer in which we ask God for some desired result. But we are often left with a sense of mystery when we attempt to understand answers to prayer in human terms. Perhaps we can be assured that prayers are answered in some way by growing closer to God.

The Eternal One hears when I call . . .
Psalm 4:3

Above all, prayer helps us enter the peace of God and constantly rediscover God's presence in the world. So we pray for peace, for *shalom,* for wholeness within ourselves, in our relationship with God, in our relationship with others.

May the words of my mouth and the meditations of my heart be acceptable before You, O Eternal One, my Rock and my Redeemer.
Psalm 19:14

Walking the Path: Renewing the Heart—Prayer

A chasid once came to Rabbi Simha Bunim of Pshischa and told him of the trouble he was having, that whenever he prayed he always got a headache from his concentration. "What has prayer to do with the head?" the *rebbe* answered in surprise. "Prayer is service of the heart, not a labor of the head."[10]

MEDITATION: BREATHING

Breathing meditation has long been practiced in Judaism as part of preparing for prayer. It calms the mind and body. Follow your breath: On the inhalation, meditate on the *Shechinah* entering your body; on the exhalation, meditate on your soul going out to God. Or you may prefer to meditate on the love of God entering your life on inhalation, and your love returning to God on exhalation.

You must be Wholehearted with the Eternal One your God.
Deuteronomy 18:13

Let everything that breathes praise the Eternal One.
Psalm 150:6

While preparing for prayer, surround your heart with a space of forgiveness. Do this by meditating on these words from Leviticus (19:18): "You shall love your neighbor as yourself." This gives your heart and mind a focus to love yourself, love God, love your neighbor—and to recognize that all three come together as Ultimate Oneness. If you are struggling with hurt or anger toward another person, visualize that person's face and extend love to that person from your heart. Forgive those who have

Create in me a clean heart, O God, and put a new and right spirit within me.
Psalm 51:12

wronged you and pray for their healing; then pray for your own for-giveness and healing while determining to make right any offense you may have committed against another person.

• • •

Prayer is another word for the ongoing dialogue between myself and the Almighty. I regularly thank angels (God's agents) for all kinds of simple interventions: an insight with a client, a red light when I'm driving too fast, an opportunity to speak to a new group. So many experiences initiate conversation with God: seeing a rainbow, arriv-ing safely from a trip, watching my children thrive. Most of these are examples of prayers of thankfulness. At this point in my life, I also whisper many prayers for guidance. So much is happening: my chil-dren are growing up, my relationship with my husband is maturing, my body is changing, my career interests are shifting, my needs for meaningful connection with friends are increasing. So these, per-haps, are the prayers of "mid-life." Time will tell what our (mine and God's) conversations will focus on in the next stage of my life. For now, my prayers are predominantly in English and mostly spon-taneous, heartfelt expressions to the Divine, punctuated with silence and listening. (kbw)

• • •

KAVANAH: AWAKENING

"You have said 'Seek My face.' My heart says to You, 'Your face, Eternal One, do I seek'" (Psalm 27:8). We seek the Eternal One through the gates of the heart—entering into the mystery of Creation, finding the sacred Truth and Divine Love that await there. Open my heart; soften my heart; hear my heart.

I keep the Eternal One before me always.
Psalm 16:8

TRADITIONAL BLESSING

"We praise You, Eternal God, Sovereign of the Universe, whose word brings on the evening. With wisdom, You open heaven's gates; and with understanding, You make the ages pass and the seasons alternate; Your will con-trols the stars as they travel through the skies.

You are Creator of day and night, rolling light away from darkness, and darkness from light; You cause day to pass and bring on the night, separating day from night; You command the hosts of heaven! May the living and eternal God rule us always, to the end of time! We praise you, O God, whose word makes evening fall. "[11]

CREATIVE BLESSING (BASED ON PSALM 141:2)

"Blessed are You, Eternal One, Compassionate Heart of the Universe. Let my prayer be as incense before You, and the lifting up of my hands be as an evening sacrifice!"

Conclusion:
Loving Ourselves, Loving Others, Loving God

Caring for our body, mind, and soul. Caring for ourselves—and for a moment, no one else. Taking the time we need for recreation, study, and prayer. These need not be solo activities, but perhaps they are the activities we do solely for ourselves. Herein lies the paradox of the spiritual path: Truly loving ourselves, caring deeply for ourselves, restoring and repairing ourselves, truly loving God and caring deeply for God, allows us to love others, to care deeply for all Creation, and to restore and repair the world.

And there shall be continuous day (it is known to the Eternal One), not day and not night, for at evening time there shall be light. On that day living waters [eternal life] shall flow from Jerusalem [the heart], half of them to the eastern sea and half of them to the western sea; it shall continue in summer as in winter. And the Eternal One will become sovereign over all the earth; on that day the Eternal One will be one and God's name will be One.

Zechariah 14:7–9

NIGHT: PAIN, LOSS, DEATH, AND HEALING

God is close to those whose hearts are broken.
—PSALM 34:19

• • •

As I laid awake in bed last night, a light shone through the loosely woven draperies that cover our windows. The light was so bright, I thought someone must have left an outside light on. With quick investigation, I found God had left the "light" on: a beautiful May full moon.

Back under the covers, I was aware of how the moonlight transformed the night into an opportunity to see what is normally hidden in darkness. As I enjoyed the silvery glow filling the room, I imagined myself a night traveler comforted by this gift of light, which gave me insight into the uncharted, unknown territory ahead. I was reminded how reassuring light can be in the darkness, how it provides guidance and hope.

The spiritual path contains both darkness and light. Even the devoted spiritual traveler faces pain, suffering, and illness, and confronts the inevitability of death. When any of these are accompanied by loss of faith or fear or confusion, it's often referred to as a "dark night of the soul."

In this chapter, we explore the darkness: illness, pain, and death. We look at anger and fear, we face doubt and guilt, we deal with enemies within and without. And then, we find healing—refu'ah—the light.

Judaism teaches that the "Eternal One leads all the night with a fiery light." In our faith we find refuge, solace, and healing; we find light even in the darkness. (kbw)

• • •

As the sun sets and the last light fades from the sky, we enter the night. Darkness may be a time of ignorance and disbelief, of adversity, of affliction, of death. In Judaism, we recognize that daily life is punctuated with pain, illness, loss, and ultimately, death. Poets often refer to sleep as the "little death" we face every day. Entering the night, the dark times, we may feel judged or abandoned by God. This can momentarily strip us of our faith. We struggle in the dark: "[F]or I am hemmed in by darkness, and thick darkness covers my face" (Job 23:17). In time, we may open to healing, for "the light," they say, "is near the darkness" (Job 17:12). And we are changed—perhaps physically, perhaps emotionally, perhaps spiritually. And we heal.

Great and Mighty One, who dwells on high,
You are Peace and Your name is Peace.
May it be Your will that You place upon us peace.
Traditional bedtime prayer

Study: Pain—Physical Illness

Pain and suffering are part of the human experience. Illness affects all of us. When we lose our health, we slow down, maybe even stop certain activities. Illness is, at least, an inconvenience and, at most, a humbling confrontation with our mortality. It can fill us with confusion, fear, and pain.

I am the Eternal One your Healer.
Exodus 15:26

128

It is understandable that the issue of physical pain and suffering is a focal point of Judaism. In the Jewish tradition, illness is seen as real, not illusory, and the art of the "physician" (the physical healer) is respected. Yet, there is a spiritual component to healing as well, one which may be as effective as medicine, or maybe even more effective. As a Jewish folktale relates,

> A sick man called a doctor. After the doctor had examined him, he said, "My friend, you, I and your disease are three. If you will take my side, the two of us will easily be able to overcome your illness, which is only one. However, should you forsake me and not cooperate with me but hold on to your disease, then I, being alone, won't be able to overcome both of you."[1]

The basis of healing within Judaism is a twofold approach of medicine and such spiritual practices as prayer. These are seen to act synergistically and not to impede each other.

Judaism does not offer a simplistic explanation for illness and other human maladies. While there are anecdotal references in Jewish religious writings to illness as punishment for misdeeds, these references are perhaps more reasonably understood today in terms of environmental stress, behaviors, beliefs, and prolonged negative feelings which may become toxic to the body. We are physical *and* spiritual beings, and the interaction between the two is just beginning to be explored in greater depth by the medical community. But whatever explanations medical science offers about illness, we must keep in mind the limits of science and maintain a deep respect for the mystery inherent in the human spirit, especially in terms of how illness manifests and how the body heals. The mystics teach that the invisible realms, which include God, deeply influence our health and well-being. What we can be certain of is that God is with us in sickness and in health.

> The Shechinah, *Divine Presence . . . is at the bedside of the sick.*
> Kitzur Shulkhan Arukh 193:4

Jewish tradition also speaks of *"yesurin shel ahava,"* the "punishments of Divine love": God afflicting the righteous as a means of purification for the afterlife or perhaps as a test of faith. But more generally, Judaism recognizes that the purpose of most illnesses may not be known to the afflicted, and that illness requires faith in God's steadfast love.

Being ill can provide us with an opportunity for reflection and evaluation. The body may be the voicebox for the spirit, crying out through illness for us to change the way we live so it is more compatible with our spiritual selves. By attempting to understand the meaning of illness, we move closer to God and we heal. Even if the very source of suffering is God, we pray that God will also heal us.

If you are experiencing serious illness, you may want to focus all your daily spiritual practice on healing. For others of us, it is important to keep in mind the full range of human experience and to recognize that, on any given day, even a cold or a headache can be a serious challenge to living mindfully and spiritually. Healing prayers, kavanot, and meditations can be adapted to address a wide variety of ailments, as well as the more spiritual and emotional malaise that also afflicts so many of us.

Walking the Path: Pain—Physical Illness

A Gentile physician believed that his wife was hopelessly ill, and in order not to witness her death agonies, he left town. When he returned a month later, he found his wife much improved, and on the way to a complete recovery. He was told that a "rebbe" had advised his family to arrange for the chanting of Psalms on behalf of her recovery—a Jewish custom of long-standing. As soon as this was done, an improvement in the sick woman's condition was noted. Later, the physician wrote a medical work concerning the ailment of his wife, and remarked at its conclusion, "If all the remedies enumerated here are of no avail, Psalms should be chanted in Hebrew."[2]

ACTIVITY

The next time you are ill, make a "recovery plan." What steps will you take to promote a cure? Will you need to see a health care provider? List your emotional needs and how you will care for them. Identify your spiritual yearnings. Which spiritual practices will help

I am utterly spent and crushed;
I groan because of the tumult of my heart.
Eternal One, all my longing is known to You,
my sighing is not hidden from You. . . .
Do not forsake me, O Eternal One!
O my God, be not far from me!
Make haste to help me,
O Eternal One, my salvation!

Psalm 38:8–9, 21–22

you regain your spiritual balance and bring you closer to God? Notice how responding to the physical, emotional, and spiritual aspects of your illness promotes an overall sense of well-being.

MEDITATION

As you recite the following Psalm, you can meditate on being both a physical and spiritual being. Our bodies are like vessels, holy containers for the soul. When the body is suffering in some way, the soul is intimately connected to the experience. We cannot separate the effect on one from the other. We pray that God's love will surround us and that we will experience healing of body and soul.

"I have become like a broken vessel. . . . But I trust in You, O Eternal One, I say, "You are my God." My times are in Your hand; . . . Let Your face shine on me; save me in Your steadfast love!" (Psalm 31:12, 14–15).

• • •

My most intense physical pain occurred when I experienced the
agony of a kidney stone. My doctor told me that this was almost as
painful as childbirth. Although the actual duration of the pain was
brief (an hour or two, since I went to a nearby hospital fairly
quickly), in that brief time all my normal inhibitions and stoicism
were absent. Just stop the pain, I demanded. It was a difficult but
worthwhile lesson in humility, and it let me know that much of the
external sense of dignity I affect can be stripped away in minutes by
my own nerve cells. (jlm)

• • •

KAVANAH: AWAKENING

"Rabbi Joshua ben Levi said . . . 'When a man feels pain in his head, let him occupy himself with Torah, since the verse (Proverbs 1:9) goes on to prescribe "for your head." When a man feels pain in his throat, let him occupy himself with Torah, for the verse likens Torah's words to "a necklace about thy throat" (Proverbs 3:3). When he feels pain in his innards, let him occupy himself with Torah, for another verse says of the Torah, that "it shall be a healing to the navel" (Proverbs 3:8). When he feels pain in his bones, let him occupy himself with Torah, since the verse also describes Torah as "marrow for thy bones" (Proverbs 3:8). When he feels pain in his entire body, let him occupy himself with Torah, since another verse speaks of it as "healing for his whole body" (Proverbs 4:22)."[3]

CREATIVE BLESSING

"Blessed are You, Eternal One, Healer of all healers, please surround me with love and light. Help me stay mindful and remember how to be well. May my bones be strong so that I can do Your will with my heart full and open and my spirit free and loving."

Study: Pain—Emotional Distress, Anger, Fear

Emotional pain can be as burdening and incapacitating as physical pain or illness. When hearts are heavy with troubling emotions, when minds are distracted with anger and fear, when we feel anxious and depressed, we are robbed of the fullness of life. Emotional pain may be the loneliest illness since there is often no outward manifestation of the painful inner world, no outward signaling system (like broken bones, wounds, fevers) to alert others to our needs. When experiencing painful emotions, it is important that we have some way to make sense out of our feelings and find constructive ways to resolve the pain. While this is not always easy, our spiritual work can strengthen our emotional resilience and expand our coping mechanisms.

Insults have broken my heart, so that I am in despair . . . you who seek God, let your hearts revive. For the Eternal One hears the needy. . . .
Psalm 69:20, 32, 33

Anger is like a fire that burns in our bellies when we feel disappointed, hurt, or betrayed. A natural and powerful response to injustice, anger can be constructive and energizing, preparing us for action. Or it can be destructive and consume our thinking, leading to impulsive actions that might be hurtful or violent. Learning to respect the power of anger and channel it constructively is an important part of the spiritual path. We can transform anger into creative problem-solving and action, but doing so requires examining our feelings and praying for wisdom and insight. It's important to assess the effects of our words and actions and determine if we are responding out of vindictiveness or out of justice.

Harboring our anger and turning it inward on itself may be toxic to the body and spirit. Being angry dramatically changes our perceptions of life, making us feel uneasy and distrustful. Like any "power," the use of anger must not be taken lightly. It requires mindfulness and deep concern for its effect on ourselves, on others, and the world.

One of the consequences of monotheism is that everything is ultimately attributed to God. While rabbinic and Christian theology envisioned Satan as a possible source of some of the "evil" in the world, the Hebrew Bible clearly asserts that God is the source of everything. But while anger is a universal human reality, another universal reality is the destructive power of nature. To the Biblical mind, the power of nature could only be attributed to a monumental divine anger. But if we read the Bible solely as theology, we make a grave mistake. The Torah is a compendium of an entire world-view, and God is its central reality, but it also consists of human perception. In the Biblical mind, everything has a justification. While God is the force behind all reality, it is people who, through their freewill, can become angry, violent, and destructive.

> And lo, the Eternal One passed by. There was a great and mighty wind, splitting mountains and shattering rocks by the power of the Eternal One; but the Eternal One was not in the wind. After the wind—an earthquake; but the Eternal One was not in the earthquake. After the earthquake—fire; but the Eternal One was not in the fire. And after the fire, a still small voice.
>
> 1 Kings 19:11–12

Another difficult, often immobilizing emotion is fear. It can keep us from creating, exploring, expressing, and loving fully. In order to be open to our potential as co-creators, to step directly into our purpose in life, we must face our fears: fears about what others think, about money, about acceptance/rejection, about ability, about making a mistake, about taking a risk, about *who we are*. We are made in the Divine image; we are children of God; we are co-creators; we are capable of living fully and mindfully in God's Light. Letting go of fear (to whatever degree we can) and trusting ourselves, trusting God, and moving forward is our spiritual work. As Psalm 23:4 states, "I fear not, for You are with me; Your guidance and blessings comfort me."

You will not fear the terror of the night. . . .
Because those who cleave to Me in love,
I will deliver them, I will protect them,
because they know My name.
Psalm 91:5, 14

Fear of God as expressed in the Bible refers to awe and reverence for the power of God, which is the power of the Life Force. This "fear" was seen as the motivation for obedience to God. Today we also may be motivated to obey Torah—the spiritual laws that guide life—out of similar awe and reverence for the Power of Creation. In prayer, we find that the word "fear" is related to separation from God since our deep love of God and our wish for closeness evoke a fear that we might be estranged from the Divine Source of Life.

When I am afraid, I put my trust in You.
In God, Whose word I praise,
in God I trust without a fear.
Psalm 56:3–4

Fear is a deeply rooted human emotion. Coupled with anxiety, it can cripple our well-being. Accepting ourselves, learning to love and honor ourselves, trusting our inner knowing, and finding security in our place in Creation will assist with decreasing fear and opening to Life—to God.

You are a protected place for me,
You save me from trouble;
You encompass me with safety.
Psalm 32:7

Walking the Path: Pain—
Emotional Distress, Anger, Fear

KAVANAH: AWAKENING

When we are emotionally distressed, our greatest challenge is seeing God's way. We may even experience God as absent or silent during these times. God's words are revealed to us through our own emotional filters—not unlike the experience of our ancestors who wrote in the Bible about God's revelations, which reflect the full spectrum of human emotion and experience. As we approach God for guidance during difficult times, we must first attempt to empty ourselves of the "voice of self"—the proud voice of ego, the hurt voice of revenge, the skeptical voice of distrust, the overly-restricting voice of fear. We must try to enter the silence with a receptive mind and an open heart. Perhaps then we can "hear" God.

• • •

They say my grandmother "died of a broken heart" after the death of her son, my uncle, in a fire during World War II. I've come to understand that the shock, anger, and sadness of the news was followed by a fatal heart attack—the literal destruction of her heart. Only God knows whether the news of my uncle's death had any bearing on her heart attack. Sometimes I hear people say, "I was scared to death" or "I was so angry I couldn't see straight." All these expressions remind me what a powerful role emotion plays in our physical, emotional, and spiritual well-being. When feelings are overwhelming, we do whatever we can to make sense out of our experience, to find cause and effect. We may try to justify how we feel; we may create stories in an attempt to relieve our fear or our pain. We might blame others or even strike out against a perceived enemy. The pain of unexamined, unresolved fear and anger is the source of much human distress. When we take the time to clear our minds, to find our center, to grieve, we often find a new perspective and begin to heal. (kbw)

• • •

PRAYER FOR RESOLVING ANGER

"Dear God, please be with me in my anger, my disappointment, my feelings of betrayal. Help me receive Your calming love and compassion. Help me calm myself so that I can clearly reflect on this experience. What can I learn here about mistakes, compassion, injustice? In what ways was *I* responsible? Is there something about myself and my own shortcomings that I should examine? As I resolve my anger, help me strengthen myself and my commitment to right living and integrity in relationships. I pray to You for the wisdom from which I can act in a way that brings holiness to this situation. Thank You, God, for listening to me and being with me in this time of anger and emotional unrest."

CREATIVE BLESSING

"Blessed are You, Eternal One, who has provided me with such color and intensity in my emotional life. I may be passionate, reflective, zealous, angry, fearful, joyful. All this provides hues and textures to my experiences. Help me recognize Your plan and Your teachings through my emotional responses, and help me care for myself so I may enjoy emotional well-being."

Study: Pain—Spiritual Doubt and Guilt

We live in a world that values (and perhaps overvalues) logic, independence, and competition. Without a meaning greater than our self and our ego-driven successes, our lives can be void of peace, happiness, and security. Coming face-to-face with our limitations often awakens the need for something "more"—a need for faith. As Rabbi Harold Kushner says,

> *The spirit of man will sustain his infirmity; but a broken spirit, who can bear?*
> Proverbs 18:14

"When problems are too hard for our minds to solve, when solutions are too long in coming for our mortal lives to encompass, we need to know there is Someone with more wisdom, more time, and more power than we have."[4]

Finding faith, having faith, maintaining faith is not always easy. One of the great gifts of the Jewish tradition is the permission to have moments of doubt and questions of faith. A Jew is weighed on the scale of action and not on the scale of faith. The great midrashic wish of the Holy One—"O that they might forsake Me and keep My commandments"—captures this reality perfectly.

Doubt is the state of mind that is the necessary companion of faith. It is twofold. Doubt can be the thought—however fleeting—that there is no God and nothing of ultimate meaning in our lives. The biblical philosopher called "Kohelet" stated this poignantly when he wrote in Ecclesiastes 1:2, "Vanity of vanities, all is vanity." The other kind of doubt is that while there *is* a God, somehow that God cares nothing about us or is even antagonistic toward us. The psalmist in agony cries out, "My God, my God why have You forsaken me?" (Psalm 22:2). Both of these varieties of doubt depress us, yet there is also something comforting in a tradition that teaches that God accepts the shortcomings of our faith.

When we feel abandoned, unprotected, uncared for by God, we may feel painfully alone. As it is written in Lamentations (3:17–18),

Do not forsake me, O Eternal One!
O my God, be not far from me!
Psalm 38:21

"[M]y soul is bereft of peace, I have forgotten what happiness is; so I say, 'Gone is my strength and my hope from the Eternal One.'"

Doubt, disconnection, spiritual despair—this is a loneliness so penetrating, it can leave a person with an unbearable sense of insignificance. As we question the meaning of life and the purpose of suffering, we struggle to make sense out of the darkness.

It is hoped that these times of spiritual despair or doubt are merely valleys in lives of faith and security. But, when despair arises, we can be comforted by knowing that there is no faith in the human condition without the great silence of *doubt*.

Guilt can also be a tremendous source of spiritual pain. Unmitigated guilt may be a cancer to the soul and eat us alive from the inside out. We have a sense of right and wrong which makes us feel guilty. We live with a sense that God is "cognizant" of our behavior and "judges" us accordingly.

The moral context of Judaism is clear and unambiguous. Human beings are given an explicit code of behavior. It is a code which, in some ways, goes against their inherent nature insofar as humans share of animal instincts. Much of the behavior which the Torah characterizes as "sinful" would be neutral if done by another creature. Other animals are not required to praise God, to refrain from taking others' property or to honor their promises. In Judaism, only because we have a higher, spiritual nature are we expected to be obedient to a set of laws (*mitzvot*) which demonstrate our respect for God, for each other, for property, and for propriety.

Judaism also embraces the concept of repentance and forgiveness: a two-pronged approach to correcting mistakes. We make *teshuvah,* or repentance, and God responds with *selikha,* forgiveness. The Hebrew word for the entire process is *kippur,* "atonement." The English word has the wonderful accident of expressing "at-one-ment"—being at one with God.

> *When one repents out of love, the previous evil acts are considered changed into good deeds.*
>
> Rabbi Levi Yitzhak of Berditchev

Without a soul, there could not be a Torah system. Without Torah, there could not be guilt. Without guilt, there could not be repentance. And without repentance, there could not be Divine forgiveness. This system establishes that we are not to live with unmitigated guilt, but to recognize and correct our wrongdoings and return to God, to the ways of Torah, so we can be "at One" and at peace with ourselves and with God.

Walking the Path:
Pain—Spiritual Doubt and Guilt

PRAYER: DOUBT

> My God, my God, why have You forsaken me?
> In my time of need, I feel so alone. I want to reach out
>   to Someone

or Something beyond myself, but at this moment I
  cannot.
Help me believe in You.
I need to feel that this universe is not cold and
  unfeeling.
I need to sense that my pain is for some higher
  purpose.
Speak to me, O Hidden One.
Answer my prayers even if I speak them with skepticism.
Touch me—just a little bit—and then I will be able to
  overcome my doubts and embrace You in love and in
  hope.
Reach out to me and I will reach out to You.

KAVANAH: AWAKENING

"The whole community broke into loud cries, and the people wept
that night. All the Israelites railed against Moses and Aaron. 'If only
we had died in the land of Egypt, if only we might die in this wilderness.' . . . And they said to one another, 'Let us head back for Egypt.'"

Numbers 14:1–2, 4

We read this painful account of "losing faith." As the enemy surrounded them, our ancient people feared that their future would be
worse than slavery. They were frightened to the point of giving up
their freedom, their faith in God's goodness, their faith in themselves, their own confidence that they would persevere and that God
would be with them.

May we be gentle with ourselves when we lose faith and be comforted by the fact that we are in the good company of our ancestors—
and that like them, we will prevail and experience what it means to
be "children of the Eternal One our God" (Deuteronomy 14:1). May
we be confident that the sun will rise with the dawn, and that we are
not alone, even though we may not understand why or how solutions
will unfold in the dark of night. *This* is called "having faith."

• • •

My husband Ron has told me that I'm not very good at saying "I'm
sorry." Well, I suppose he is right. To say "I'm sorry" presupposes

that I was wrong—and I don't like being wrong! I look for ways to explain my behavior, to justify my thinking, to protect my self-esteem. To say "I'm sorry" means that, first, I have to recognize I've done something wrong. Then, I have to go to the person (or to God) and say, "I'm sorry. Will you forgive me?" I've never questioned God's forgiveness. I rarely question whether those who love me will forgive me. So, what's the big deal? The truth is, I've had a hard time forgiving myself—and because of this, it hasn't mattered what others (even God) think. I've been my worst enemy and my harshest judge in this way. Learning to have more compassion and understanding for myself has allowed me to "feel" the forgiveness available from others and from God. The external result of learning to forgive myself and to feel forgiveness has been an increase in audible, heartfelt "I'm sorry's" to those I've hurt. The internal result has been a much greater sense of peace and closeness to those I love— and to God. (kbw)

. . .

MEDITATION: ATONEMENT AND RECONCILIATION

When we atone, we are offered the opportunity to return to "at-one-ment" with ourselves and with our God, and to know peace, shalom.

If a person incurs guilt . . . when the guilt is recognized . . . it shall be confessed . . . the priest shall make expiation on behalf of the sin and it shall be forgiven.

Leviticus 5:5–6

Study: Pain—Enemies

The prototype of the enemy of our ancient people is Amalek: "Remember what Amalek did to you on your journey, after you left Egypt—how, undeterred by awe and reverence for God, he surprised you on the march, when you were famished and weary, and cut down all the stragglers in your rear. . . . Do not forget" (Deuteronomy 25:17–19). According to the Torah, this

Is the Eternal One present among us or not?
Deuteronomy 17:7

enmity will last in perpetuity: "The Eternal One will be at war with Amalek throughout the ages" (Exodus 17:16).

Amalek represents the enemy. Many groups have tried to destroy the Jewish faith and the Jewish people. On a day-to-day basis, we may also face enemies who threaten our integrity, our reputation, our personhood, our professionalism, our state of well-being, or our personal safety. Confronting an enemy can be painful.

Pray for your enemies as for yourself.
The Baal Shem Tov

The issue of God's silence or apparent lack of intervention emerges when we attempt to understand how personal assaults or war or the Holocaust can happen in a world governed by a *just* God. Anger at God or at our enemies or at injustice can harden our hearts.

Pain can spread throughout the body from unresolved anger at a personal enemy, just as pain spreads throughout the body of the People Israel from unresolved anger at a collective enemy. Such pain resonates in the collective unconscious and limits our ability to fully live in the present with a sense of blessing. The anger cries out for the healing which is necessary if we are to reclaim our rightful place in the holiness of Creation. As David Ariel wrote,

> God did not permit Auschwitz or the death of a child. Humanity lives in a world in which God does not relate directly to individuals. Human destiny rests entirely in the hands of humanity. God assumes whatever form or manifestation our actions dictate. Yet, at the same time, we are bound to God by a common being that challenges us to act according to His moral attributes. Our failure to do so results in a catastrophe of our own making.[5]

Perhaps this is too simplistic an explanation of how catastrophe happens. In the case of the Holocaust, we will never have a satisfying answer for its occurrence. What's important is how we live in a world that allows such enemies to exist.

If we let hatred cloud our perception of others, of God, of life, do *we*, then, *become the enemy*? According to Victor Frankl, this is possible, but the choice is ours:

> In the concentration camps . . . we watched and witnessed some of our comrades behave like swine while others behaved like saints.

Man has both potentialities within himself; which one is actualized depends on decisions but not on conditions.[6]

Looking deeply into this dilemma, we realize that the only true enemy we must be aware of throughout time is *ourselves* since the eternal enemy, Amalek, is within. Amalek is our weaknesses, our *yetser ha-rah,* the "evil impulse." When all other enemies have been removed, we have ourselves to deal with. The internal enemy is the voice of indifference. "Who cares? God is unimportant" is the voice that encourages us to stray from the path of Right Living. It can sneak up from behind us and insidiously erode our commitment to Truth and Justice.

Within us is the ever-present battle between evil and good, dark and light, curse and blessing, death and life, oppression and freedom.

How we live day-to-day depends on the decisions we make, not on the conditions we face. This is a very difficult spiritual truth to swallow. Decisions to resolve differences and anger, to forgive and heal, all require faith—and all require God.

Yet we can transform the energy of anger into the energy of justice. "Never again!" becomes the slogan personally and collectively of the Jewish commitment to confront oppression, refusing to create or passively allow new victims anywhere in our global community. Doing this requires daily awareness, concern, and action.

Walking the Path: Pain—Enemies

MEDITATION

"Go you forth" (Genesis 12:1) are the words that God spoke to Abram. They can be interpreted to mean "Go to yourself, know yourself, fulfill yourself." In Deuteronomy 21:10, we read: "When you go forth to war against your enemies . . . ," which we may interpret to

> Hear, O Israel, you draw near this day to battle against your enemies: let not your heart faint; do not fear, or tremble, or be in dread of them; for the Eternal One your God is the One who goes with you, to fight for you against your enemies, to give you the victory.
>
> Deuteronomy 20:3–4

mean, "Go to yourself to war against the enemies within; know yourself, know your enemies within, fulfill yourself; heal your enemies within." Amen, may it be so.

• • •

For a peace-loving person, I have had my share of enemies. These are people whom I have hated, and who, in turn, have hated me. Most of them, I now realize, were similar to me in many ways. They were more threatening because I saw in them traits that I disliked in myself. However intense the negative feelings, as I changed or as my circumstances changed most of the hatred diminished, and my feelings of enmity for most of these people were put aside, almost forgotten. My next goal in life is to learn how to transform my enmity into friendship. But that may be beyond my capacity. (jlm)

• • •

KAVANAH: AWAKENING

"Why am I so hated and despised by my enemies?
What have I done to be so attacked and persecuted?
God be with me and help me remember that when I ask
    questions like these I fall into the trap that my
    enemies have set for me.
I have done nothing to deserve enmity. While I
    acknowledge my shortcomings and mistakes, I know
    that I am worthy of love and respect.
Let me not internalize my enemies' irrational and
    destructive feelings for me.
Let me remember that it is *their* need to hate that
    motivates them.
They may hurt me, they may slay me—but only if I let
    their view of me become my own can they defeat me.
If my enemies make me become self-hating, bitter,
    angry, or cynical—then they have won.
Let me rise above their anger and help me to keep in
    mind Your Eternal Love for me which will sustain me
    even if I am disdained and ridiculed.
Help me to affirm: I am a child of God and worthy of
    Love—Divine and human."

CREATIVE BLESSING

"Blessed are You, Eternal One, Creator of Freedom and Choice, stay near me as I make my choices. Help me know the value of freedom and honor freedom for all people. May my choices reflect awareness of how exercising freedom may oppress others so that I can minimize such outcomes. Help me never forget that my ultimate goal is to have faith in You and Your love—and that no circumstances can take that away from me."

Study: Pain—Death and Loss

The midrash about the death of Moses is one of the longest. The Torah tells us, "And the Eternal One said to Moses: Behold your days approach that you must die." According to the midrash, Moses ascended to heaven to plead his cause against this decree of mortality. Moses vowed not to budge until God rescinded the sentence of death, and called upon heaven and earth to voice his cause. But nothing availed.

I responded to those who did not ask,
I was at hand to those who did not seek Me;
I said, 'Here I am, here I am' . . .

Isaiah 65:1

Moses' unwillingness to accept his own mortality, and his tremendous struggle to remain alive, is the Rabbis' way of affirming that even the most righteous and faithful of us fear death—even with the knowledge that an eternal reward awaits. In this way, they give permission for us lesser mortals to fear death. The life force is so powerful that, under most circumstances, even the most accepting of human beings may seem anxious as death approaches.

Blessed shall you be when you come in and blessed shall you be when you go out.

Deuteronomy 22:6

In the midrash, God finally appeals to the soul of Moses. Only after God promises heavenly reward to Moses does his soul depart with a kiss from God. In Rabbinic theology, this is the most perfect of all deaths. Even so, all Creation mourns the death of a nearly perfect human being.

144

According to the mystics, death is the soul's return to its Source. The soul is eternal. It was implanted in the body and will return to the Source from which it came. Some mystics would encourage a sense of honoring, even celebrating the transition from this life to the "next life"—the time of returning Home.

> *Rav Nachman showed himself to Rava [in a dream after his death]; Rava asked him, "Was death painful?" Rav Nachman replied, "It was as painless as lifting a hair from a cup of milk. But were the Holy One . . . to say to me, 'You may return to that world where you were before,' I would not wish to do it. The fear of death is too great."*
> Talmud: *Mo'ed Katan* 28a

Everything we love, everything to which we are attached, carries the seed of painful loss. Rabbi David Wolpe referred to this when he wrote,

> This is the pain of love and the check on joy. At moments of intense love there is also an ache somewhere in the center of the soul. Because the beloved will, like the lover, not always stay. Because attachment carries with it the whispered prefiguration of loss. Because before even love itself, the first fact is impermanence.[7]

Whether due to death or to a momentary loss of self-esteem, loss interrupts our everyday life. How we ordinarily experience life stops. We feel alone. We withdraw from the source of pain toward an inner world often filled with even more pain and confusion. While the experience of loss is etched deeply in the human psyche, the continuation of life depends on the ability to

> *Dust you are and dust you will be.*
> Genesis 3:19

reemerge from the darkness and live again with faith and optimism. Elie Wiesel alluded to this when he noted that the real wonder of Adam and Eve is that they lost both their children

> *There are three ascending levels of how one mourns: With tears—that is the lowest. With silence—that is higher. And with a song—that is the highest.*
> A Chasidic teaching

in one cruel blow—one became a victim and the other became a fugitive. They then had every reason to be bitter and withdraw into themselves. Instead, they began their family life over again.

Following the shock (and often the disbelief) of loss, we enter into a period of grief and mourning. This is an essential step toward healing and returning to life.

We may go through many cycles of grief and healing before we feel we have resolved ourselves to the loss. The mourning rituals are straightforward: the funeral procession, the turning of the earth at the cemetery, the simple prayers at the service, the movement from death back into life. Yet for every mourner, there comes the ultimate moment of truth. At night, alone in bed, the terrible reality sinks in: We will never again see or hear our loved one in this life. Only memories remain, and they bring painful reminders of loss. We weep, pray, remember, and wish we could turn back time. We examine regrets, go over mistakes, replay moments like movies in our minds. We cry out to God, but even God cannot bring our loved one back to us.

I am weary with my moaning;
every night I flood my bed with tears;
I drench my couch with my weeping.
My eye wastes away because of grief,
it becomes weak because of all my pain.
Psalm 6:6–7

As the nights pass, one after another, mourning progresses and the darkness and the pain begin to abate. Our faith can assist us during this process: "Share your burden with God and the Holy One will sustain you" (Psalm 55:23). Memory becomes the beautiful gift that allows us to cherish in our hearts that which is lost. As Proverbs (10:7) assures us, "The memory of the righteous is a blessing."

For some, memory itself is immortality. Still, we wonder, "Is there life after life?" Judaism is clear about this: Death is not the end, but the veil that separates this life from the next that cannot be pierced in this lifetime. Judaism envisions loved ones in the heavenly "Garden of Eden," and certain mystical Jewish traditions promise reincarnation or the transmigration of the soul. In the Talmud, there is even a

[God] sets on high those who are lowly,
and those who mourn are lifted to safety.
Job 5:11

firm promise of *techiat ha maytim,* the physical resurrection of the body in post-Messianic times. While the Rabbis developed an entire cosmology about the afterlife (which was adopted full-cloth by Christianity), we need not be concerned with the details of soul, resurrection, judgment, and heaven. We know that these are human metaphors of a reality that is purely mysterious.

While we are alive, the idea that loved ones taken by death are cognizant of our thoughts and love and still care about us is perfectly acceptable in Judaism, as long as those loved ones do not become substitutes for God. Medieval Jews believed we are surrounded by the souls of loved ones, as well as by angels and demons—but all prayers are directed to the Holy One, who created all of these and more.

> This *world is an inn,*
> *and* that *world is the permanent house.*
> Talmud, *Moed Katan*, 9b

Death will never be conquered. But we experience immortality in so many ways that death need not be victorious. One of those paths to immortality is Judaism's promise that after death on this earth, we will continue to live in another realm.

> *Sarah died . . .*
> *and Abraham went in*
> *to mourn for Sarah*
> *and to weep for her.*
> Genesis 23:2

Walking the Path: Pain—Death and Loss

KAVANAH: AWAKENING

"O God, help me live with my grief. Someone who was so dear to me is gone. I feel sad and alone. Help me affirm life for I want to live and that is what my dear would have wanted for me. Now I need You more than ever before. Help me live with my grief and not become bitter. You are my Shepherd. Lead me by the hand to the valley of healing and help me overcome my grief."

• • •

Death is a constant companion in my work as a rabbi, yet it never fails to arouse in me a deep sense of fear. Of course, it reminds me of my own mortality. Even more poignantly, it points to the loss of those I love, should I outlive them. One criticism of Judaism (and of religion, in general) is that it provides the myth of eternal life to soothe the harsh reality of permanent loss that death brings. I've struggled with that. I attempt to be honest in my agnosticism—we do not know what lies beyond the grave—but something deep inside of me wants to believe that death is not the end. But whatever the future, the pain of loss is real and enduring. (jlm)

. . .

MEDITATION

Al tira ki imcha Ani.
"Don't be afraid for I Am with you, and above all do not fear.
Don't be afraid for I Am with you, I am always here."[8]

CREATIVE BLESSING

"Blessed are You, the Eternal One, Home to the soul, assist me with my pain. Help me live in the fullness of Your love even as I suffer from my loss. Comfort me as I mourn and recreate my life. Relieve me of the painful memories and help me find forgiveness for past hurts and mistakes. May the memories precious to my heart remind me that life is to be lived fully. Thank you for my life, O God."

Study: Healing the Pain—*Refu'ah*

We live for moments of consciousness and awareness when we can touch holiness, when we are in the blessing of the Eternal One's Light, when we walk in the ways of the Holy One. In this way, we heal our inner world, which is an essential step toward repairing and healing the outer world.

In each incarnation we weave or unravel a few more stitches in the garment of Light. At a certain point one has finished and can go Home.

Rabbi Jonathan Omer-Man

The process often begins with how we perceive ourselves to be or life to be. As we surrender to Divine Will, as we let go of the struggle to control life and all its ups and downs, we open ourselves to healing.

The ultimate goal of the life of the spirit is the ability to accept whatever is placed before us. Accep-

You will find refuge under God's wings . . . you need not fear the terror by night . . . God's angels will guard you wherever you go and carry you in their hands.

Psalm 91:4–5, 11

tance does not mean resignation. Judaism emphasizes the moral responsibility to act with integrity in the face of injustice wherever it is found. The Torah teaching "Do not stand by the blood of your neighbor" (Leviticus 19:16) is the clearest commandment to provide caring action whatever the consequences. There are no innocent bystanders in life. Yet on a deeper level, God has created a world in which life ends with death—and mortality is symbolic of aspects of the world which cannot be changed. No one can possibly offer a rational explanation for all the unfairness we experience each day. And even if many illnesses are curable, there is no moral vocab- ulary to help us understand why "innocent" people are pained in so many ways. When tragedy strikes, we are sad, even angry. But ulti- mately, we must learn to accept reality if we are to go on with our lives.

Accepting the Mystery gives us permission to accept all of life, and frees us to live with holiness and continue to see beauty in the world. For many, this is a process of sig- nificant inner transformation.

O Eternal One, by these things humanity lives, and in all these is the life of my spirit. Oh, restore me to health and make me live!

Isaiah 38:16

The next step, perhaps the next *layer* of the healing process, involves forgiving ourselves and others. Forgiveness does not require us to "forget" or "condone" behaviors or offenses. It acknowledges that we've learned all we can from the experience. By forgiving, we refuse to let past experiences drain our life energy and taint the present. Holding on to hurts and wrongdoings keeps our spirit in the past and prevents us from being present, from living fully and peacefully in *this* mo- ment, which is the only moment we have and is filled with opportu- nities for creating, repairing, and healing. Stephen Levine, author of *Who Dies,* knew this when he wrote,

Finishing business means that I open my heart to you, that whatever blocks my heart with resentment or fear, whatever I still want from you is let go of and I just send love. . . . I open to you as you are . . . not as I wish you to be or as I wish me to be . . . no longer looking to be forgiven or to show others how unfair they were. To finish our business we must begin to stop holding back.[9]

Stepping into the light of forgiveness relieves us of many burdens, and we move from harboring ill-will, anger, resentment, or fear to understanding, compassion, lovingkindness. That heals our body, mind, and soul.

When we forgive ourselves and others, when we let go of fear and the past, a sense of resolve follows. We can be mindful of ourselves, of one another, of our purpose. By healing our true nature, we restore ourselves to the Divine image, just as Deena Metzger describes through the bird who is restored by the light:

Sometimes the bird turns away. Sometimes it does not open its mouth to sing. Sometimes it is afraid. Sometimes it is afraid of the dark. But when it forgets it is afraid and opens its mouth to sing, it fills with light.[10]

Healing is a lifelong process. It involves all the ways we mend the separation between ourselves and the Holy One. Healing is living in awareness of the Oneness of Creation. It is living with a sense of blessing—and striving to *be* a blessing.

Heal me, O Eternal One, and let me be healed.
Save me and let me be saved;
For You are my glory.
Jeremiah 17:14

The mystics teach that the word for "created" in the first line of Genesis—"In the beginning, God created"—can be plausibly translated as "In the beginning, God *healed* the heaven and the earth." As we move through life, healing, growing, experiencing, may we know the power we call God, the Eternal Light, who brings healing to "heaven and earth"—and to you and to me.

The Eternal One leads all the night with a fiery light.
Psalm 78:14

Walking the Path: Healing the Pain—*Refu'ah*

KAVANAH: AWAKENING

"I am the Eternal One your God, and I will bring you out
from under the burdens of your pain and oppression,
and I will heal your spirit from the bondage of affliction,
and I will restore you with an outstretched arm . . ."
(Based on Exodus 6:6).

Through healing, we live as fully and as presently as we can in
the Light of God's Creation. It is a way to reach for God while we repair the world, and to be holy with one another.

• • •

*I had a dream that gave me a glimpse into death. I was on a boat
with my family going on a tour from an island to an unknown destination. As the dream progressed, I watched my children from behind
and then saw past them through a porthole that was just above the
water line. The sense of calm changed as we moved toward open
sea. On some level, I recognized potential danger; at the same time,
I knew that our course had been set and could not be changed.
Whatever was ahead was meant to be. Out of this awareness, I
began to say the Sh'ma quietly to myself. My daughter, Ali, calmly
reached out to take my hand, communicating that she too recognized
our situation. As I took her hand and felt my love for her, a wall of
water caused the entire vessel to turn. I awoke with my heart beating
wildly. I quietly observed my heart rate slowing and felt elated by the
comfort and acceptance, the peace and love that had surrounded this
dream of sure death. And then it occurred to me: it's a fine line between birth, death, and rebirth. It was a beautiful dream—a healing
dream—a God-filled dream. (kbw)*

• • •

GUIDED MEDITATION

"Holy One of Healing—Eternal Physician of my body and
soul—I am in need of healing."

- Focus on the pain/disease/distress/crisis that you are experiencing.

- Focus on those aspects which you can imagine being cured or alleviated.

- Focus on those aspects which probably cannot be healed in your lifetime.

"I am doing everything in my power to lift myself up from my distress."

- Focus on what you are doing to alleviate your pain/disease/distress/crisis.

"I need Your help."

- Focus on how you envision Divine healing coming to you.

"Let us be partners in my healing process and let us create an environment for healing. If we are successful, please remind me to express gratitude in acts of lovingkindness and mercy to all beings in many meaningful ways."

- Identify acts of lovingkindness that you can do now. Know that silently celebrating life or sending love to others is a beautiful gift and your being is a blessing.

For you who honor My name the saving sun will rise, with healing on its wings.
Malachi 3:20

CREATIVE BLESSING (BASED ON MALACHI 3:20)

"Blessed are You, Eternal Light of Healing, may You bring healing and may Your Light illuminate this time of darkness."

Conclusion: Out of Our Darkness

Darkness is a metaphor for pain, confusion, loneliness, and hopelessness: "Weeping tarries for the night—joy comes in the morning" (Psalm 30:5).

Judaism does not see physical death as the eternal darkness of the grave. Instead, it is a transition to a world in which suffering does not exist, a world of constant light. Yet while we are alive, we often ask, "Watchman—what of the night?" (Isaiah 21:11). That is to say, how much longer will we suffer before we find relief? Sadly, the duration of the metaphorical darkness in our lives is yet another aspect of life which is a deep and abiding mystery: "The night of watching is the Eternal One's" (Exodus 12:42). As Rabbi David Wolpe writes,

My soul yearns for You in the night, my spirit within me earnestly seeks You.

Isaiah 26:9

> Like Abraham before him, Jacob is confronted in the night, facing the elements inside of himself that stir and surprise him, calling up reserves of strength he did not know he had. . . . That is why, like Jacob, we hope that the night will release its mystery to us, and the dawn will come.[11]

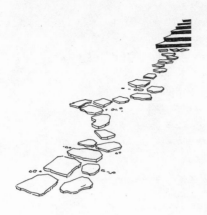

Midnight: Mysticism, Sexuality, and Creation

I arise at midnight to praise you.
—Psalm 119:62

• • •

There is a well-known legend that speculates on the many worlds
that God created before this one. It seems that the Rabbis envisioned
even God's creative process as a matter of trial and error. This idea
is also a metaphor for the life of the individual. Spiritually, we as-
cend and descend every day searching for the proper balance in our
lives. We suspect that we are, in essence, spiritual beings, but we
are constantly being tugged by physical and ego needs. The journey
of the human soul is the most exhilarating flight of all. What we fail
to accomplish today may be realized tomorrow or the day after. (jlm)

• • •

In the dark of midnight, we are freed from our normal vision so we
can look within: Midnight is like the womb that envelops mystery

Then the mystery was revealed to Daniel
in a vision of the night.
Then Daniel blessed the God of heaven. Daniel said:
"Blessed be the name of God for ever and ever,
to whom belong wisdom and might.
God changes times and season;
God removes kings and sets up kings;
God gives wisdom to the wise and knowledge to those
who have understanding;
God reveals deep and mysterious things;
God knows what is in the darkness,
and the light dwells with God."

Daniel 2:19–22

and Creation. It represents a time when we can prepare to bring new life to old forms. To paraphrase Genesis (49:25), "Be blessed by the God of your father and mother who will help you, by God Almighty who will bless you with blessings of heaven above, blessings of the deep mysteries below, blessings of spiritual nourishment, and blessings of Creation." We now enter midnight—a time of gestation and promise, the time before awakening the dawn, before the birthing of a new day.

Study: Mysticism—Turning Prophecy into Action

Mysticism is the sum total of all the ways that we seek knowledge of God through insight or intuition, in ways other than ordinary sensory perception and logical reasoning. Mysticism often speaks in a language of poetry and metaphor, addressing the part of us that wants to transcend rational limits, that

The king said to Daniel,
"Truly, your God is God of gods and Lord of kings,
and a revealer of mysteries . . ."

Daniel 2:47

seeks to enter unbounded awareness and see from one end of the world to the other. This is the part that wants to soar—to dream of other worlds, to live with angels, to prophesy with Divine inspiration.

As Rabbi Lawrence Kushner has written, "We choose our truth by the scope of our vision."[1] The mystic sees the world through intuition, which is often called "spiritual sight," "symbolic sight," the "sight that comes from behind the eyes." Learning to see experiences as both physical and spiritual opens us to the intuitive self. Intuition helps us see the world differently and interpret cues on a spiritual as well as physical level. We begin to look at all interactions as learning experiences; we may "see" people differently (even seeing "auras" or energy fields or receiving pictures about them in our minds that give us insights into them); we recognize synchronicity as more than coincidence; and we honor the knowing that defies logic. Intuition is not reserved for a gifted few; it is a skill we can all develop. And over time and with practice and understanding, we see the miracle of Creation, and of God, everywhere.

Such was the appearance of the likeness of the glory of the Eternal One. And when I saw it, I fell upon my face, and I heard the voice of One speaking.

Ezekiel 1:28

An important mystical moment of the day might occur while sleeping or dreaming. "And God spoke to Israel in visions of the night, and God said, 'Jacob, Jacob.' And Jacob said, 'Here I am'" (Genesis 42:2). While waking visions may be rare, all of us have visions (which we call "dreams") in the night.

The ancient Hebrews had a great regard for dreams and sought the counsel of those who could explain

The visions of my head as I lay in bed were these: I saw, and behold, a tree in the midst of the earth; and its height was great. The tree grew and became strong, and its top reached to heaven, and it was visible to the end of the whole earth. Its leaves were fair and its fruit abundant, and in it was food for all. The beasts of the field found shade under it, and the birds of the air dwelt in its branches, and all flesh was fed from it.

Daniel 4:10–12

them. However, the Israelites were forbidden to let dreams and dream interpretation cross over into idol worship or magic.

The Bible has many accounts of dreams and their interpretations. Jacob dreamed and saw a stairway to heaven. Joseph dreamed and found his destiny. Some of these offer mystical insight into the nature of the universe; others are prophetic.

And God said, "Hear my words: If there is a prophet among you, I the Eternal One make Myself known to you in a vision, I speak with you in a dream."

Numbers 12:6

Dreams speak in symbolic language, which is the language of the unconscious, individual and collective. Like "symbolic sight," dreams provide inroads to our deeper thoughts and feelings. Dreams, even when strictly about ourselves, contain the seeds of mystical insight and prophecy. They are ours to interpret and learn from. As the Zohar says, "A dream uninterpreted is like a letter unopened." Pay attention to your dreams. Write them down. Discuss them. Contemplate them. In them, you may find answers you have been seeking, answers which may help you enter into a partnership with God to create our world that is constantly evolving. Following in the footsteps of the ancient prophets, Hillel said we are all "apprentice prophets." We are the ones listening, hearing, trusting, and following the Truth. We can be the ones who, through our work, fulfill the Eternal Laws of transformation and creation. According to Jeremiah (1:5), God said, "Before you were born I consecrated you; I appointed you a prophet to the nations."

The Holy One called me from the womb,
from the body of my mother,
God named my name. . . ." I will give you
as a light to the nations, that my salvation may
reach to the ends of the earth."

Isaiah 49:1, 6

Judaism is about translating ideas and beliefs into action. We can take the poetry of faith and mysticism, and apply its wisdom and insights to everyday life. To manifest the Mystery in the physical world, knowing is not enough; we must act in ways commensurate with our abilities to bring Light into the world. As Rabbi David Wolpe has noted,

> The normal mystic in the Jewish tradition was one whose life was devoted to the "repairing imperative," that things must be mended, a sense livened by the constant perception of God's presence and concern behind all things.[2]

Walking the Path: Mysticism—
Turning Prophecy into Action

ACTIVITY

Keep your journal next to your bed so you can easily write down your dreams. It is important that you write down the details of a dream as soon as you wake up, or it may quickly fade back into your unconscious. Reread what

"And it shall come to pass afterward, that I will pour out My spirit on all flesh; your sons and your daughters shall prophesy, your old ones shall dream dreams, and your young people shall see visions."

Joel 3:1

you've written that same day and let your intuitive mind interpret the message. What was the feeling of your entry? What was the dream telling you?

If you are interested in dream interpretation, you may find a "dream group" very useful. This is a small group that gathers to explore dreams. But even when consulting others, it is important to know that *you* are the final interpreter of your dreams.

MEDITATION

"When I go forth to find You, I find You seeking me."
Yehuda Halevy

Mysticism is the sum total of all the ways in which we seek knowledge of God—and in which we discover that God is seeking us.

KAVANAH: AWAKENING

"Behold, I am preparing myself to open my soul to the Mysteries of the Universe which lie beyond my five senses. Help me see with my Inner Eye the splendor of Your Creation and the invisible marvels of spirit that surround me.

Help me hear with my Mystical Ear the music and the sounds of the spirit that are more beautiful than any symphony.

Help me inhale with my Spiritual Sense of Smell the sweet incense of the soul, of the Garden of Eden which revives my flagging spirit when I feel faint or weary.

Help me taste with the Tongue of Mystery the sweet spiritual honey from the rock of Your Divine bounty, which sustains my inner life.

Help me feel with the Invisible Hands of Spirit the spiritual sensuality of Your Holy Being, soft and gentle, which comforts even as it is comforted.

Open to me the potential to become a Higher Being truer to my Inner Self and alive to all the mysteries of the Universe."

• • •

Two or three times in my life, I have experienced a sense of spiritual transformation: at the birth of my children, at the death of my father, perhaps at the height of romantic infatuation. These experiences convinced me that the world cannot be contained in the physical interaction of molecules. God breaks into our lives, and we are overwhelmed. Mysticism is the idea that these peak experiences are the essence of existence, and that our everyday "normal" activities are simply the gaps between true living. But those gaps (which may last for years) are necessary components of the peak experiences which follow. We live on the other side of Divine Light, separated from it by an opaque wall. But a mere pinprick is able to penetrate that wall. When that happens, we are bathed in a Light so powerful that everything else is obscured. (jlm)

• • •

CREATIVE BLESSING

"Blessed are You, Source of Mystery, I am learning to listen with the ears of a mystic and to see with the eyes of a mystic. Help me expand my awareness so I can encounter You in my every way. Help me be open to Your messages—whether through dreams, or the people I meet, or the experiences I have, or the 'still small voice within.' I'm seeking You. And I know You're seeking me."

Study: Living with Angels

An angel, or *malakh* in Hebrew, is a force that operates within and around us, inspired by God. It does God's will and acts as God's messenger, just as Jacob dreamed (Genesis 28:12) "that there was a ladder set up on the earth, and the top of it reached to heaven; and behold, the angels of God were ascending and descending on it!"

In Judaism, the most famous angels are Michael, the guardian angel whose quality is holiness, and whose earthly manifestation is fire; Gabriel, the angel of strength whose quality is courage and whose earthly manifestation is water; Raphael, the angel of healing whose quality is charity and whose earthly manifestation is air; Uriel, the angel of light whose quality is knowledge and whose earthly manifestation is earth itself; and Elijah, the prophet of peace and the angel of the Covenant, who is responsible for recording in heaven all human deeds.[3] *Kabbalah,* the Jewish mystical tradition, further elaborates on angels and their hierarchies.

> "May Michael be at my right hand,
> Gabriel at my left,
> Uriel before me, Raphael behind me
> and above my head
> the presence of God."
>
> A Chasidic prayer for summoning the angels

> And the angel of the Eternal One appeared to him [Moses] in a flame of fire out of the midst of a bush; and he looked, and lo, the bush was burning, yet it was not consumed.
>
> Exodus 3:2

Angels are also discussed in the Apocrypha (writings from biblical times, excluded from the Hebrew Bible), the Dead Sea Scrolls, the Talmud, the Zohar, Chasidic writings, and present-day Jewish lore. Nevertheless, many of us still wonder, "Do angels exist?" They are no more illogical than any other aspect of creation. Like the concept of "soul," they are not part of the material world and so they can be perceived only in visions or in the imagination. For some people, angels are only a metaphor for Divine intervention in our world.

In the Bible, angels are often disguised as strangers. Usually, these are people who appear unexpectedly, bring an important message, and disappear again. Morris Margolies writes in A *Gathering of Angels* that Elijah, for instance, is a "champion of underdogs and innocents, a friend of those in need, and, especially . . . the guardian of good and pious folk in the face of serious dangers. He appears in an impressive variety of guises, depending on his particular mission."[4]

And the angel who talked with me came again, and waked me, like a man
that is wakened out of his sleep.
Then he said to me, "This is the word of the Eternal One: Not by might, nor by force, but by my Spirit, says the Eternal One of hosts."
Zechariah 4:1, 6

Earlier in the Bible, three strangers appeared at Abraham's tent; later a man came to wrestle Jacob unexpectedly in the night; and finally Joshua was confronted by a man carrying a sword outside Jericho. Joshua asked the stranger, "'Are you for us, or for our adversaries?' And he said, 'No, but as commander of the army of the Eternal One I have now come'" (Joshua 5:13–14).

Much Jewish folklore describes how humans create angels through our own actions. With each misdeed, we create a bad angel, a demon, or serpent; with each good deed, we create a good angel, a guardian, or protector. We create our company as we move through life—bad angels or good angels—depending on our actions in the world. According to Rabbi Abraham Isaac Kook,

We concern ourselves with the pursuit of Torah and wisdom, and good deeds, with the cultivation of good character traits, to tie the holy angels to ourselves, to strengthen ourselves with the strength of the gracious God, who reveals Himself to us with His light and deliverance.[5]

Another way to think of angels is to see them as metaphors for describing the emotions and the forces within us. Since we are both physical and spiritual beings, perhaps "angels" communicate between our physical and spiritual selves as we attempt to bring the heavenly down to earth and raise the earthly up toward heaven.

We may also think of angels as prayers from our hearts which take wing toward heaven. Jews may pray to angels, while acknowledging they are nothing but the personification of the Divine will. Many Jewish authorities caution against evoking angelic assistance because angels might then be seen as independent beings and this can engender a type of polytheism that is antithetical to monotheistic Judaism.

No matter how we conceptualize or perceive angels today, they have played a central role in traditional Judaism from the beginning of the religion. One of the most common Sabbath table songs—indeed, *the* quintessential *Shabbat* song—is *"Shalom Aleichem,"* which addresses angels directly: "Peace to you O guardian angels, angels on high who have come from the King—the King of Kings—the Holy One Blessed be He." Angels and the Sabbath are connected also in this story from the second century that is related by Rabbi Yose ben Yehuda:

> [T]wo angels accompany every man from synagogue to home on the eve of the Sabbath, one good and one bad. If he enters his house and finds the candles lit, the table set, and his bed made, the good angel exclaims: "May it be thus next Sabbath as well!" and the bad angel responds, "Amen" in spite of himself. If the case is otherwise (a messy household), the bad angel exclaims: "May it be thus next Sabbath as well." and the good angel responds "Amen" in spite of himself.[6]

Thinking of angels watching over us can be an easier way of thinking of God as a Divine guardian. If the idea of angels appeals to you, then they can be fully embraced as part of the Jewish tradition while keeping in mind that angels are compelled to do God's will—not our own.

"Behold, I sent an Angel before you, to guard you on the way and to bring you into the place which I have prepared."

Exodus 23:20–21

Walking the Path: Living with Angels

ACTIVITY

You may have thought of someone you know as an "angel in the flesh." You may never know if this person was an agent of God, but you know that he or she was someone special.

The morning stars sang together and all the divine beings shouted for joy.

Job 38:7

Think about a person who has entered your life, done something for you or "delivered a message" which has allowed you to take a new, life-changing path. Was he or she an angel? Have you ever felt that perhaps you have functioned as an angel for someone else?

• • •

This week on the news there was a story about a man hallucinating— or maybe it was about an angel intervening. A hiker had been lost in the Olympic National Forest for eight days. He'd wandered aimlessly without food, losing twenty-five pounds and nearly losing his mind. On his eighth day in the woods, he began hearing bagpipes and flutes. Without questioning why he was doing it, he followed the sound through the forest. When the music stopped, he was in the company of a forest ranger. His life was saved. The forest ranger knew nothing about bagpipes and flute music. All the hiker's family knew was that they had prayed daily for Divine intervention. A woman told me in a class that I taught the night this came on the news that there's a tale about another hiker who used to go to the same area to play his bagpipes. He, too, had been lost, but was never found. I don't know if it's true. What do you think? (kbw)

• • •

KAVANAH: AWAKENING

"Angels, Messengers, Faces of God, Divine Attributes, Spiritual Guides, Guardians of my waking and sleeping: I invoke you by the Names by which we give you life:

God's Healer: Give me health.
God's Champion: Give me strength.
God's Mercy: Give me comfort.
God's Consort: Give me pleasure.
God's Guardian: Give me safety.
God's Womb: Give me creativity.
God's Redeemer: Give me salvation."

164

PRAYING WITH ANGELS

Focus on one deep, abiding need in your life and consider doing the following:

- State your need in the form of a petitionary prayer to God, such as, "O God, I need physical healing of my cancer."

- Imagine a Messenger of God who could bring you an answer to your need. Select a name for your Angel. (It can either be a traditional name, such as Raphael, or one that has special meaning to you.) One way to do this is to say, "I call upon you, O Raphael, Messenger of God's healing."

- Reach out and embrace the image/Angel with words and feelings. "I embrace you, Raphael. I feel your warm presence close to me, holding my hand and stroking my head."

- Share your pain and needs with the Angel/Messenger and ask that your words and feelings be taken to God: "I pray for healing from Your Creator and Master—take these words on High and be my intercessor."

- Take leave of the Angel/Messenger with words and feelings of affirmation and gratitude: "Go in peace, O Angel of Peace, Messenger of the Most High. Thank you for being with me in my time of need. Return to me when I call upon you. May I be worthy of your attention and companionship."

CREATIVE BLESSING (BASED ON PSALM 121)

"Blessed are You, Eternal One our God, Divine Presence in Heaven and on earth, be my Keeper—my Guardian. Protect me from hurt. Keep me from all evil. Keep my life in Your hands as I go out into the world until I come back Home, from this time forth and forevermore. Amen."

Study: Mysticism—The Tree of Life

God is as different from the spiritual as God is from the physical. *Ein Sof*, a Hebrew term which refers to God, means "without end" or "eternal" and is considered incomprehensible to the human mind. Kabbalah teaches that the ten *sefirot*, the stages of emanation through which the Unknown becomes known, exist to allow the energy of God and humanity to meet. Each *sefirah* manifests God's creative force through humanity into the world.[7]

Oh, that I knew how to reach God, how to get to the Eternal One's dwelling place.

Job 23:3

The Tree of Life, depicted as an inverted tree, is the kabbalistic symbol for the connection of humanity with God. The roots of the tree are planted in "heaven" (with God) and the branches reach into the physical world. The Tree of Life is also depicted as the human body, which is said to contain the full mystery of Creation (because humanity was made in the image of God). We are patterned after the forces of Creation—our thoughts and feelings reflect the qualities of the *sefirot*, which are aspects of God translated into human terms and human logic. God shares these Divine qualities with us; our task is to manifest with balance and harmony the *sefirot* through our spiritual journey, which will bring us closer to our true nature.

The Tree of Life is also thought of as a spiritual ladder in the center of the Garden of Eden. Through contemplation and spiritual practice, we can climb the ladder and return to God. Each rung on the ladder represents a more powerful understanding or revelation of the essence of God. Our task is to develop the Divine attributes in our daily life and bring heaven and earth closer through our actions. However, the Eternal One remains beyond any attributes or qualities contained in the *sefirot*. Consequently, we can never "become" God; we can only seek God, reach for God, become closer to God in our devotion and practice by emulating Divine qualities.

Along with coming closer to God, we can actually affect the flow of creation by returning energy back up the ladder toward *Ein Sof*. We call this energy "return evolution," which is one way to think about how we co-create with the Eternal One. According to E. J. Holmyard,

What is below is like that which is above and what is above is like that which is below. . . . Ascend with the greatest sagacity from the earth to heaven and then again descend to earth. And unite together the powers of things superior and inferior. Thus you will obtain the glory of the whole world and obscurity will fly away from you.[8]

The Tree of Life teaches us to seek balance and harmony in our relationships with ourselves, with others, and with the Universe. It reaches toward this harmony at many levels since, as Ann Williams-Heller wrote,

[T]he Tree of Life is a way of life, a way of living, a way of thinking, a way of relating, a way of awakening, a way of self-discovery, a way of sharing. Its wisdom-path is ready to lead the human mind from personal to universal awareness, and to direct the soul from a magnetic earth-consciousness to the cosmic consciousness of the heart.[9]

Walking the Path: Mysticism: The Tree of Life

ACTIVITY:

The Tree of Life is part of a mystical tradition which has several layers of meaning and esoteric wisdom. We will now take you through each of the levels, starting at the lowest and ascending toward God. Each step introduces a particular

Hear, O Israel, the Eternal One is our God, the Eternal One is One.

Deuteronomy 6:4

sefirah (an aspect of God), describes the spiritual work necessary at that level, and offers a passage of scripture upon which to meditate. Notice that as we climb the ladder—as we ascend toward the Source—we're focusing on many aspects of daily life discussed in previous chapters. Exploring the Tree of Life, then, synthesizes the principles that are throughout this book.

Malkhut, "Kingship": *Malkhut* is experienced at either the bottom of our feet or the base of our spine. This is our base in the world.

Our souls are born into physical bodies which function in the world of action. The action occurs in the context of community and we are grounded physically and emotionally by the earth and by our families. Here, we receive God's Presence into our everyday lives; we study and practice Torah, God's operating manual for living with holiness in the world; and we seek to understand what it means to be holy, to repair the world, to serve the Holy One.

Ceremonies and rituals help securely root us in community. They unite us with our ancestors so we know what it means to be Jewish and what it means to be human. It is said that every Jewish soul from all time was present when God appeared at Sinai: "And they shall be my community, and I will be their God" (Jeremiah 32:38). This is our covenant with God. We are God's community and we are a manifestation of God in community, just as God is manifest in all aspects of Creation and all Creation is God's Community.

And the Eternal One will become sovereign over all the earth; on that day the Eternal One will be one and God's name One.

Zechariah 14:9

From this place, we transform our relationship of separateness into unity; we begin to see beyond *self* into the greater Self, the Eternal Oneness of all Creation. Our spiritual task involves examining those beliefs and practices that separate us from Oneness of Creation and from God's holy community.

Yesod, "Foundation": *Yesod* is the procreative, harmonizing life force. It corresponds to the genitals.

Each aspect of creation has masculine and feminine forces underpinning its existence. In *yesod,* these forces come together in balance and harmony. Here we examine how we relate to money and power, and how we give *tsedakah,* which is money or goods that we donate to others as our social

Thus says the Eternal One of hosts, render true judgments, show compassion and mercy each to God's children, do not oppress the widow, the fatherless, the sojourner, or the poor; and let none of you devise evil against any of God's children in your heart.

Zechariah 7:9–10

responsibility to the community. Here, we consider the laws of *kashrut* and become more compassionate toward animals. We are also conscious about how our

For I am the Eternal One your God; honor yourself, therefore, and be holy, for I am holy.
Leviticus 11:44

livelihood and the way we live affects the earth, which is God's holy ground. And we examine our relationships with our parents, siblings, lovers, friends, neighbors, strangers, enemies, striving to honor all of them. Every person carries a spark of the Divine and our interactions with others reflect our respect and honor for God.

Netzach, "Endurance/Eternity": *Netzach* is dominance, permanence, overcoming adversity, drawing closer to Truth. It is associated with the masculine and corresponds to the right leg.

Hod, "Splendor": *Hod* is submission to the Divine principles that organize the universe. It is associated with the feminine and corresponds to the left leg.

You shall be holy unto your God.
Numbers 15:40

These are the points where the ego's wish to dominate meets the spirit's wish to submit to eternal Truth. How we resolve these two forces determines our personal code of honor.

Here, we can step into the Divine flow and let prophecy emerge. We can develop the freedom to follow without fear. The balance we achieve lets us be responsible for our lives while recognizing that life itself is a gift from God.

T'feret, "Beauty": *T'feret* is compassion. The "heart" or the trunk of the Tree of Life, it connects the five metaphysical *sefirot* above with the four earthly *sefirot* below. It corresponds to the

[P]ower belongs to God; and to You, O Eternal One, belongs steadfast love.
Psalm 62:11–12

Sun, which is the sustainer of life.

In the spiritual journey, the heart is the gateway to the sacred, to

And you shall love the Eternal One your God with all your heart and with all your soul, and with all your might.
Deuteronomy 6:5

compassion, beauty, harmony, and forgiveness of self and others. The heart is God's resting place

169

within us. Through acts of love, we bring balance to that which is above and that which is below, uniting heaven and earth.

Chesed, "Love": *Chesed* is unlimited giving and grace. It is associated with the masculine and corresponds to the right arm and the right side of the throat.

Gevurah, "Strength/Power": *Gevurah* is limitations, barriers, and good judgment. It is associated with the feminine and corresponds to the left arm and the left side of the throat.

Here, again, we are faced with the possible tension between our will and God's will. When we choose to live by Torah, our lives can be transformed in unimaginable ways. But this requires faith, commitment, balance, and self-examination.

> *Teach me to do Your will, for You are my God!*
> *Let Your good spirit lead me on a level path!*
> Psalm 143:10

Every choice we make each day has the possibility to return us to God. At the level of the throat, we can examine communications, especially those of love and judgment. Our potential to speak with love and truth should not be underestimated. Negative judgment and harsh criticism can be destructive. Each word we speak reflects our awareness (or our lack of awareness) of God.

Hokhmah, "Wisdom": *Hokhmah* is the intermediary point between Divine mind and human thought. It is associated with the masculine and corresponds to the right brain and to pure abstract power.

Binah, "Understanding": *Binah* is the womb. It is where all thought is made ready for birth. It is associated with the feminine and corresponds to the left brain and to pure intuitive power.

At this level, we attempt to marry human thought with Divine reasoning, to explore the points where logic meets mystery. This is the birthplace of the mystic, of intuitive intelligence, of the ability to discern between good and evil. Energy at this level is felt in the head behind the spiritual eye.

Here, rather than struggle with needing to know the workings of the Universe in rational terms, we open ourselves to trust in Divine reasoning.

> *Love the truth and peace.*
> Zechariah 8:19

Keter, "Crown": *Keter* is the "Divine Mind," the part of God that inspires physical manifestation. It is associated with eternity, and corresponds to the top of the head—the "crown."

The Eternal God is your dwelling place.
Deuteronomy 33:27

Here, no time or place restricts the spirit. There is no past and no future, only the Eternal boundless God.

When we sense the Eternal, we feel infinitely connected with all creation. King David's exclamation, "Now I know that You are the Eternal One," really means, "Now, in this eternal moment, *I know in a way I have never known before, that* You are God."

Like David, our spirit cries out to live in the Eternal now, to freely and joyously offer ourselves to God.

In the light of the King's face, there is life.
Proverbs 16:15

• • •

While a dear friend of mine was recuperating from a severe sprained ankle, he wrote in his journal about lessons from his situation. He realized that he was unnecessarily holding himself back from what he truly wanted to do and recognized his fear of disappointing others.
He understood that he could either continue with his current professional path or explore new directions. When we looked at the Tree of Life for insights, he recognized that the expectations and perceptions of family and religious community played a part in his dilemma.
With new insight into his struggle, he knew he could start becoming a counselor for other people who wanted to pursue nontraditional spiritual paths. The Tree of Life had offered confirmation and an ancient schema to understand his current situation. (kbw)

• • •

KAVANAH: AWAKENING

At midnight, the mystery emerges and the stirrings of the soul may be deeply felt. The yearning to be spiritually unbound may rise up more now than during the light of day. We study, we pray, we imagine climbing the ladder to Heaven. We experience our spirit seeking God: "My soul yearns for You in the night; my spirit within me earnestly seeks You" (Isaiah 26:9).

Study: Creation and Sexuality

Creation—new life, new form, or bringing new life to old forms—brings into being the world that is constantly coming. Creation allows God's Eternal Light to become life, it lets the Force of Creation take form. We are continuously renewing Creation through our thoughts, words, actions. Everything, in fact, is changing—except God, who is constant, eternal, infinite. Realizing that God is the Source of all Creation can produce, as Rabbi Abraham Isaac Kook counseled, an epiphany that "transports you from a place where there is nothing new to a place where there is nothing old, where everything renews itself, where heaven and earth rejoice as at the moment of Creation."[10]

You were the same before the universe was created;
You have been the same since the universe has been created;
You are the same in this universe,
You will be the same in the universe to come.
Traditional Jewish morning prayer

Sexuality enters the Creation story first through Adam, who is both masculine and feminine, then through Adam *and* Eve, both of whom were created in God's image. "Honor your father and your mother" (Exodus 20:12) tells us to honor the masculine and feminine embodied in our parents. Each of us has masculine and feminine traits—action and restraint, giving and receiving, doing and being. Sexuality is an explicit part of the Life Force of Creation. Through balancing masculine and feminine *sefirot,* God was able to manifest in the world. And by balancing the masculine and feminine in ourselves, we move toward spiritual wholeness.

Sexual energy can connect us with the sustaining energy of the universe, yet one of the greatest mysteries is the relationship between sexuality and creation. On the surface, it seems to be one of the major paradoxes of God's divine plan since God's Creation is a singular act of a singular and unique Creator, while the earthly act of procreation originates from the dualism of male and female.

One way that Judaism explains this apparent discontinuity is to refer to the Creation myth itself: "And God created humanity in God's image—male and female, God created them" (Genesis 1:27).

The Rabbis see in this ambiguous locution an important underlying reality: that the original human was singular and androgynous and was later separated into two halves—male and female. The sexual act, then is a return to this primordial unity. In this ideal state, "Adam," who represents all humanity, can emulate God through procreation. The Rabbis are telling us, in essence, that sexual union is the holiest moment in earthly life: it is when we truly find ourselves in the image of God, and as a Creator.

> *A man shall leave his father and mother, and attach himself to his wife, and they shall become one flesh.*
> Genesis 2:24

Mystics believe that only when a soul enters a body does it split into male or female. Consequently, sexual union allows for us to form "one body" and to unite two souls into one. Mystics saw this reunion as the highest form of human love and used sexual metaphors to describe how sexual union between man and woman unite *t'feret* (the Husband) and *shechinah* (the Bride). These represent the union of the masculine and feminine aspects of God as experienced in the world. When this is accomplished, heaven and earth will be "one" and the world will be governed by harmony as God's everlasting abundance illuminates the world with peace.[11]

> *I am my beloved's, and his desire is for me. Come, my beloved, let us go forth into the fields, and lodge in the villages; let us go out early to the vineyards. . . . There I will give you my love.*
> Song of Songs 7:10, 12

The Bible offers guidelines for enhancing marital and sexual relations. Some of these may seem odd. For example, "If a man and woman have sexual relations, they shall bathe in water and remain *tamey*, 'unclean' until evening" (Leviticus 15:18). Rabbi Levi Meier suggests that the Hebrew word *tamey*, which is translated as "unclean" in the previous sentence, can be plausibly translated as "private."[12] This yields an alternative translation of the previous passage: "If a man and woman have sexual relations, they shall bathe in water and remain *private* until evening"—being together, sharing, extending the beauty of sexual intimacy into the evening. This translation gives us a different understanding of the biblical directive.

> *And in that day, says the Eternal One, you will call me, "My husband" . . .*
> Hosea 2:16

This same issue of "uncleanness" prohibits sexual union during menstruation. If we substitute the word "private" for "unclean" in this commandment, we relate to a woman's menstrual time quite differently. It then becomes a time for privacy, reflection, and withdrawal, a time to abstain from "routine" activities and to instead honor the sacred mysteries of life and death.

By examining the essential qualities of masculinity and femininity, we realize that masculine sexual response is usually strong, active, forthright, and can result in dominance over a partner if not balanced. The feminine sexual response is usually powerful, open, surrendering, and can result in passiveness if not balanced. Each of us brings our own balance of masculine and feminine qualities to our sexual relationships. Through trust, love, and consideration, partners can seek the spiritual wholeness inherent (but often hidden) in sexual union, and can experience a profound sense of "oneness" and holiness. Abraham Abulafia, the thirteenth-century mystic, realized this when he wrote:

> The purpose of the marriage of a woman and a man is union.
> The purpose of union is fertilization.
> The purpose of fertilization is giving birth.
> The purpose of birth is learning.
> The purpose of learning is to grasp the divine.
> The purpose of apprehending the divine is to maintain the endurance of the one who apprehends with the joy of apprehension.[13]

Walking the Path: Creation and Sexuality

For many, the single most important prerequisite to a fulfilling sexual relationship is for your lover to also be your best friend. The Bible talks of sexual intercourse as "knowing": "Now Adam knew Eve his wife, and she conceived and bore Cain" (Genesis 4:1). (We assume that Eve also knew Adam!) In Jewish spiritual-based sexuality, we keep in mind the important tenets of loving friendship, of *knowing* one another in

This is my beloved and this is my friend.
Song of Songs 5:16

the full sense of the word: discovering, honoring, cherishing, caring for, admiring, respecting, and wanting the best for each other.

Intimacy occurs in the larger context of our lives beyond sexuality. Creating a daytime of lovingness, of listening to words that are spoken and unspoken enhances the emotional, physical, and spiritual connection available through sex. Also, being in tune with our own relationship with God helps prepare for the physical union through sex.

MEDITATION BEFORE MAKING LOVE

"Holy One, I thank you for the many blessings and gifts you have given me in my life. Foremost among them is the person and love of my dear _____, who has brought me happiness beyond measure.

_____'s beauty and sensuality is a foretaste of the world to come.

As I prepare to join with _____ in a time of intimacy, help me keep in mind that _____ reflects your Divine glory. Let me be aware of _____'s needs and concerns. Let not the urgency of my own needs cause _____ pain or dissatisfaction. May all my expressions to _____ be loving and gentle.

Help me keep in mind the fullness of the sexual encounter. May it be loving and compassionate, sweet and exciting, strong and fulfilling, physical and spiritual.

May it help me to remember to express my love and gratitude in words as well as actions. I thank You, Holy One, for the gifts of body and spirit."

• • •

The Rabbis equate the male sexual drive with the yetser ha'rah—*the evil instinct which is necessary for procreation and other worldly acts of progress. In this way, they anticipated today's radical feminists. In my own life, I've tried not to objectify women, while maintaining a loving and physical relationship with my partner. Given these complex and often bewildering tensions, sexuality remains the single most exciting and creative aspect of my day-to-day life, and I hope it will remain so until the day I die. (jlm)*

KAVANAH: AWAKENING

The sexual metaphor reenacts creation and foreshadows the coming of a repaired and perfected world. This was apparent to Rabbi Abraham Isaac Kook:

> I love you, my people and nation; I desire you with my heart and all my soul, with all the warmth of my heart I want you. With all the fire in my bones I long to see your glory, your beauty and splendor; when you will be exalted and arise; when you will develop your beautiful character; when all your qualities and hidden wonders will be actualized; when you will be planted in your land, the land of your splendor, and your magnificent strength and exalted glory will appear in the north and south, the east and west.[14]

CREATIVE BLESSING (BASED ON PSALM 42:8)

"Blessed are You, the Eternal One our God, Infinite and Eternal Source of Creative Life Energy. I feel surrounded by Your love all day; I am embraced by Your song at night. You are the God of my life!"

Study: The Power of Love

We cannot talk about the mystical—or about Creation and sexuality—without also talking about love. As Aryeh Kaplan writes, "Love is the power that breaks down barriers and unifies opposites."[15] A central tenet in Judaism is love: love of God, love of neighbor, love of self, love of stranger, and God's love for Creation.

By day the Eternal One will enjoin love; and at night God's song is with me, a prayer to the God of my life.

Psalm 42:8

[L]ove is the great all-sustaining power that moves the sacred music of creation into its most sacred space—the human heart.

Ann Williams-Heller

Love is fuel to the soul. The basis of Creation is God's love

The heart must be filled with love for all. . . .
The flame of the holy fire of the love of God
is always burning in the human heart.
Rabbi Abraham Isaac Kook

flowing into the world. Without Divine love, there would be no existence. Since Jews are instructed to emulate God in every way possible, the primary way to be like God is to be loving—both to God and to Creation.

On a practical level, Judaism teaches that even if love is not manifest—for whatever reason—each of us is required to act justly according to the highest level of fairness and equity. Perhaps Judaism does not *require* that we show love to our enemy, but the Rabbis teach that the highest aspiration of the human spirit is to love all of God's creation, even our enemies: "The degree of love in the soul of the righteous," stated Rabbi Abraham Isaac Kook, "embraces all creatures, it excludes nothing, and no people or tongue."[16] Psychiatrist Victor Frankl understood the power of love this way:

Say, You are our brother, to those who hate you.
Isaiah 66:5

> A thought transfixed me: for the first time in my life I saw the truth as it is set into song by so many poets, proclaimed as the final wisdom by so many thinkers. The truth—that love is the ultimate and the highest goal to which man can aspire. Then I grasped the meaning of the greatest secret that human poetry and human thought and belief have to impart: *The salvation of man is through love and in love*.[17]

Evil comes when humanity fails to manifest the Divine within. Aspiring to love our enemies does not mean that we condone wrongdoing or that we love evil. By loving all humanity, we show our love for God. According to Deuteronomy (6:5), "You shall love the Eternal One your God with all your heart, and with all your soul, and will all your might." The Rabbis interpreted this as meaning that we should act out of love, and that whatever we do, we do with love for God with "our

The Eternal One will love you and bless you.
Deuteronomy 7:13

whole heart." And even if God takes our soul—our life—we still love God fully, with all our strength.

Even more important than our love of humanity, of Creation, and of God is God's love for us, specifically through Torah, which helps us understand the ways of God. As we say in our daily prayers, "You love us with a monumental love, O Eternal One our God."

God's compassion is over all God's works.

Psalm 145:9

While Judaism does not distinguish between spiritual and romantic love, there are different words for "love" in Hebrew: *ahava, chesed,* and *rachamim.* These are often translated as "love," "kindness," and "mercy," but each manifests feelings that, in English, we call "love."

The future of the world depends on our ability to love. Love will heal the world; coupled with truth and justice, love lights the Jewish path. May we walk in this Light with our hearts full of love, acting out of love, to all and to God. Rabbi Abraham Isaac Kook summed this up when he said, "It will be love without cause that will save Israel and all mankind."[18]

Then you shall see and be radiant, your heart shall thrill and be enlarged; because the abundance of the sea of love shall be turned to you . . .

Psalm 60:5

Walking the Path: The Power of Love

KAVANAH: AWAKENING

"O my heart, be open to the potential for Love which flows through you each and every moment. Help me be more loving to myself, to others, to the Universe, and to the Creator. Open the eyes of my soul so I can perceive the goodness in every being and every moment. When pain or doubt assail me, help me see that the world is pure blessing, but let me not be blind to the physical and spiritual needs of my fellow creatures. May my love constantly express itself through acts of kindness, affirmation, and healing. May my passion and love for justice equal my passion and love for peace. May I approach every living thing with the knowledge that I stand before a manifestation of God's loving Creation."

• • •

There are many kinds of love. Waking up in the morning to the sun rising, I feel energizing love. Once at work, a client turns to me at the door after a difficult therapy session and says, "Thank you"— understanding love. When I drive into the garage from work, my children are often yelling before I open the car door to tell me something exciting about their day—overflowing love. I get in the house and our 110-pound dog, Moshe, leans into my knee and says, "Welcome home—pet me NOW"—big love. Upstairs my husband, Ron, is looking at the mail and stops for a moment to give me a kiss—steady love. I notice that the three roses I tend on our deck off the family room are blooming—bursting love! Later that evening, I'm struck by the beautiful sunset—awesome love. Before going to sleep, I review the day—grateful love. God's love surrounds—in nature, in animals, in people, in myself. (kbw)

• • •

MEDITATION

When heaven and earth become one . . . And in that day the mountains shall drip sweet wine—*Mercy,* and the hills shall flow with milk—*Kindness,* and all the stream beds of Judah shall flow with water—*Compassion;* and a fountain *of love* shall come forth from the house of the Eternal One and water the valley of Shittim—*Creation.*

Adapted from Joel 3:18

The Eternal One appeared to me from afar.
"I have loved you with an everlasting love; therefore, I continue my faithfulness to you."
Jeremiah 31:3

Study: Sabbath/*Shabbat,* Wholeness/*Shalom,* Messiah/*Mashiach*

God created for six days, and on the seventh day, rested. Every week, we are offered a taste of the world to come: *Shabbat.* Traditionally, we rest from our work so we can enter into a time of *shalom*—of wholeness, completeness, of Godfulness. When we finish the work

On the seventh day God finished the work which God was doing, and ceased on the seventh day from all the work which was created.

Genesis 2:2

that God created for us, life will be a continuous *Shabbat:* a time of harmony and wholeness, a time of union with God's true nature.

In Judaism, society's goal is to create the world to come: a world of universal peace, freedom, and Divine love. Then, the cosmos will be in harmony and God's true nature will be fully manifest. We carry the seed of *yom she-kulo Shabbat,* "the day that is all *Shabbat,*" within us each

What was created on the seventh day? Tranquility, serenity, peace, and repose.

Genesis *Rabbah* 10,9

and every day. And we continue the work of *tikkun olam,* of repairing the world, until the end of all days when there will be no work, only *shalom,* only wholeness.

For the sake of Creation, I will not keep silent, and for the sake of Peace in the world, I will not rest, until the ultimate purpose of humanity goes forth as brightness, And shalom, *peace for all is a burning torch.*

Isaiah 62:1

Peace, or *shalom,* can come by following the ways of Torah. *Shalom* can be translated as "peace." In English, this can mean "freedom from war," but *shalom* means more than this. Rabbi Stephen S. Wise taught that war "is the supreme repudiation and negation of religion forasmuch as war commands men to kill, to hate, to lie, to covet, to steal . . ."[19]

Shalom refers to the ultimate peace, to the wholeness of heaven and earth, to the transformation of all that is unholy into holiness. To achieve *shalom,* we must act in the Light of our true nature—our Divine nature—

And they shall beat their swords into plow shares, and their spears into pruning hooks; nation shall not lift up sword against nation, neither shall they learn war anymore.

Isaiah 2:4

with each step we take. Life's most important lessons are learning to trust God's ways, to harness the power of God's love, to give expression to it, to act faithfully in God's spirit. Then, and only then, will we complete the work that God created and the time of the *Mashiach,* the Messiah, will arrive.

One of the deepest desires of the Jewish people—and of all humanity—is a world free from pain and sorrow. On one level, this is manifest in the promise of an afterlife—a spiritual haven for the soul. But Judaism also envisions this as a possibility for this world in the mythic future. The Messiah is thought to be a messenger sent by God to raise humanity's consciousness. It is said that every year a certain number of people are born with the potential to fulfill this role.

The wolf shall dwell with the lamb; and the leopard shall lie down with the kid, and the calf and the lion and the fatling together and a little child shall lead them. The cow and the bear shall feed; their young shall lie down together; and the lion shall eat straw like the ox. They shall not hurt or destroy in all My holy mountain; for the earth shall be full of the knowledge of the Holy One as the waters cover the sea.

Isaiah 11:6–9

Judaism speaks of the Messianic Age that will be brought about by the collective spiritual and intellectual energies of all humanity. Together, we can perfect life in ways that are unimaginable. Every prayer, every scientific discovery, every act of kindness can become a stone along the path to *mashiach tseiten,* the Messianic times that will be "heaven on earth." With this vision, every positive act has cosmic significance.

When man shall live each under his vine and under his fig tree, with none to make him afraid.

Micah 4:4

Walking the Path: Sabbath/*Shabbat*, Wholeness/*Shalom*, Messiah/*Mashiach*

KAVANAH: AWAKENING

A PRAYER FOR PEACE
by Rabbi Nachman of Breslov

May we see the day when war and bloodshed cease,
when a great peace will embrace the whole world.
Then nation will not threaten nation
and mankind will not again know war.
For all who live on earth shall realize
we have not come into being to hate or to destroy.
We have come into being
to praise, to labor, and to love.
Compassionate God, bless the leaders of all nations
with the power of compassion.
Fulfill the promise conveyed in Scripture:
I will bring peace to the land,
and you shall lie down and no one shall terrify you.
I will rid the land of vicious beasts
and it shall not be ravaged by war.
Let love and justice flow like a mighty stream.
Let peace fill the earth as the waters fill the sea
And let us say: Amen.[20]

ACTIVITY: LIGHTING CANDLES

One of the simplest yet most profound spiritual acts is creating fire.
Fire is the symbol par excellence of the presence of God/Divine/Holiness in our lives. We are taught by the sages that "humanity's spirit is God's light." That is, we are the flint that allows

May the Eternal One give strength to humanity,
May the Eternal One bless humanity with peace.
Psalm 29:11

God to make flame. Lighting candles on *Shabbat*, on Holy Days, at *Havdalah* (the service marking the end of the Sabbath), at the wedding canopy and the funeral bier, and around the conjugal bed reminds us of God's presence. When Jews need to feel the light of God's presence, we light candles or oil wicks. In the synagogue, the focal point is the *ner tamid*, the eternal light over the Holy Ark.

Yea, You light my candle;
the Eternal One my God lightens
my darkness.

Psalm 18:28

Light your own candles to manifest the everpresent light of God. Be aware that the candle light connects to the light of holiness in your own heart and soul.

TRADITIONAL *BRAKHA* FOR LIGHTING SABBATH CANDLES

Baruch atah Adonai, Eloheinu melech ha-olam, asher kid'shanu b'mitzvotav v'tzivanu l'hadlik ner shel Shabbat.

"Blessed are You, Eternal One, Divine Presence in the Universe, You have made us holy with Your commandments and commanded us to kindle the Sabbath lights."

• • •

Each of us has delusions of grandeur. We want to believe that we are so special that the world will become a better place because of our presence in it. This aspect of the process of Creation is a hallmark of our species. Each one of us partakes, therefore, of the Messianic spirit. Part of my reason for being a partner in writing this book is to make my mark in this world and play a transformative role in the lives of others whom I will never meet. What my legacy in this life will be, I do not know. Some part of me wants to be a messiah (with a small "m"): someone who made a difference, with the help of God, each and every day. (jlm)

• • •

CREATIVE BLESSING

"Blessed are You, Eternal One, whose name is Peace. I pray for the day when all the people of the earth know Your name in whatever tongue they speak, and all live in Your spirit, and there is peace."

The Holy One forms the great lights,
for God's lovingkindness endures forever.

Psalm 136:7

Conclusion: Awakening the Dawn!

"Then the Eternal One awoke us from sleep . . ." (Psalm 78:65). Thus we pray that we will awaken to the Eternal Oneness, to the blessings of Life, to the holiness of our true nature. This is our hope that we will awaken today and every day to hear the Eternal Oneness echoing in the gift of life.

Awake, my soul!
Awake O harp and lyre!
I will awake the dawn!
Psalm 57:8

Recently a Jewish writer summed up the underlying philosophy of Judaism in the single Hebrew word *le-chayim*, "to life." So, too, do we offer a summary of our approach to the Jewish tradition as a spiritual path to self/Self: *hineni*, "Here I am." This was the response of Abraham, Jacob, Moses, Samuel, and Elijah to the urgent call of the One whom they called *Adonai*, the Eternal. The call was heard once (or perhaps twice) during their lifetime; they heard it and responded to it because they had walked the path of holiness each and every day.

Hineni is the ultimate Jewish response to those rare, life-changing encounters with the Divine, to moments of catharsis ("life-changing") or theophany ("God-meeting"), which can only occur within a daily life lived mindfully. We live, some might say, so we can recognize these transcendent moments and be prepared to utter that single *hineni* which can connect us to our historical knights of faith: Abraham and Sarah, Rachel and Jacob, Moses and Miriam, Hannah and Samuel, Ruth, Elisha, and Elijah.

The One who called them may call to us as well. May we also be able to respond: *Hineni*, "Here I am."

As daylight approaches, we are renewed, as are our opportunities to create a world of Godfulness. We pray that the mystic within us sees deeply into the mystery and wonder that surrounds us. We pray for the opportunity to soar with angels, to dream, to prophesy; to access our spiritual nature so we may live in the everyday world more fully and consciously. We pray for *shalom*, for wholeness. We pray to manifest

And Moses said, "I will turn aside and see this
great sight. . . ." When the Eternal One saw that
he turned aside to see, God called to him out of
the bush, "Moses, Moses!"
And Moses said, hineni, "Here I am."
Exodus 3:3–4

184

the light of *Shabbat* as we move through the other six days repairing, creating, bringing into being the world that is constantly coming. And we pray that the days of the *Mashiach,* the Messiah, will be soon. And let us say: Amen, may it be so.

I will meditate on all Your work,
and gaze meditatively on Your mighty deeds.
Your way, O God, is holy.
What God is great like our God?
You are the God that works wonders,
who has manifested Your might
among the peoples.

Psalm 77:12–14

Epilogue

I try to walk the road of Judaism. Embedded in the road there are many jewels. One is marked "Sabbath" and one "Civil Rights" and one "Kashruth" and one "Honor Your Parents" and one "Study of Torah" and one "You Shall Be Holy." There are at least 613 of them and they are of different shapes and sizes and weights. Some are light and easy for me to pick up, and I pick them up. Some are too deeply embedded for me, so far at least, though I get a little stronger by trying to extricate the jewels as I walk the street. Some, perhaps, I shall never be able to pick up. I believe that God expects me to keep on walking Judaism Street and to carry away whatever I can of its commandments. I do not believe that God expects me to lift what I cannot, nor may I condemn my fellow Jew who may not be able to pick up even as much as I can.

Rabbi Arnold Jacob Wolf

When we began this book, we were hoping that it would become a useful, inspirational way to bring Jewish spirituality into everyday life. We hope we have succeeded. Ideally, life should be permeated with a constant sense of wonder and an ever-present gratitude. We recognize that, very often, there are impediments to being at one with ourselves and with God. We hope we have addressed these areas of conflict in a caring and thoughtful way.

The psalmist who exclaimed, "Bless God O my soul—and let all that is within me Praise God's Holy Name," expressed for us the ground of all religious and spiritual journeys. Within the overwhelming mystery of Being, we hope that we can acknowledge the sense of God's presence, the *Shechinah,* through which we exist and find meaning. Judaism recognizes that very often it is through our relationships with animals, nature, and other people that the holy is most clearly demonstrated.

We deeply hope that this book has been a beacon for you, guiding you to your own potential as a holy being in a holy universe. As we hold out the candle of our souls to you, our reader and our friend, we trust that, with God's help, our souls may meet in this life or the next. For you we offer this prayer:

May the One who fashions Peace
   throughout the Universe
   send Peace to you, and to this place.
And we say: Amen—may it be so.

Shalom,
Jim Mirel Karen Bonnell Werth

Acknowledgments

The process of conceiving, writing, and publishing a book is one of the most exhilarating experiences in life. We are grateful to God for our lives and for the opportunity to share our ideas and struggles.

We deeply appreciate the many wonderful people who support us, encourage us, and provide inspiration: The team of caring people at Jewish Lights Publishing have been more than helpful. They are co-creators with us in this venture. We humbly thank Stuart Matlins, who has changed the entire field of Jewish publishing with his vision; Arthur Magida, thoughtful and respectful editor; Jennifer Goneau, who provided the necessary electronic hand-holding along the way; and Richard Fumosa whose creative spirit found us the right title and more.

We also wish to acknowledge the caring community at our synagogue, Temple B'nai Torah in Bellevue, Washington, who encouraged us over many months as we tried to formulate the ideas that are in this book in our sermons, study groups, and seminars. We also thank our dear friends of many faiths whose interest and critical feedback added immense value to these pages.

Each of us has been blessed with inspiring, yet constructively critical teachers and mentors over the years. We mention by name and for blessing Rabbi William Cutter, Rabbi Harold Saperstein, Rabbi Norman Mirsky, Rabbi Alfred Gottschalk, and Cantor David Serkin-Poole. We thank Thich Nhat Hanh, Zen master and author, whose dedication to making Buddhist spiritual practices accessible to practitioners of all religions inspired our writing. We also recognize the important contribution of the many authors we've studied, many of whom we've quoted. Their work has significantly enlightened and challenged our minds.

Finally, we are grateful to our families who, each and every day, provide sustenance, love, and joy. To Ruth Bonnell, and Ron, Ali, and Ben Werth, and to Joan Greenberg and Julie, Chava, and Shoshana Mirel, we give our deepest thanks and most heartfelt appreciation.

Notes

Cornerstones and Fundamentals

1. Joseph Gikatilla, *Sha'aray Orah,* quoted in Matt, *The Essential Kabbalah* (San Francisco: HarperCollins, 1995), p. 67.

2. *Merriam-Webster's Collegiate Dictionary, 9th ed.,* s.v. "kabbalah."

3. The Baal Shem Tov, quoted in David Ariel, *The Mystic Quest* (New York: Schocken Books, 1988), p. 12.

Sunrise: Dawn—Awakening to Life

1. Z'ev ben Shimon Halevi, *Kabbalah* (York Beach, Maine: Samuel Weiser, Inc., 1976), p. 27.

2. Abraham Joshua Heschel, quoted in John C. Merkle, *Heschel's Attitude toward Religious Pluralism* (New York: Free Press), p. 102.

3. Abraham Joshua Heschel, quoted in Murray Poiner and Naomi Goodman, *The Challenge of Shalom* (Philadelphia, Pa.: New Society Publishers, 1994), p. 209.

4. Quoted in Matt, *The Essential Kabbalah,* p. 31.

5. Lawrence Kushner, *The Book of Words: Talking Spiritual Life, Living Spiritual Talk* (Woodstock, Vt.: Jewish Lights Publishing, 1993), p. 28.

6. Research has shown the relaxation response brought about by meditation has multiple positive influences on the health and well-being of the practitioner. See Herbert Benson's *Timeless Healing* (New York: Scribner, 1996) for details.

7. Abraham Isaac Kook, *Orot ha-Qodesh* 3:270, quoted in Matt, *The Essential Kabbalah,* p. 124.

8. *Mishnah Sanhedrin,* IV, 5.

9. Aryeh Kaplan, *Jewish Meditation* (New York: Schocken Books, 1985), p. 51.

10. Ibid., p. 52.

11. Hayyim Vital, *Sha'arei Qe-dushah,* quoted in Matt, *The Essential Kabbalah,* p. 123.

12. *Taldot Yaakov Yosef, VaYakhel,* p. 67d, quoted in Kaplan, *Meditation and Kabbalah,* p. 294.

13. Reuven Hammer, *Entering Jewish Prayer* (New York: Schocken Books, 1994), pp. 154, 155.

Morning: Going On Our Way, Doing Our Work

1. Based on Chasidic prayers quoted in Yitzhak Buxbaum, *Jewish Spiritual Practices* (Northvale, N.J.: Jason Aronson Inc., 1990), p. 201.

2. *Kodesh Hillulim,* pp. 150–151, quoted in Buxbaum, *Jewish Spiritual Practices,* pp. 202–203.

3. Abraham Joshua Heschel, *I Asked for Wonder: A Spiritual Anthology* (New York: Crossroads, 1993), p. ix.

4. Ibid., p. 67.

5. Arthur Waskow, *Down-to-Earth Judaism: Food, Money, Sex, and the Rest of Life* (New York: William Morrow & Co., 1995), p. 182.

6. Ibid., p. 187.

7. Ibid.

Noon: Mealtime, Gratitude, Hospitality

1. Michael Lerner, *Jewish Renewal: A Path to Healing and Transformation* (New York: HarperCollins, 1995), p. 339.

2. *Ohalei Shem,* p. 26, #45, quoted in Buxbaum, *Jewish Spiritual Practices,* p. 227.

3. Quoted in Ari Goldman, *The Search for God at Harvard* (New York: Ballantine Books, 1991), p. 113.

4. *Kitzur Shnei Luchot ha-Brit, Inyanei tefillat yud-chet,* p. 121, quoted in Buxbaum, *Jewish Spiritual Practices,* p. 233.

Afternoon: Relationships—Family, Friends, Community, God

1. Matt, *The Essential Kabbalah,* p. 16.

2. Heschel, *I Asked for Wonder,* p. 12.

3. David Wolpe, *The Healer of Shattered Hearts* (New York: Penguin Books, 1990), p. 51.

4. Moses Cordovero, *Or Ne'erav,* quoted in Matt, *The Essential Kabbalah,* p. 22.

5. Elie Wiesel, *From the Kingdom of Memory* (New York: Schocken Books, 1990), p. 62.

6. Abraham Joshua Heschel, *God in Search of Man* (New York: Farrar, Straus & Giroux, Inc., 1976), p. 50.

7. Wolpe, *The Healer of Shattered Hearts,* p. 165.

8. Rabbi Abraham Isaac Kook, source unknown.

9. Moses Cordovero, *The Palm Tree of Deborah,* quoted in Matt, *The Essential Kabbalah,* p. 86.

10. *Sefer Yetsirah,* quoted in Matt, *The Essential Kabbalah,* p. 102.

11. Sheldon Kramer, "Jewish Meditation," in *Opening the Inner Gates,* edited by Edward Hoffman (Boston: Shambhala, 1995), p. 235.

12. Three is an important number representing God's connection with the world of duality. It represents the unity of *time* through past, present and future, and the unity of *space* through length, height and width. Three represents balance and stability.

13. Elie Wiesel, *Sages and Dreamers* (New York: Simon & Schuster, 1991), p. 54.

14. Wiesel, *From the Kingdom of Memory,* p. 75.

15. The *minyan* consists of ten people who have reached the age of maturity, traditionally the age of thirteen, though a Torah scroll can sometimes be substituted for the tenth person. Some Jewish traditions still require that only men be counted for a *minyan,* but most Reform and Conservative Jews include women.

16. Abraham Joshua Heschel, quoted in Polner and Goodman, *The Challenge of Shalom,* p. 151.

17. Albert Einstein, quoted ibid., p. 204.

18. Abraham Isaac Kook, *Orat ha-Qodesh,* quoted in Matt, *The Essential Kabbalah,* p. 154.

19. Abraham Isaac Kook, quoted in Ariel, *The Mystic Quest,* p. 184.

20. Rabbi Adin Steinsaltz, *The Thirteen Petalled Rose* (Northvale, N.J.: Jason Aronson Inc., 1992), p. 97.

Evening: Leisure—Recreation, Study, and Prayer

1. *Webster's New Collegiate Dictionary, 11th Edition,* s.v. "recreation."
2. *Ish ha-Pele,* quoted in Buxbaum, *Jewish Spiritual Practices,* p. 481.
3. Weisel, *Sages and Dreamers,* p. 21.
4. Chaim Stern, ed., *Gates of Prayer for Shabbat and Weekdays* (New York: Central Conference of American Rabbis, 1994), pp. 12–13.
5. Baal Shem Tov, *Tzavaat ha-Rabash,* quoted in Buxbaum, *Jewish Spiritual Practices,* p. 5.
6. Meditation based on *Or ha-Gamuz l'Tzaddikim,* p. 10; cf. pp. 11 and 22. Quoted ibid., p. 325.
7. Martin Buber, *Tales of the Hasidim: The Early Masters* (New York: Random House Inc., 1991), p. 69–70.
8. Midrash on Psalms 4:4.
9. Hammer, *Entering Jewish Prayer,* p. 29.
10. *Midor Dor,* vol. 1, p. 212, quoted in Buxbaum, *Jewish Spiritual Practices,* p. 137.
11. Stern, ed., *Gates of Prayer for Shabbat and Weekdays,* 1994.

Night: Pain, Loss, Death, and Healing

1. Nathan Ausubel, ed., *A Treasury of Jewish Folklore* (New York: Crown Publishing Group, 1989), p. 53.
2. Louis Newman, *The Hasidic Anthology* (Northvale, N.J.: Jason Aronson Inc., 1990), p. 64.
3. Talmud, *Eruvin* 54a.
4. Harold Kushner, *Who Needs God?* (New York: Summit Books, 1989), p. 64.
5. Ariel, *The Mystic Quest,* p. 204.
6. Victor Frankl, *Man in Search of Meaning* (New York: Washington Square Press, 1984), p. 157.
7. Wolpe, *The Healer of Shattered Hearts,* p. 30.
8. Rabbi Ted Falcon, Ph.D., ed., in *Siddur* (Bet Alef: A Center for Meditative Judaism, 1997).
9. Stephen Levine, quoted in Anne Brener, *Mourning & Mitz-*

vah: A Guided Journal for Walking the Mourner's Path Through Grief to Healing (Woodstock, Vt.: Jewish Lights Publishing, 1993), p. 148.

10. Deena Metzger, quoted in Brener, *Mourning & Mitzvah,* p. 163.

11. Wolpe, *The Healer of Shattered Hearts,* p. 28.

Midnight: Mysticism, Sexuality, and Creation

1. Lawrence Kushner, *The Book of Words: Talking Spiritual Life, Living Spiritual Talk* (Woodstock, Vt.: Jewish Lights Publishing, 1993), p. 115.

2. Wolpe, *The Healer of Shattered Hearts,* p. 93.

3. Talmud *Kidushin* 70.

4. Morris Margolies, *A Gathering of Angels* (New York: Ballantine Books, 1994), p. 202.

5. *Abraham Isaac Kook,* Classics of Western Spirituality, (Mahwah, N.J.: 1978), p. 213.

6. Talmud Sabbath 119b.

7. Daniel Matt, *Zohar: The Book of Enlightenment* (Ramsey, N.J.: Paulist Press, 1983), p. 221.

8. E. J. Holmyard (source unknown).

9. Ann Williams-Heller, *Kabbalah: Your Inner Path to Freedom* (Wheaton, Ill.: The Theosophical Publishing House, 1990), p. 7.

10. Abraham Isaac Kook, *Orot ha-Qodesh* 2:517, quoted in Matt, *The Essential Kabbalah,* p. 99.

11. Ariel, *The Mystic Quest,* pp. 101–102.

12. Levi Meier, *Ancient Secrets* (New York: Villard, 1996), p. 140.

13. Abraham Abulafia, quoted in Matt, *The Essential Kabbalah,* p. 21.

14. Abraham Isaac Kook, *Olat Re'iyah II,* p. 211 (Jerusalem: Genesis Jerusalem Press, 1992), quoted in Moshe Zvi Neriyah *Celebration of the Soul,* p. 19.

15. Aryeh Kaplan, *Jewish Meditation* (New York: Schocken Books, 1985), p. 127.

16. *Abraham Isaac Kook,* Classics of Western Spirituality, p. 137.

17. Frankl, *Man in Search of Meaning,* p. 57.

18. Abraham Isaac Kook, quoted in Kasimow & Sherwin, eds., *No Religion Is an Island* (Maryknoll, N.Y.: Orbis Books, 1991), p. 101.

19. Rabbi Stephen S. Wise, quoted in Polner and Goodman, *The Challenge of Shalom*, p. 171.

20. Quoted in Polner and Goodman, *The Challenge of Shalom*, p. 7. Adapted and translated by Rabbi Jules Harlow from the Hebrew of Rabbi Nathan Sternhartz (1780–1845), whose work was based on the teachings of Rabbi Nachman of Bratslav.

Sources

The many quotes that appear throughout this book came from the following sources. We are grateful to these authors and these sacred texts for their wisdom which has enriched our lives and, we hope, yours as well.

Ariel, David. *The Mystic Quest* (New York: Schocken Books, 1988).

Bokser, Ben Zion. *Abraham Isaac Kook,* Classics of Western Spirituality (Mahwah, N.J.: Paulist Press, 1978).

Brener, Anne. *Mourning & Mitzvah: A Guided Journal for Walking the Mourner's Path Through Grief to Healing* (Woodstock, Vt.: Jewish Lights Publishing, 1993).

Buber, Martin. *Tales of the Hasidim: The Early Masters* (New York: Random House Inc., 1991).

Buxbaum, Yitzhak. *Jewish Spiritual Practices* (Northvale, N.J.: Jason Aronson Inc., 1990).

Frankl, Victor. *Man in Search of Meaning* (New York: Washington Square Press, 1984).

Goldman, Ari. *The Search for God at Harvard* (New York: Ballantine Books, 1991).

Halevi, Z'ev ben Shimon. *Kabbalah* (York Beach, Maine: Samuel Weiser Inc., 1976).

Hammer, Reuven. *Entering Jewish Prayer* (New York: Schocken Books, 1994).

Heschel, Abraham Joshua. *God in Search of Man* (New York: Farrar, Straus, & Giroux Inc., 1976).

Heschel, Abraham Joshua. *I Asked for Wonder: A Spiritual Anthology* (New York: Crossroads, 1993).

Hoffman, Edward, ed. *Opening the Inner Gates,* (Boston: Shambhala, 1995).

Kaplan, Aryeh. *Jewish Meditation* (New York: Schocken Books, 1985).

Kaplan, Aryeh. *Meditation and Kabbalah* (Northvale, N.J.: Jason Aronson Inc., 1995).

Kasimow and Sherwin, eds. *No Religion Is an Island* (Maryknoll, N.Y.: Orbis Books, 1991).

Kushner, Harold. *Who Needs God?* (New York: Summit Books, 1989).

Kushner, Lawrence. *The Book of Words: Talking Spiritual Life, Living Spiritual Talk* (Woodstock, Vt.: Jewish Lights Publishing, 1993).

Lerner, Michael. *Jewish Renewal: A Path to Healing and Transformation* (New York: Harper Perrenial, 1995).

Margolies, Morris. *A Gathering of Angels* (New York: Ballantine Books, 1994).

Matt, Daniel. *The Essential Kabbalah* (San Francisco: HarperSan-Francisco, 1995).

Matt, Daniel. *Zohar: The Book of Enlightenment* (Ramsey, N.J.: Paulist Press, 1983).

Meier, Levi. *Ancient Secrets* (New York: Villard, 1996).

Newman, Louis. *The Hasidic Anthology* (Northvale, N.J.: Jason Aronson Inc., 1990).

Polner, Murray and Naomi Goodman. *The Challenge of Shalom* (Philadelphia, Pa.: New Society Publishers, 1994).

Steinsaltz, Adin. *The Thirteen Petalled Rose* (Northvale, N.J.: Jason Aronson Inc., 1992).

Waskow, Arthur. *Down-to-Earth Judaism: Food, Money, Sex, and the Rest of Life* (New York: William Morrow & Co., 1995).

Wiesel, Elie. *From the Kingdom of Memory* (New York: Schocken Books, 1990).

Wiesel, Elie. *Sages and Dreamers* (New York: Simon & Schuster, 1991).

Williams-Heller, Ann. *Kabbalah: Your Inner Path to Freedom* (Wheaton, Ill.: The Theosophical Publishing House, 1990).

Wolpe, David. *The Healer of Shattered Hearts* (New York: Penguin Books, 1990).

Recommended Reading

We also offer the following list as recommended reading to futher your study in areas of Jewish spirituality.

Kabbalah

Addison, Howard. *The Enneagram and Kabbalah: Reading Your Soul* (Woodstock, Vt.: Jewish Lights Publishing, 1998).

Ariel, David. *The Mystic Quest* (New York: Schocken, 1988).

Halevi, Z'ev ben Shimon. *Kabbalah* (York Beach, Maine: Samuel Weiser Inc., 1976).

Kushner, Lawrence. *Honey from the Rock: An Easy Introduction to Jewish Mysticism* (Woodstock, Vt.: 1994).

Labowitz, Shoni. *Miraculous Living* (New York: Simon & Schuster, 1996).

Matt, Daniel. *The Essential Kabbalah* (San Francisco: HarperSanFrancisco, 1995).

Matt, Daniel. *Zohar: The Book of Enlightenment* (Ramsey, N.J.: Paulist Press, 1983).

Edward Hoffman, ed. *Opening the Inner Gates* (Boston: Shambhala, 1995).

Steinsaltz, Adin. *The Thirteen Petalled Rose* (Northvale, N.J.: Jason Aronson Inc., 1992).

Williams-Heller, Ann. *Kabbalah: Your Inner Path to Freedom* (Wheaton, Ill.: The Theosophical Publishing House, 1990).

Jewish Meditation

Cooper, David. *God Is a Verb* (New York: Riverhead, 1997).

Davis, Avram, ed. *Meditation from the Heart of Judaism: Today's Teachers Share Their Practices, Techniques, and Faith* (Woodstock, Vt.: Jewish Lights Publishing, 1997).

Kaplan, Aryeh. *Jewish Meditation* (New York: Schocken Books, 1985).

Kaplan, Aryeh. *Meditation and Kabbalah* (Northvale, N.J.: Jason Aronson, 1998).

Daily Jewish Practices

Brener, Anne. *Mourning & Mitzvah: A Guided Journal for Walking the Mourner's Path Through Grief to Healing* (Woodstock, Vt.: Jewish Lights Publishing, 1993).

Green, Arthur & Barry Holtz. *Your Word Is Fire: The Hasidic Masters on Contemplative Prayer* (Woodstock, Vt.: Jewish Lights Publishing, 1993).

Greenfield, Judy, and Tamar Frankiel. *Minding the Temple of the Soul: Balancing Body, Mind, and Spirit throught Traditional Jewish Prayer, Movement, and Meditation* (Woodstock, Vt.: Jewish Lights Publishing, 1997).

Hammer, Reuven. *Entering Jewish Prayer* (New York: Schocken Books, 1994).

Hoffman, Lawrence. *My People's Prayer Book: Traditional Prayers, Modern Commentaries* (Woodstock, Vt.: Jewish Lights Publishing, 1997).

Lerner, Michael. *Jewish Renewal: A Path to Healing and Transformation* (New York: Harper Perrenial, 1995).

Polner, Murray and Naomi Goodman, *The Challenge of Shalom* (Philadelphia, Pa.: New Society Publishers, 1994).

Salkin, Jeffrey. *Being God's Partner: How to Find the Hidden Link between Spirituality and Your Work* (Woodstock, Vt.: Jewish Lights Publishing, 1997).

Waskow, Arthur. *Down-to-Earth Judaism: Food, Money, Sex, and the Rest of Life* (New York: William Morrow & Co., 1995).

God in Judaism

Goldman, Ari. *The Search for God at Harvard* (New York: Ballantine Books, 1991).

Heschel, Abraham Joshua. *God in Search of Man* (New York: Farrar, Straus & Giroux Inc., 1976).

Heschel, Abraham Joshua. *I Asked for Wonder: A Spiritual Anthology* (New York: Crossroads, 1993).

Kasimow, Harold, and Byron L. Sherwin, eds. *No Religion Is an Island* (Maryknoll, N.Y.: Orbis Books, 1991).

Kushner, Harold. *Who Needs God?* (New York: Summit Books, 1989).

Matt, Daniel. *God & the Big Bang: Discovering Harmony Between Science and Spirituality* (Woodstock, Vt.: Jewish Lights Publishing, 1996).

Wolpe, David. *The Healer of Shattered Hearts* (New York: Penguin Books, 1990).

Jewish Spiritual Teachings

Buber, Martin. *Tales of the Hasidim: The Early Masters* (New York: Random House Inc., 1991).

Buxbaum, Yitzhak. *Jewish Spiritual Practices* (Northvale, N.J.: Jason Aronson Inc., 1990).

Classics of Western Spirituality, *Abraham Isaac Kook* (Mahwah, N.J., 1978).

Frankl, Victor. *Man in Search of Meaning* (New York: Washington Square Press, 1984).

Kushner, Lawrence. *The Book of Words: Talking Spiritual Life, Living Spiritual Talk* (Woodstock, Vt.: Jewish Lights Publishing, 1993).

Kushner, Lawrence. *God Was in This Place, and I, i Did Not Know: Finding Self, Spirituality, and Ultimate Meaning* (Woodstock, Vt.: Jewish Lights Publishing, 1991).

Kushner, Lawrence. *The River of Light: Spirituality, Judaism, Consciousness* (Woodstock, Vt.: Jewish Lights Publishing, 1990).

Margolies, Morris. *A Gathering of Angels* (New York: Ballantine Books, 1994).

Meier, Levi. *Ancient Secrets* (New York: Villard, 1996).

Newman, Louis. *The Hasidic Anthology* (Northvale, N.J.: Jason Aronson Inc., 1990).

Schwartz, Dannel, and Mark Hass. *Finding Joy: A Practical Spiritual Guide to Happiness* (Woodstock, Vt.: Jewish Lights Publishing, 1996).

Waskow, Arthur. *Godwrestling—Round 2: Ancient Wisdom, Future Paths* (Woodstock, Vt.: Jewish Lights Publishing, 1996).

Wiesel, Elie. *From the Kingdom of Memory* (New York: Schocken Books, 1990).

Wiesel, Elie. *Sages and Dreamers* (New York: Simon & Schuster, 1991).

About JEWISH LIGHTS Publishing

People of all faiths and backgrounds yearn for books that attract, engage, educate and spiritually inspire.

Our principal goal is to stimulate thought and help all people learn about who the Jewish People are, where they come from, and what the future can be made to hold. While people of our diverse Jewish heritage are the primary audience, our books speak to people in the Christian world as well and will broaden their understanding of Judaism and the roots of their own faith.

We bring to you authors who are at the forefront of spiritual thought and experience. While each has something different to say, they all say it in a voice that you can hear.

Our books are designed to welcome you and then to engage, stimulate and inspire. We judge our success not only by whether or not our books are beautiful and commercially successful, but by whether or not they make a difference in your life.

We at Jewish Lights take great care to produce beautiful books that present meaningful spiritual content in a form that reflects the art of making high quality books. Therefore, we want to acknowledge those who contributed to the production of this book.

PRODUCTION
Bronwen Battaglia

EDITORIAL & PROOFREADING
Jennifer Goneau, Martha McKinney

COVER DESIGN
Bronwen Battaglia

COVER PRINTING
Phoenix Color Corp., Taunton, Massachusetts

PRINTING AND BINDING
Royal Book, Norwich, Connecticut

Personal Stepping Stones

Spirituality

HOW TO BE A PERFECT STRANGER, In 2 Volumes
A Guide to Etiquette in Other People's
Religious Ceremonies
Edited by *Stuart M. Matlins* & *Arthur J. Magida*

> *"A book that belongs in every living room,*
> *library and office!"*

Explains the rituals and celebrations of America's major religions/denominations, helping an interested guest to feel comfortable, participate to the fullest extent possible, and avoid violating anyone's religious principles. Answers practical questions from the perspective of *any* other faith.

•AWARD WINNER•

VOL. 1: America's Largest Faiths

VOL. 1 COVERS: Assemblies of God • Baptist • Buddhist • Christian Science • Churches of Christ • Disciples of Christ • Episcopalian • Greek Orthodox • Hindu • Islam • Jehovah's Witnesses • Jewish • Lutheran • Methodist • Mormon • Presbyterian • Quaker • Roman Catholic • Seventh-day Adventist • United Church of Christ

6" x 9", 432 pp. Hardcover, ISBN 1-879045-39-7 **$24.95**

VOL. 2: Other Faiths in America

VOL. 2 COVERS: African American Methodist Churches • Baha'i • Christian and Missionary Alliance • Christian Congregation • Church of the Brethren • Church of the Nazarene • Evangelical Free Church of America • International Church of the Foursquare Gospel • International Pentecostal Holiness Church • Mennonite/Amish • Native American • Orthodox Churches • Pentecostal Church of God • Reformed Church of America • Sikh • Unitarian Universalist • Wesleyan

6" x 9", 416 pp. HC, ISBN 1-879045-63-X **$24.95**

GOD & THE BIG BANG
Discovering Harmony Between Science & Spirituality
by *Daniel C. Matt*

Mysticism and science: What do they have in common? How can one enlighten the other? By drawing on modern cosmology and ancient Kabbalah, Matt shows how science and religion can together enrich our spiritual awareness and help us recover a sense of wonder and find our place in the universe.

> "This poetic new book...helps us to understand the human meaning of creation."
> —*Joel Primack, leading cosmologist, Professor of*
> *Physics, University of California, Santa Cruz*

•AWARD WINNER•

6" x 9", 216 pp. Quality Paperback, ISBN 1-879045-89-3 **$16.95** HC, ISBN-48-6 **$21.95**

MINDING THE TEMPLE OF THE SOUL
Balancing Body, Mind, & Spirit through Traditional Jewish
Prayer, Movement, & Meditation
by *Tamar Frankiel* and *Judy Greenfeld*

This new spiritual approach to physical health introduces readers to a spiritual tradition that affirms the body and enables them to reconceive their bodies in a more positive light. Relying on Kabbalistic teachings and other Jewish traditions, it shows us how to be more responsible for our own psychological and physical health. Focuses on the discipline of prayer, simple Tai Chi–like exercises and body positions, and guides the reader throughout, step-by-step, with diagrams, sketches and meditations.

7"x 10", 184 pp. Quality Paperback Original, illus., ISBN 1-879045-64-8 **$16.95**

Audiotape of the Blessings, Movements & Meditations (60-min. cassette) **$9.95**
Videotape of the Movements & Meditations (46-min. VHS) **$20.00**

Spirituality

MEDITATION FROM THE HEART OF JUDAISM
Today's Teachers Share Their Practices, Techniques, and Faith
Edited by *Avram Davis*

A "how-to" guide for both beginning and experienced meditators, it will help you start meditating or help you enhance your practice.

Twenty-two masters of meditation explain why and how they meditate. *A detailed compendium of the experts' "Best Practices"* offers practical advice and starting points.

"A treasury of meditative insights and techniques....Each page is a meditative experience that brings you closer to God."
—*Rabbi Shoni Labowitz, author of* Miraculous Living: A Guided Journey in Kabbalah through the Ten Gates of the Tree of Life
6" x 9", 256 pp. Hardcover, ISBN 1-879045-77-X **$21.95**

SELF, STRUGGLE & CHANGE
Family Conflict Stories in Genesis and Their Healing Insights for Our Lives
by *Norman J. Cohen*

How do I find greater wholeness in my life and in my family's life?

The people described by the biblical writers of Genesis were in situations and relationships very much like our own. We identify with them. Their stories still speak to us because they are about the same problems we deal with every day. Here a modern master of biblical interpretation brings us greater understanding of the ancient text and of ourselves in this intriguing re-telling of conflict between husband and wife, father and son, brothers, and sisters.

"Delightfully written...rare erudition, sensitivity and insight." —*Elie Wiesel*
6" x 9", 224 pp. Quality Paperback, ISBN 1-879045-66-4 **$16.95**; HC, ISBN-19-2 **$21.95**

ECOLOGY & THE JEWISH SPIRIT
Where Nature & the Sacred Meet
Edited and with Introductions by *Ellen Bernstein*

What is nature's place in our spiritual lives?

A focus on nature is part of the fabric of Jewish thought. Here, experts bring us a richer understanding of the long-neglected themes of nature that are woven through the biblical creation story, ancient texts, traditional law, the holiday cycles, prayer, *mitzvot* (good deeds), and community.

For people of all faiths, all backgrounds, this book helps us to make nature a sacred, spiritual part of our own lives.

"A great resource for anyone seeking to explore the connection between their faith and caring for God's good creation, our environment."
—*Paul Gorman, Executive Director, National Religious Partnership for the Environment*
6" x 9", 288 pp. HC, ISBN 1-879045-88-5 **$23.95**

ISRAEL—A SPIRITUAL TRAVEL GUIDE
A Companion for the Modern Jewish Pilgrim
by *Rabbi Lawrence A. Hoffman*

Be spiritually prepared for your journey to Israel.

A Jewish spiritual travel guide to Israel, helping today's pilgrim tap into the deep spiritual meaning of the ancient—and modern—sites of the Holy Land. Combines in quick reference format ancient blessings, medieval prayers, biblical and historical references, and modern poetry. The only guidebook that helps readers to prepare spiritually for the occasion. More than a guide book: It is a spiritual map.

"To add spiritual dimension to your journey, pack this extraordinary new guidebook to Israel. I'll be bringing it on my next visit."
—*Gabe Levenson, travel columnist for* The New York Jewish Week
4 3/4" x 10 1/8", 256 pp. Quality Paperback Original, ISBN 1-879045-56-7 **$18.95**

Spirituality

MY PEOPLE'S PRAYER BOOK
Traditional Prayers, Modern Commentaries
Vol. 1—The Sh'ma and Its Blessings
Edited by *Rabbi Lawrence A. Hoffman*

Provides a diverse and exciting commentary to the traditional liturgy, written by 10 of today's most respected scholars and teachers from all perspectives of the Jewish world.

This groundbreaking first of seven volumes examines the oldest and best-known of Jewish prayers. Often the first prayer memorized by children and the last prayer recited on a deathbed, the *Sh'ma* frames a Jewish life.

"This book engages the mind and heart....It challenges one's assumptions at whatever level of understanding one brings to the text."
—*Jewish Herald-Voice*

7" x 10", 168 pp. HC, ISBN 1-879045-79-6 **$19.95**

FINDING JOY
A Practical Spiritual Guide to Happiness
by *Dannel I. Schwartz* with *Mark Hass*

Searching for happiness in our modern world of stress and struggle is common; *finding* it is more unusual. This guide explores and explains how to find joy through a time-honored, creative—and surprisingly practical—approach based on the teachings of Jewish mysticism and Kabbalah.

"Lovely, simple introduction to Kabbalah....a singular contribution...."
—*American Library Association's* Booklist

•AWARD WINNER•

6" x 9", 192 pp. HC, ISBN 1-879045-53-2 **$19.95**

THE DEATH OF DEATH
Resurrection and Immortality in Jewish Thought
by *Neil Gillman*

Noted theologian Neil Gillman explores the original and compelling argument that Judaism, a religion often thought to pay little attention to the afterlife, not only offers us rich ideas on the subject—but delivers a deathblow to death itself. By exploring Jewish thought about death and the afterlife, this fascinating work presents us with challenging new ideas about our lives.

"Enables us to recover our tradition's understanding of the afterlife and breaks through the silence of modern Jewish thought on immortality.... A work of major •AWARD WINNER• significance."
—*Rabbi Sheldon Zimmerman, President, Hebrew Union College–Jewish Institute of Religion*

6" x 9", 336 pp., HC, ISBN 1-879045-61-3 **$23.95**

THE EMPTY CHAIR: FINDING HOPE & JOY
Timeless Wisdom from a Hasidic Master,
Rebbe Nachman of Breslov
Adapted by Moshe Mykoff and the Breslov Research Institute

A "little treasure" of aphorisms and advice for living joyously and spiritually today, written 200 years ago, but startlingly fresh in meaning and use. Challenges and helps us to move from stress and sadness to hope and joy.

Teacher, guide and spiritual master—Rebbe Nachman provides vital words of inspiration and wisdom for life today for people of any faith, or of no faith.

•AWARD WINNER•

"For anyone of any faith, this is a book of healing and wholeness, of being alive!"
— *Bookviews*

4" x 6", 128 pp., 2-color text, Deluxe Paperback, ISBN 1-879045-67-2 **$9.95**

Spirituality—The Kushner Series

INVISIBLE LINES OF CONNECTION
Sacred Stories of the Ordinary
by *Lawrence Kushner*

Through his everyday encounters with family, friends, colleagues and strangers, Kushner takes us deeply into our lives, finding flashes of spiritual insight in the process. This is a book where literature meets spirituality, where the sacred meets the ordinary, and, above all, where people of all faiths, all backgrounds can meet one another and themselves.

"Does something both more and different than instruct—it inspirits. Wonderful
•AWARD WINNER• stories, from the best storyteller I know."
— *David Mamet*

5 1/2" x 8 1/2", 160 pp. Quality Paperback, ISBN 1-879045-98-2 **$15.95** HC, -52-4 **$21.95**

HONEY FROM THE ROCK
An Easy Introduction to Jewish Mysticism
by *Lawrence Kushner*

"Quite simply the easiest introduction to Jewish mysticism you can read."

An introduction to the ten gates of Jewish mysticism and how it applies to daily life.

"Captures the flavor and spark of Jewish mysticism. . . . Read it and be rewarded." —*Elie Wiesel*

6" x 9", 168 pp. Quality Paperback, ISBN 1-879045-02-8 **$14.95**

THE BOOK OF WORDS
Talking Spiritual Life, Living Spiritual Talk
by *Lawrence Kushner*

In the incomparable manner of his extraordinary *The Book of Letters,* Kushner now lifts up and shakes the dust off primary religious words we use to describe the spiritual dimension of life. For each word Kushner offers us a startling, moving and insightful explication, and pointed readings from classical Jewish sources that further illuminate the concept. He concludes with a short exercise that helps unite the spirit of the word with our actions in the world.

"This is a powerful and holy book."
—*M. Scott Peck, M.D., author of* The Road Less Traveled *and other books*

"What a delightful wholeness of intellectual vigor and meditative playfulness, and all in a tone of gentleness that speaks to this gentile."
—*Rt. Rev. Krister Stendahl, formerly Dean, Harvard Divinity School/Bishop of Stockholm*

6" x 9", 152 pp. HC, beautiful two-color text, ISBN 1-879045-35-4 **$21.95**

THE BOOK OF LETTERS
A Mystical Hebrew Alphabet
by *Rabbi Lawrence Kushner*

In calligraphy by the author. Folktales about and exploration of the mystical meanings of the Hebrew Alphabet. Open the old prayerbook-like pages of *The Book of Letters* and you will enter a special world of sacred tradition and religious feeling. Rabbi Kushner draws from ancient Judaic sources, weaving talmudic commentary, Hasidic folktales, and kabbalistic mysteries around the letters.

"A book which is in love with Jewish letters."
— *Isaac Bashevis Singer* (ה)

•AWARD WINNER•

• **Popular Hardcover Edition** 6"x 9", 80 pp. HC, two colors, inspiring new Foreword.
ISBN 1-879045-00-1 **$24.95**

• **Deluxe Gift Edition** 9"x 12", 80 pp. HC, four-color text, ornamentation, in a beautiful slipcase.
ISBN 1-879045-01-X **$79.95**

• **Collector's Limited Edition** 9"x 12", 80 pp. HC, gold-embossed pages, hand-assembled slipcase. With silkscreened print. **Limited to 500 signed and numbered copies.** ISBN 1-879045-04-4 **$349.00**

To see a sample page at no obligation, call us

Spirituality

GOD WAS IN THIS PLACE & I, i DID NOT KNOW
Finding Self, Spirituality & Ultimate Meaning
by Lawrence Kushner

Who am I? Who is God? Kushner creates inspiring interpretations of Jacob's dream in Genesis, opening a window into Jewish spirituality for people of all faiths and backgrounds.

In this fascinating blend of scholarship, imagination, psychology and history, seven Jewish spiritual masters ask and answer fundamental questions of human experience.

"Rich and intriguing."
—M. Scott Peck, M.D., *author of* The Road Less Traveled *and other books*

6" x 9", 192 pp. Quality Paperback, ISBN 1-879045-33-8 **$16.95**

THE RIVER OF LIGHT
Spirituality, Judaism, Consciousness
by Lawrence Kushner

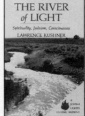

A "manual" for all spiritual travelers who would attempt a spiritual journey in our times. Taking us step by step, Kushner allows us to discover the meaning of our own quest: "to allow the river of light—the deepest currents of consciousness—to rise to the surface and animate our lives."

"Philosophy and mystical fantasy....Anybody—Jewish, Christian, or otherwise...will find this book an intriguing experience."
—*Kirkus Reviews*

6" x 9", 180 pp. Quality Paperback, ISBN 1-879045-03-6 **$14.95**

GODWRESTLING—ROUND 2
Ancient Wisdom, Future Paths
by *Arthur Waskow*

• AWARD WINNER •

This 20th-anniversary sequel to a seminal book of the Jewish renewal movement deals with spirituality in relation to personal growth, marriage, ecology, feminism, politics, and more. Including new chapters on recent issues and concerns, Waskow outlines original ways to merge "religious" life and "personal" life in our society today.

BEST RELIGION BOOK OF THE YEAR

"A delicious read and a soaring meditation."
—*Rabbi Zalman M. Schachter-Shalomi*

"Vivid as a novel, sharp, eccentric, loud....An important book for anyone who wants to bring Judaism alive."
—*Marge Piercy*

6" x 9", 352 pp. Quality Paperback, ISBN 1-879045-72-9 **$18.95** HC, ISBN-45-1 **$23.95**

BEING GOD'S PARTNER
How to Find the Hidden Link Between Spirituality and Your Work
by *Jeffrey K. Salkin* Introduction by *Norman Lear*

Will challenge people of every denomination to reconcile the cares of work and soul. A groundbreaking book about spirituality and the work world, from a Jewish perspective. Helps the reader find God in the ethical striving and search for meaning in the professions and in business and offers practical suggestions for balancing your professional life and spiritual self.

"This engaging meditation on the spirituality of work is grounded in Judaism but is relevant well beyond the boundaries of that tradition."
—Booklist *(American Library Association)*

6" x 9", 192 pp. Quality Paperback, ISBN 1-879045-65-6 **$16.95** HC, ISBN-37-0 **$19.95**

Healing/Recovery/Wellness

Experts Praise *Twelve Jewish Steps to Recovery*

"Recommended reading for people of all denominations."
—*Rabbi Abraham J. Twerski, M.D.*

TWELVE JEWISH STEPS TO RECOVERY
A Personal Guide to Turning from Alcoholism & Other Addictions...Drugs, Food, Gambling, Sex...
by *Rabbi Kerry M. Olitzky & Stuart A. Copans, M.D.*
Preface by *Abraham J. Twerski, M.D.*; Intro. by *Rabbi Sheldon Zimmerman*; "Getting Help" by *JACS Foundation*

A Jewish perspective on the Twelve Steps of addiction recovery programs with consolation, inspiration and motivation for recovery. It draws from traditional sources and quotes from what recovering Jewish people say about their experiences with addictions of all kinds. Inspiring illustrations of the twelve gates of the Old City of Jerusalem introduce each step.

6" x 9", 136 pp. Quality Paperback, ISBN 1-879045-09-5 **$13.95**

Recovery from Codependence: A Jewish Twelve Steps Guide to Healing Your Soul
by Rabbi Kerry M. Olitzky

6" x 9", 160 pp. Quality Paperback Original, ISBN 1-879045-32-X **$13.95**   HC, ISBN-27-3 **$21.95**

Renewed Each Day: Daily Twelve Step Recovery Meditations Based on the Bible
by Rabbi Kerry M. Olitzky & Aaron Z.

6" x 9", Quality Paperback Original, **V. I**, 224 pp. **$14.95**   **V. II**, 280 pp. **$16.95**
Two-Volume Set ISBN 1-879045-21-4   **$27.90**

One Hundred Blessings Every Day: Daily Twelve Step Recovery Affirmations, Exercises for Personal Growth & Renewal Reflecting Seasons of the Jewish Year
by Rabbi Kerry M. Olitzky

4 1/2" x 6 1/2", 432 pp. Quality Paperback Original, ISBN 1-879045-30-3   **$14.95**

HEALING OF SOUL, HEALING OF BODY
Spiritual Leaders Unfold the Strength and Solace in Psalms
Edited by *Rabbi Simkha Y. Weintraub, CSW, for The Jewish Healing Center*

A source of solace for those who are facing illness, as well as those who care for them. The ten Psalms which form the core of this healing resource were originally selected 200 years ago by Rabbi Nachman of Breslov as a "complete remedy." Today, for anyone coping with illness, they continue to provide a wellspring of strength. Each Psalm is newly translated, making it clear and accessible, and each one is introduced by an eminent rabbi, men and women reflecting different movements and backgrounds. To all who are living with the pain and uncertainty of illness, this spiritual resource offers an anchor of spiritual comfort.

"Will bring comfort to anyone fortunate enough to read it. This gentle book is a luminous gem of wisdom."
—*Larry Dossey, M.D., author of* Healing Words: The Power of Prayer & the Practice of Medicine

6" x 9", 128 pp. Quality Paperback Original, illus., 2-color text, ISBN 1-879045-31-1 **$14.95**

Theology/Philosophy

•Award Winner•

A LIVING COVENANT
The Innovative Spirit in Traditional Judaism
by *David Hartman*

WINNER,
National Jewish
Book Award

The Judaic tradition is often seen as being more concerned with uncritical obedience to law than with individual freedom and responsibility. Hartman challenges this approach by revealing a Judaism grounded in a covenant—a relational framework—informed by the metaphor of marital love rather than that of parent-child dependency.

"Jews and non-Jews, liberals and traditionalists will see classic Judaism anew in these pages."
— *Dr. Eugene B. Borowitz, Hebrew Union College–Jewish Institute of Religion*

6" x 9", 368 pp. Quality Paperback, ISBN 1-58023-011-3 **$18.95**

THE SPIRIT OF RENEWAL
Finding Faith after the Holocaust
by *Edward Feld*

•Award Winner•

Trying to understand the Holocaust and addressing the question of faith after the Holocaust, Rabbi Feld explores three key cycles of destruction and recovery in Jewish history, each of which radically reshaped Jewish understanding of God, people, and the world.

"A profound meditation on Jewish history [and the Holocaust]....Christians, as well as many others, need to share in this story."
— *The Rt. Rev. Frederick H. Borsch, Ph.D., Episcopal Bishop of L.A.*

6" x 9", 224 pp. Quality Paperback, ISBN 1-879045-40-0 **$16.95**

•Award Winner•

SEEKING THE PATH TO LIFE
Theological Meditations On God
and the Nature of People, Love, Life and Death
by *Rabbi Ira F. Stone*

For people who never thought they would read a book of theology—let alone understand it, enjoy it, savor it and have it affect the way they think about their lives. In 45 intense meditations, each a page or two in length, Stone takes us on explorations of the most basic human struggles: Life and death, love and anger, peace and war, covenant and exile.

"A bold book....The reader of any faith will be inspired...."
— *The Rev. Carla V. Berkedal, Episcopal Priest*

6" x 9", 132 pp. Quality Paperback, ISBN 1-879045-47-8 **$14.95** HC, ISBN-17-6 **$19.95**

CLASSICS BY ABRAHAM JOSHUA HESCHEL

The Earth Is the Lord's: The Inner World of the Jew in Eastern Europe
5 1/2" x 8", 112 pp, Quality Paperback, ISBN 1-879045-42-7 **$13.95**

Israel: An Echo of Eternity with new Introduction by Susannah Heschel
5 1/2" x 8", 272 pp, Quality Paperback, ISBN 1-879045-70-2 **$18.95**

A Passion for Truth: Despair and Hope in Hasidism
5 1/2" x 8", 352 pp, Quality Paperback, ISBN 1-879045-41-9 **$18.95**

THEOLOGY & PHILOSOPHY...Other books—Classic Reprints

Aspects of Rabbinic Theology by Solomon Schechter, with a new Introduction by Neil Gillman 6" x 9", 440 pp, Quality Paperback, ISBN 1-879045-24-9 **$18.95**

The Last Trial: On the Legends and Lore of the Command to Abraham to Offer Isaac as a Sacrifice by Shalom Spiegel, with a new Introduction by Judah Goldin 6" x 9", 208 pp, Quality Paperback, ISBN 1-879045-29-X **$17.95**

Judaism and Modern Man: An Interpretation of Jewish Religion by Will Herberg; new Introduction by Neil Gillman 5.5" x 8.5", 336 pp, Quality Paperback, ISBN 1-879045-87-7 **$18.95**

Tormented Master: The Life and Spiritual Quest of Rabbi Nahman of Bratslav by Arthur Green 6" x 9", 408 pp, Quality Paperback, ISBN 1-879045-11-7 **$18.95**

Your Word Is Fire Ed. and trans. with a new Introduction by Arthur Green and Barry W. Holtz 6" x 9", 152 pp, Quality Paperback, ISBN 1-879045-25-7 **$14.95**

Life Cycle

GRIEF IN OUR SEASONS
A Mourner's Kaddish Companion
by *Rabbi Kerry M. Olitzky*

Strength from the Jewish tradition for the first year of mourning.

Provides a wise and inspiring selection of sacred Jewish writings and a simple, powerful ancient ritual for mourners to read each day, to help hold the memory of their loved ones in their hearts. It offers a comforting, step-by-step daily link to saying *Kaddish*.

"A hopeful, compassionate guide along the journey from grief to rebirth from mourning to a new morning."
> —*Rabbi Levi Meier, Ph.D., Chaplain, Cedars–Sinai Medical Center, Los Angeles*

4 1/2" x 6 1/2", 448 pp., Quality Paperback Original, ISBN 1-879045-55-9 **$15.95**

MOURNING & MITZVAH   • WITH OVER 60 GUIDED EXERCISES •
A Guided Journal for Walking the Mourner's Path Through Grief to Healing
by *Anne Brener, L.C.S.W.;* Foreword by *Rabbi Jack Riemer;* Introduction by *Rabbi William Cutter*

"Fully engaging in mourning means you will be a different person than before you began." **For those who mourn a death, for those who would help them,** for those who face a loss of any kind, Brener teaches us the power and strength available to us in the fully experienced mourning process. Guided writing exercises help stimulate the processes of both conscious and unconscious healing.

"A stunning book! It offers an exploration in depth of the place where psychology and religious ritual intersect, and the name of that place is Truth."
> —*Rabbi Harold Kushner, author of* When Bad Things Happen to Good People

7 1/2" x 9", 288 pp. Quality Paperback Original, ISBN 1-879045-23-0 **$19.95**

A TIME TO MOURN, A TIME TO COMFORT
A Guide to Jewish Bereavement and Comfort
by *Dr. Ron Wolfson*

A guide to meeting the needs of those who mourn and those who seek to provide comfort in times of sadness. While this book is written from a layperson's point of view, it also includes the specifics for funeral preparations and practical guidance for preparing the home and family to sit *shiva*.

"A sensitive and perceptive guide to Jewish tradition. Both those who mourn and those who comfort will find it a map to accompany them through the whirlwind."
> —*Deborah E. Lipstadt, Emory University*

7" x 9", 320 pp. Quality Paperback, ISBN 1-879045-96-6 **$16.95**

WHEN A GRANDPARENT DIES
A Kid's Own Remembering Workbook for Dealing with Shiva and the Year Beyond
by *Nechama Liss-Levinson, Ph.D.*

Drawing insights from both psychology and Jewish tradition, this workbook helps children participate in the process of mourning, offering guided exercises, rituals, and places to write, draw, list, create and express their feelings.

"Will bring support, guidance, and understanding for countless children, teachers, and health professionals."
> —*Rabbi Earl A. Grollman, D.D., author of* Talking about Death

8" x 10", 48 pp. HC, illus., 2-color text, ISBN 1-879045-44-3 **$15.95**

Art of Jewish Living Series for Holiday Observance

THE SHABBAT SEDER
by *Dr. Ron Wolfson*

A concise step-by-step guide designed to teach people the meaning and importance of this weekly celebration, as well as its practices.

Each chapter corresponds to one of ten steps which together comprise the Shabbat dinner ritual, and looks at the *concepts, objects,* and *meanings* behind the specific activity or ritual act. The blessings that accompany the meal are written in both Hebrew and English, and accompanied by English transliteration. Also included are craft projects, recipes, discussion ideas and other creative suggestions for enriching the Shabbat experience.

"A how-to book in the best sense...."
—Dr. David Lieber, President, University of Judaism, Los Angeles

7" x 9", 272 pp. Quality Paperback, ISBN 1-879045-90-7 **$16.95**

Also available are these helpful companions to *The Shabbat Seder*:
- Booklet of the Blessings and Songs   ISBN 1-879045-91-5 $5.00
- Audiocassette of the Blessings   DNO3 $6.00
- Teacher's Guide   ISBN 1-879045-92-3 $4.95

HANUKKAH
by *Dr. Ron Wolfson*
Edited by *Joel Lurie Grishaver*

Designed to help celebrate and enrich the holiday season, *Hanukkah* discusses the holiday's origins, explores the reasons for the Hanukkah candles and customs, and provides everything from recipes to family activities.

There are songs, recipes, useful information on the arts and crafts of Hanukkah, the calendar and its relationship to Christmas time, and games played at Hanukkah. Putting the holiday in a larger, timely context, "December Dilemmas" deals with ways in which a Jewish family can cope with Christmas.

"Helpful for the family that strives to induct its members into the spirituality and joys of Jewishness and Judaism...a significant text in the neglected art of Jewish family education."
—Rabbi Harold M. Schulweis, Cong. Valley Beth Shalom, Encino, CA

7" x 9", 192 pp. Quality Paperback, ISBN 1-879045-97-4 **$16.95**

THE PASSOVER SEDER
by *Dr. Ron Wolfson*

Explains the concepts behind Passover ritual and ceremony in clear, easy-to-understand language, and offers step-by-step procedures for Passover observance and preparing the home for the holiday.

Easy-to-Follow Format: Using an innovative photo-documentary technique, real families describe in vivid images their own experiences with the Passover holiday. **Easy-to-Read Hebrew Texts:** The Haggadah texts in Hebrew, English, and transliteration are presented in a three-column format designed to help celebrants learn the meaning of the prayers and how to read them. **An Abundance of Useful Information:** A detailed description of how to perform the rituals is included, along with practical questions and answers, and imaginative ideas for Seder celebration.

"A creative 'how-to' for making the Seder a more meaningful experience."
—Michael Strassfeld, co-author of The Jewish Catalog

7" x 9", 336 pp. Quality Paperback, ISBN 1-879045-93-1 **$16.95**

Also available are these helpful companions to *The Passover Seder*:
- Passover Workbook   ISBN 1-879045-94-X $6.95
- Audiocassette of the Blessings   DNO4 $6.00
- Teacher's Guide   ISBN 1-879045-95-8 $4.95

Life Cycle

A HEART OF WISDOM
Making the Jewish Journey from Midlife Through the Elder Years
Edited by *Susan Berrin*

We are all growing older. *A Heart of Wisdom* shows us how to understand our own process of aging—and the aging of those we care about—from a Jewish perspective, from midlife through the elder years.

How does Jewish tradition influence our own aging? How does living, thinking and worshipping as a Jew affect us as we age? How can Jewish tradition help us retain our dignity as we age? Offers insights and enlightenment from Jewish tradition.

"A thoughtfully orchestrated collection of pieces that deal candidly and compassionately with a period of growing concern to us all: midlife through old age."
—*Chaim Potok*

6" x 9", 384 pp. HC, ISBN 1-879045-73-7 **$24.95**

•AWARD WINNER•

LIFECYCLES
V. 1: Jewish Women on Life Passages & Personal Milestones
Edited and with Introductions by *Rabbi Debra Orenstein*
V. 2: Jewish Women on Biblical Themes in Contemporary Life
Edited and with Introductions by
Rabbi Debra Orenstein and *Rabbi Jane Rachel Litman*

This unique multivolume collaboration brings together over one hundred women writers, rabbis, and scholars to create the first comprehensive work on Jewish life cycle that fully includes women's perspectives.

"Nothing is missing from this marvelous collection. You will turn to it for rituals and inspiration, prayer and poetry, comfort and community. *Lifecycles* is a gift to the Jewish woman in America."
—*Letty Cottin Pogrebin, author of* Deborah, Golda, and Me: Being Female and Jewish in America

V. 1: 6" x 9", 480 pp. HC, ISBN 1-879045-14-1, **$24.95**; V. 2: 6" x 9", 464 pp. HC, ISBN 1-879045-15-X, **$24.95**

LIFE CYCLE— The Art of Jewish Living Series for Holiday Observance
by Dr. Ron Wolfson

Hanukkah—7" x 9", 192 pp. Quality Paperback, ISBN 1-879045-97-4 **$16.95**

The Shabbat Seder—7" x 9", 272 pp. Quality Paperback, ISBN 1-879045-90-7 **$16.95**; Booklet of Blessings **$5.00**; Audiocassette of Blessings **$6.00**; Teacher's Guide **$4.95**

The Passover Seder—7" x 9", 336 pp. Quality Paperback, ISBN 1-879045-93-1 **$16.95**; Passover Workbook, **$6.95**; Audiocassette of Blessings, **$6.00**; Teacher's Guide, **$4.95**

LIFE CYCLE...Other Books

Bar/Bat Mitzvah Basics: A Practical Family Guide to Coming of Age Together
Ed. by Cantor Helen Leneman 6" x 9", 240 pp. Quality Paperback, ISBN 1-879045-54-0 **$16.95**

Embracing the Covenant: Converts to Judaism Talk About Why & How
Ed. and with Intros. by Rabbi Allan L. Berkowitz and Patti Moskovitz
6" x 9", 192 pp. Quality Paperback, ISBN 1-879045-50-8 **$15.95**

The New Jewish Baby Book: Names, Ceremonies, Customs—A Guide for Today's Families by Anita Diamant 6" x 9", 328 pp. Quality Paperback, ISBN 1-879045-28-1 **$16.95**

Putting God on the Guest List, 2nd Ed.: How to Reclaim the Spiritual Meaning of Your Child's Bar or Bat Mitzvah by Rabbi Jeffrey K. Salkin 6" x 9", 224 pp. Quality Paperback, ISBN 1-897045-59-1 **$16.95**; HC, ISBN 1-879045-58-3 **$24.95**

So That Your Values Live On: Ethical Wills & How to Prepare Them
Ed. by Rabbi Jack Riemer & Professor Nathaniel Stampfer
6" x 9", 272 pp. Quality Paperback, ISBN 1-879045-34-6 **$17.95**

Children's Spirituality

A PRAYER FOR THE EARTH
The Story of Naamah, Noah's Wife

For ages 4 and up

by *Sandy Eisenberg Sasso*

Full-color illustrations by *Bethanne Andersen*

NONDENOMINATIONAL, NONSECTARIAN

This new story, based on an ancient text, opens readers' religious imaginations to new ideas about the well-known story of the Flood. When God tells Noah to bring the animals of the world onto the ark, God *also* calls on Naamah, Noah's wife, to save each plant on Earth.

> "A lovely tale....Children of all ages should be drawn to this parable for our times."
>
> —*Tomie dePaola, artist/author of books for children*

•AWARD WINNER•

9" x 12", 32 pp. HC, Full-color illus., ISBN 1-879045-60-5 **$16.95**

THE 11TH COMMANDMENT
Wisdom from Our Children

For all ages

by The Children of America

MULTICULTURAL, NONDENOMINATIONAL, NONSECTARIAN

"If there were an Eleventh Commandment, what would it be?"

Children of many religious denominations across America answer this question—in their own drawings and words—in *The 11th Commandment*.

> "Wonderful....This unusual book provides both food for thought and insight into the hopes and fears of today's young."
>
> —*American Library Association's* Booklist

8" x 10", 48 pp. HC, Full-color illus., ISBN 1-879045-46-X **$16.95**

SHARING BLESSINGS
Children's Stories for Exploring the Spirit of the Jewish Holidays

For ages 6 and up

by *Rahel Musleah* and *Rabbi Michael Klayman*

Full-color illustrations by *Mary O'Keefe Young*

What is the spiritual message of each of the Jewish holidays? How do we teach it to our children?

Many books tell children about the historical significance and customs of the holidays. Now, through engaging, creative stories about one family's spiritual preparation, *Sharing Blessings* explores ways to get into the *spirit* of 13 different holidays.

> "A beguiling introduction to important Jewish values by way of the holidays."
>
> —*Rabbi Harold Kushner, author of* When Bad Things Happen to Good People *and* How Good Do We Have to Be?

7" x 10", 64 pp. HC, Full-color illus., ISBN 1-879045-71-0 **$18.95**

THE BOOK OF MIRACLES

For ages 9–13

A Young Person's Guide to Jewish Spiritual Awareness

by *Lawrence Kushner*

With a Special 10th Anniversary Introduction and all new illustrations by the author.

From the miracle at the Red Sea to the miracle of waking up this morning, this intriguing book introduces kids to a way of everyday spiritual thinking to last a lifetime. Kushner, whose award-winning books have brought spirituality to life for countless adults, now shows young people how to use Judaism as a foundation on which to build their lives.

6" x 9", 96 pp. HC, 2-color illus., ISBN 1-879045-78-8 **$16.95**

Children's Spirituality

For ages 8 and up

BUT GOD REMEMBERED
Stories of Women from Creation to the Promised Land
by *Sandy Eisenberg Sasso*
Full-color illustrations by *Bethanne Andersen*

NONDENOMINATIONAL, NONSECTARIAN

A fascinating collection of four different stories of women only briefly mentioned in biblical tradition and religious texts, but never before explored. Award-winning author Sasso brings to life the intriguing stories of Lilith, Serach, Bityah, and the Daughters of Z, courageous and strong women from ancient tradition. All teach important values through their faith and actions.

•AWARD WINNER•

"Exquisite....a book of beauty, strength and spirituality."
—*Association of Bible Teachers*

9" x 12", 32 pp. HC, Full-color illus., ISBN 1-879045-43-5 **$16.95**

IN GOD'S NAME
by *Sandy Eisenberg Sasso*
Full-color illustrations by *Phoebe Stone*

For ages 4 and up

MULTICULTURAL, NONDENOMINATIONAL, NONSECTARIAN

Like an ancient myth in its poetic text and vibrant illustrations, this modern fable about the search for God's name celebrates the diversity and, at the same time, the unity of all the people of the world. Each seeker claims he or she alone knows the answer. Finally, they come together and learn what God's name really is, sharing the ultimate harmony of belief in one God by people of all faiths, all backgrounds.

•AWARD WINNER•

"I got goose bumps when I read *In God's Name,* its language and illustrations are that moving. This is a book children will love and the whole family will cherish for its beauty and power."
—*Francine Klagsbrun, author of* Mixed Feelings: Love, Hate, Rivalry, and Reconciliation among Brothers and Sisters

"What a lovely, healing book!"
—*Madeleine L'Engle*

Selected by
Parent Council, Ltd.™

9" x 12", 32 pp. HC, Full color illus., ISBN 1-879045-26-5 **$16.95**

For ages 4 and up

GOD'S PAINTBRUSH
by *Sandy Eisenberg Sasso*
Full-color illustrations by *Annette Compton*

MULTICULTURAL, NONDENOMINATIONAL, NONSECTARIAN

Invites children of all faiths and backgrounds to encounter God openly in their own lives. Wonderfully interactive, provides questions adult and child can explore together at the end of each episode.

"An excellent way to honor the imaginative breadth and depth of the spiritual life of the young."
—*Dr. Robert Coles, Harvard University*

•AWARD WINNER•

11" x 8 1/2", 32 pp. HC, Full-color illus., ISBN 1-879045-22-2 **$16.95**

Also Available!
Teacher's Guide: A Guide for Jewish & Christian Educators and Parents
8 1/2" x 11", 32 pp. PB, ISBN 1-879045-57-5 **$6.95**

AVAILABLE FROM BETTER BOOKSTORES.
TRY YOUR BOOKSTORE FIRST.

Order Information

# of Copies	Book Title / ISBN (Last 3 digits)	$ Amount
_____	_____	_____
_____	_____	_____
_____	_____	_____
_____	_____	_____
_____	_____	_____
_____	_____	_____
_____	_____	_____
_____	_____	_____
_____	_____	_____
_____	_____	_____
_____	_____	_____
_____	_____	_____
_____	_____	_____

For shipping/handling, add $3.50 for the first book, $2.00 each
add'l book (to a max of $15.00)   **$ S/H** _____

TOTAL _____

Check enclosed for $_____ *payable to:* JEWISH LIGHTS Publishing

Charge my credit card: ❐ MasterCard   ❐ Visa

Credit Card #_____Expires _____

Signature _____Phone (_____)_____

Your Name _____

Street_____

City / State / Zip _____

Ship To:

Name _____

Street_____

City / State / Zip _____

Phone, fax or mail to: **JEWISH LIGHTS Publishing**
Sunset Farm Offices, Route 4 • P.O. Box 237 • Woodstock, Vermont 05091
Tel (802) 457-4000   Fax (802) 457-4004   www.jewishlights.com
Credit card orders **(800) 962-4544** (9AM–5PM ET Monday–Friday)
Generous discounts on quantity orders. SATISFACTION GUARANTEED. Prices subject to change.

New from Jewish Lights

"WHO IS A JEW?"
Conversations, Not Conclusions
by *Meryl Hyman*

Who is "Jewish enough" to be considered a Jew? And by whom?

Meryl Hyman courageously takes on this timely and controversial question to give readers the perspective necessary to draw their own conclusions. With the skill of a seasoned journalist, she weaves her own life experiences into this complex and controversial story. Profound personal questions of identity are explored in conversations with Jew and non-Jew in the U.S., Israel and England. *"Who Is a Jew?"* is a book for those who seek to understand the issue, and for those who think they already do.

6" x 9", 272 pp. HC, ISBN 1-879045-76-1 **$23.95**

THE JEWISH GARDENING COOKBOOK
Growing Plants and Cooking for Holidays & Festivals
by *Michael Brown*

Through gardening and cooking for holiday and festival use, we can recover and discover many exciting aspects of Judaism to nourish both the mind and the spirit. Whether you garden in an herb garden, on a city apartment windowsill or patio, or on an acre, with the fruits and vegetables of your own gardening labors, the traditional repasts of Jewish holidays and celebrations can be understood in many new ways!

Gives easy-to-follow instructions for raising foods that have been harvested since ancient times. Provides carefully selected, tasty and easy-to-prepare recipes using these traditional foodstuff for holidays, festivals, and life cycle events. Clearly illustrated with more than 30 fine botanical illustrations. For beginner and professional alike.

6" x 9", 208 pp (est). HC, ISBN 1-58023-004-0 **$21.95**

WANDERING STARS
An Anthology of Jewish Fantasy & Science Fiction
Edited by *Jack Dann; with an Introduction by Isaac Asimov*

Jewish science fiction and fantasy? *Yes!*

Here is the distinguished list of contributors to *Wandering Stars*, originally published in 1974 and the only book of its kind, anywhere: Bernard Malamud, Isaac Bashevis Singer, Isaac Asimov, Robert Silverberg, Harlan Ellison, Pamela Sargent, Avram Davidson, Geo. Alec Effinger, Horace L. Gold, Robert Sheckley, William Tenn and Carol Carr. Pure enjoyment. We laughed out loud reading it. A 25th Anniversary Classic Reprint.

"It is delightful and deep, hilarious and sad." —*James Morrow, author,* Towing Jehovah

6" x 9", 272 pp. Quality Paperback, ISBN 1-58023-005-9 **$16.95**

THE ENNEAGRAM AND KABBALAH
Reading Your Soul
by *Rabbi Howard A. Addison*

What do the Enneagram and *Kabbalah* have in common? Together, can they provide a powerful tool for self-knowledge, critique, and transformation?

How can we distinguish between acquired personality traits and the essential self hidden underneath?

6" x 9", 176 pp. Quality Paperback Original, ISBN 1-58023-001-6 **$15.95**